W9-BAJ-021

Also by James Alan McPherson

Crabcakes

Elbow Room

Railroad: Trains and Train People
in American Culture

Hue and Cry: Short Stories

A Region Not Home

Reflections from Exile

James Alan McPherson

Simon & Schuster
New York London Sydney Singapore

SIMON & SCHUSTER
Rockefeller Center
1230 Avenue of the Americas
New York, NY 10020

Copyright © 2000 by James A. McPherson

All rights reserved, including the right of reproduction
in whole or in part in any form.

Simon & Schuster and colophon are registered trademarks
of Simon & Schuster, Inc.

Permissions Acknowledgments for the essays appear on page 317.

Lyrics from "Jim Dean of Indiana," "The War Is Over," and "When I'm Gone,"
by Phil Ochs, copyright © 1968 (renewed) Barricade Music, Inc. (ASCAP). All rights
for world administered by Almo Music Corp. (ASCAP). All rights reserved. Used
by permission. Warner Bros. Publications U.S. Inc., Miami FL 33014.

Designed by Jeanette Olender
Manufactured in the United States of America

1   3   5   7   9   10   8   6   4   2

Library of Congress Cataloging-in-Publication Data
McPherson, James Alan, date.
A region not home : reflections from exile / James Alan McPherson.
p. cm.
I. Title.
PS3563.A325 R4 1999
813'54—dc21   99-056063
ISBN 0-684-83464-2

Acknowledgments

With loving memories of Eleanor Simmons, mentor in art, in class, and in talking trash.

To Ralph and Benjamin,
to history and destiny

Contents

A Region Not Home

On Becoming an American Writer

In 1974, during the last months of the Nixon administration, I lived in San Francisco, California. My public reason for leaving the East and going there was that my wife had been admitted to the San Francisco Medical Center School of Nursing, but my private reason for going was that San Francisco would be a very good place for working and for walking. Actually, during that time San Francisco was not that pleasant a place. We lived in a section of the city called the Sunset District, but it rained almost every day. During the late spring Patricia Hearst helped to rob a bank a few blocks from our apartment, a psychopath called "the Zebra Killer" was terrorizing the city, and the mayor seemed about to declare martial law. Periodically the FBI would come to my apartment with pictures of the suspected bank robbers. Agents came several times, until it began to dawn on me that they had become slightly interested in why, of all the people in a working-class neighborhood, I alone sat at home every day. They never asked any questions on this point, and I never volunteered that I was trying to keep my sanity by working very hard on a book dealing with the relationship between folklore and technology in nineteenth-century America.

In the late fall of the same year a friend came out from the East to give a talk in Sacramento. I drove there to take him back to San Francisco. This was an older black man, one whom I respect a great deal, but during our drive an argument developed between us. His major worry was the recession, but eventually his focus shifted to people in my age group and our failures. There were a great many of these, and he listed them point by point. He said, while we drove through a gloomy evening rain, "When the smoke clears and you start counting, I'll bet you won't find that many more black doctors, lawyers, accountants, engineers, dentists. . . ." The list went on. He remonstrated a bit more, and said, "White people are very generous. When they start a thing they usually finish it. But after all this chaos, imagine how mad and tired they must be. Back in the fifties, when this thing started, they must have known anything could happen. They must have said, 'Well, we'd better settle in and hold on tight. Here come the niggers.'" During the eighteen months I spent in San Francisco, this was the only personal encounter that really made me mad.

In recent years I have realized that my friend, whom I now respect even more, was speaking from the perspective of a tactician. He viewed the situation in strict bread-and-butter terms: a commitment had been made to redefine the meaning of democracy in this country, certain opportunities and the freedom they provided. From his point of view, it was simply a matter of fulfilling a contractual obligation: taking full advantage of the educational opportunities that had been offered to achieve middle-class status in one of the professions. But from my point of view, one that I never shared with him, it was not that simple. Perhaps it was because of the differences in our generations and experiences. Or perhaps it was because each new generation, of black people at least, has to redefine itself even while it attempts to grasp the new opportunities, explore the new freedom. I can speak for no one but myself, yet maybe in trying to preserve the uniqueness of my experience, as I tried to do in *Elbow Room,* I can begin to set the record straight for my friend, for myself, and for the sake of the record itself.

In 1954, when *Brown* v. *Board of Education* was decided, I was eleven years old. I lived in a lower-class black community in Savannah, Georgia, attended segregated public schools, and knew no white people socially. I can't remember thinking of this last fact as a disadvantage, but I do know that early on I was being conditioned to believe that I was not *supposed* to know any white people on social terms. In our town the children of the black middle class were expected to aspire to certain traditional occupations; the children of the poor were expected not to cause too much trouble.

There was in those days a very subtle, but real, social distinction based on gradations of color, and I can remember the additional strain under which darker-skinned poor people lived. But there was also a great deal of optimism, shared by all levels of the black community. Besides a certain reverence for the benign intentions of the federal government, there was a belief in the idea of progress, nourished, I think now, by the determination of older people not to pass on to the next generation too many stories about racial conflict, their own frustrations and failures. They censored a great deal. It was as if they had made basic and binding agreements with themselves, or with their ancestors, that for the consideration represented by their silence on certain points they expected to receive, from either Providence or a munificent federal government, some future service or remuneration, the form of which would be left to the beneficiaries of their silence. Lawyers would call this a contract with a condition precedent. And maybe because they did tell us less than they knew, many of us were less informed than we might have been. On the other hand, because of this same silence many of us remained free enough of the influence of negative stories to take chances, be ridiculous, perhaps even try to form our own positive stories out of whatever our own experiences provided. Though ours was a limited world, it was one rich in possibilities for the future.

If I had to account for my life from segregated Savannah to this place and point in time, I would probably have to say that the contract would be no bad metaphor. I am reminded of Sir Henry Maine's observation that the progress of society is from status to contract. Although he was writing about the development of English common law, the reverse of his generalization is most applicable to my situation: I am the beneficiary of a number of contracts, most of them between the federal government and the institutions of society, intended to provide people like me with a certain status.

I recall that in 1960, for example, something called the National Defense Student Loan Program went into effect, and I found out that by my agreeing to repay a loan plus some little interest, the federal government would back my enrollment in a small Negro college in Georgia. When I was a freshman at that college, disagreement over a seniority clause between the Hotel & Restaurant Employees and Bartenders Union and the Great Northern Railway Company, in St. Paul, Minnesota, caused management to begin recruiting temporary summer help. Before I was nineteen I was encouraged to move from a segregated Negro college in the South and through that very beautiful part of the country that lies between Chicago and the Pacific Northwest. That year—1962—the World's Fair was in Seattle, and it was a magnificently diverse panorama for a young man to see. Almost every nation on earth was represented in some way, and at the center of the fair was the Space Needle. The theme of the U.S. exhibit, as I recall, was drawn from Whitman's *Leaves of Grass:* "Conquering, holding, daring, venturing as we go the unknown ways."

When I returned to the South, in the midst of all the civil rights activity, I saw a poster advertising a creative-writing contest sponsored by *Reader's Digest* and the United Negro College Fund. To enter the contest I had to learn to write and type. The first story I wrote was lost (and very badly typed); but the second, written in 1965, although also badly typed, was awarded first prize by Edward Weeks and his staff at the *Atlantic Monthly.* That same year I was offered the opportunity to enter Harvard Law School. During my second year at law school, a third-year man named Dave Marston (who was in a contest with Attorney General Griffin Bell earlier that year) offered me, through a very conservative white fellow student from Texas, the opportunity to take over his old job as a janitor in one of the apartment buildings in Cambridge.

There I had the solitude, and the encouragement, to begin writing seriously. Offering my services in that building was probably the best contract I ever made.

I have not recalled all the above to sing my own praises or to evoke the black American version of the Horatio Alger myth. I have recited these facts as a way of indicating the haphazard nature of events during that ten-year period. I am the product of a contractual process. To put it simply, the 1960s were a crazy time. Opportunities seemed to materialize out of thin air; and if you were lucky, if you were in the right place at the right time, certain contractual benefits just naturally accrued. You were assured of a certain status; you could become a doctor, a lawyer, a dentist, an accountant, an engineer. Achieving these things was easy, if you applied yourself.

But a very hard price was extracted. It seems to me now, from the perspective provided by age and distance, that certain institutional forces, acting impersonally, threw together black peasants and white aristocrats, people who operated on the plane of the intellect and people who valued the perspective of the folk. There were people who were frightened, threatened, and felt inferior; there were light-skinned people who called themselves "black," and there were dark-skinned people who could remember when this term had been used negatively; there were idealists and opportunists, people who seemed to want to be exploited and people who delighted in exploiting them. Old identities were thrown off, of necessity, but there were not many new ones of a positive nature to be assumed. People from backgrounds like my own, those from the South, while content with the new opportunities, found themselves trying to make sense of the growing diversity of friendships, of their increasing familiarity with the various political areas of the country, of the obvious differences between their values and those of their parents. We *were* becoming doctors, lawyers, dentists, engineers; but at the same time our experiences forced us to begin thinking of ourselves in new and different ways. We never wanted to be "white," but we never wanted to be "black" either. And back during that period there was the feeling that we could be whatever we wanted. But, we discovered, unless we joined a group, subscribed to some ideology, accepted some provisional identity, there was no contractual process for defining and stabilizing what it was we wanted to be. We also found that this was an individual problem, and in order to confront it one had to go inside one's self.

Now I want to return to my personal experience, to one of the contracts that took me from segregated Savannah to the Seattle World's Fair. There were many things about my earliest experiences that I liked and wanted to preserve, despite the fact that these things took place in a context of segregation; and there were a great many things I liked about the vision of all those nations interacting at the World's Fair. But the two seemed to belong to separate realities, to represent two different worldviews. Similarly, there were some things I liked about many of the dining-car waiters with whom I worked, and some things I liked about people like Dave Marston whom I met in law school. Some of these people and their values were called "black" and some were called "white," and I learned very quickly that all of us tend to wall

ourselves off from experiences different from our own by as-
signing to these terms greater significance than they should
have. Moreover, I found that trying to maintain friendships
with, say, a politically conservative white Texan, a liberal-to-
radical classmate of Scottish-Italian background, my oldest
black friends, and even members of my own family introduced psychological contradictions that became tense and
painful as the political climate shifted. There were no contracts covering such friendships and such feelings, and in order to keep the friends and maintain the feelings I had to
force myself to find a basis other than race on which contradictory urgings could be synthesized. I discovered that I had
to find, first of all, an identity as a writer, and then I had to
express what I knew or felt in such a way that I could make
something whole out of a necessarily fragmented experience.

While in San Francisco, I saw in the image of the nineteenth-century American locomotive a possible cultural
symbol that could represent my folk origins and their values,
as well as the values of all the people I had seen at the World's
Fair. During that same time, unconsciously, I was also beginning to see that the American language, in its flexibility and
variety of idioms, could at least approximate some of the
contradictory feelings that had resulted from my experience.
Once again, I could not find any contractual guarantee that
this would be the most appropriate and rewarding way to
hold myself, and my experience, together. I think now there
are no such contracts.

I quoted earlier a generalization by Sir Henry Maine to the
effect that human society is a matter of movement from status to contract. Actually, I have never read Sir Henry Maine.

I lifted his statement from a book by a man named Henry Allen Moe—a great book called *The Power of Freedom*. In that book, in an essay entitled "The Future of Liberal Arts Education," Moe goes on to say that a next step, one that goes beyond contract, is now necessary, but that no one seems to know what that next step should be. Certain trends suggest that it may well be a reversion to status. But if this happens it will be a tragedy of major proportions, because most of the people in the world are waiting for some nation, some people, to provide the model for the next step. And somehow I felt, while writing the last stories in *Elbow Room,* that what the old folks in my hometown wanted in exchange for their censoring was not just status of a conventional kind. I want to think that after having waited so long, after having seen so much, they must have at least expected some new stories that would no longer have to be censored to come out of our experience. I felt that if anything, the long experience of segregation could be looked on as a period of preparation for a next step. Those of us who are black and who have had to defend our humanity should be obliged to continue defending it, on higher and higher levels—not of power, which is a kind of tragic trap, but on higher levels of consciousness.

All of this is being said in retrospect, and I am quite aware that I am rationalizing many complex and contradictory feelings. Nevertheless, I do know that early on, during my second year of law school, I became conscious of a model of identity that might help me transcend, at least in my thinking, a provisional or racial identity. In a class in American constitutional law taught by Paul Freund, I began to play with the idea that the Fourteenth Amendment was not just a legislative instrument devised to give former slaves legal equality with other Americans. Looking at the slow but steady way in which the basic guarantees of the Bill of Rights had, through judicial interpretation, been incorporated into the clauses of that amendment, I began to see the outlines of a new identity.

You will recall that the first line of Section 1 of the Fourteenth Amendment makes an all-inclusive definition of citizenship: "All persons born or naturalized in the United States, and subject to the jurisdiction thereof, are citizens of the United States. . . ." The rights guaranteed to such a citizen had themselves traveled from the provinces to the World's Fair: from the trial and error of early Anglo-Saxon folk rituals to the rights of freemen established by the Magna Carta, to their slow incorporation into early American colonial charters, and from these charters (especially Virginia's Bill of Rights, written by George Mason) into the U.S. Constitution as its first ten amendments. Indeed, these same rights had served as the basis for the Charter of the United Nations. I saw that through the protean uses made of the Fourteenth Amendment, in the gradual elaboration of basic rights to be protected by federal authority, an outline of something much more complex than "black" and "white" had been begun.

It was many years before I was to go to the Library of Congress and read the brief of the lawyer-novelist Albion W. Tourgee in the famous case *Plessy* v. *Ferguson*. Argued in 1896 before the United States Supreme Court, Tourgee's brief was the first meaningful attempt to breathe life into the amendment. I will quote here part of his brief, which is a very beautiful piece of literature:

> This provision of Section 1 of the Fourteenth Amendment *creates* a new citizenship of the United States embracing *new* rights, privileges and immunities, derivable in a *new* manner, controlled by *new* authority, having a *new* scope and extent, depending on national authority for its existence and looking to national power for its preservation.

Although Tourgee lost the argument before the Supreme Court, his model of citizenship—and it is not a racial one—is still the most radical idea to come out of American constitutional law. He provided the outline, the clothing, if you will, for a new level of status. What he was proposing in 1896, I think, was that each United States citizen would attempt to approximate the ideals of the nation, be on at least conversant terms with all its diversity, carry the mainstream of the culture inside himself. As an American, by trying to wear these clothes he would be a synthesis of high and low, black and white, city and country, provincial and universal. If he could live with these contradictions, he would be simply a representative American.

This was the model I was aiming for in my book of stories. It can be achieved with or without intermarriage, but it will cost a great many mistakes and a lot of pain. It is, finally, a product of culture and not of race. And achieving it will require that one be conscious of America's culture and the complexity of all its people. As I tried to point out, such a perspective would provide a minefield of delicious ironies. Why, for example, should black Americans raised in southern culture *not* find that some of their responses are geared to country music? How else, except in terms of cultural diversity, am I to account for the white friend in Boston who taught me much of what I know about black American music? Or the white friend in Virginia who, besides developing a homegrown aesthetic he calls "crackertude," knows more about black American folklore than most black people? Or the possibility that many black people in Los Angeles have been just as much influenced by Hollywood's "star system" of the forties and fifties as they have been by society's response to the color of their skins? I wrote about people like these in *Elbow Room* because they interested me, and because they help support my belief that most of us are products of much more complex cultural influences than we suppose.

What I have said above will make little sense until certain contradictions in the nation's background are faced up to, until personal identities are allowed to partake of the complexity of the country's history as well as of its culture. Some years ago, a very imaginative black comedian named Richard Pryor appeared briefly on national television in his own show. He offended a great many people, and his show was canceled after only a few weeks. But I remember one episode that may emphasize my own group's confusion about its historical experience. This was a satiric takeoff on the popular television movie *Roots,* and Pryor played an African tribal historian who was selling trinkets and impromptu history to black American tourists. One tourist, a middle-class man, approached the tribal historian and said, "I want you to tell me who my great-great-granddaddy was." The African handed him a picture. The black American looked at it and said, "But that's a *white* man!" The tribal historian said, "That's right." Then the tourist said, "Well, I want you to tell me where I'm from." The historian looked hard at him and said, "You're from Cleveland, nigger." I think I was trying very hard in my book to say the same thing, but not just to black people.

Today I am not the lawyer my friend in San Francisco thought I should be, but this is the record I wanted to present to him that rainy evening back in 1974. It may illustrate why the terms of my acceptance of society's offer had to be modified. I am now a writer, a person who has to learn to live with contradictions, frustrations, and doubts. Still, I have another quote that sustains me, this one from a book called *The Tragic Sense of Life,* by the Spanish philosopher Miguel de Unamuno. In a chapter called "Don Quixote To-day," Unamuno asks, "How is it that among the words the English have borrowed from our language there is to be found this word *desperado?*" And he answers himself: "It is despair, and despair alone, that begets heroic hope, absurd hope, mad hope."

I believe that the United States is complex enough to induce that sort of despair that begets heroic hope. I believe that if one can experience its diversity, touch a variety of its people, laugh at its craziness, distill wisdom from its tragedies, and attempt to synthesize all this inside oneself without going crazy, one will have earned the right to call oneself "citizen of the United States," even though one is not quite a lawyer, doctor, engineer, or accountant. If nothing else, one will have learned a few new stories and, most important, one will have begun on that necessary movement from contract to the next step, from province to the World's Fair, from a hopeless person to a desperado. I wrote about my first uncertain steps in this direction in *Elbow Room* because I have benefited from all the contracts, I have exhausted all the contracts, and at present it is the only new direction I know.

Foreword to the Collected Stories
of Breece Pancake

I think you should come over (drive or train, I'll pay your expenses and "put you up") because if you do the preface I feel you should be more familiar with this valley and [my son] Breece's surroundings as well as what you knew of him in Charlottesville.

Letter from Mrs. Helen Pancake, February 10, 1981

He never seemed to find a place
With the flatlands and the farmers
So he had to leave one day
He said, To be an Actor.

He played a boy without a home
Torn, with no tomorrow
Reaching out to touch someone
A stranger in the shadows.

Then Marcus heard on the radio
That a movie star was dying.
He turned the treble way down low
So Hortense could go on sleeping.

"Jim Dean of Indiana," Phil Ochs

In late September of 1976, in the autumn of the Bicenten-
nial year, I began my career as a teacher at the University of
Virginia. I had been invited to join the writing program
there by John Casey, who was then on leave. I had been lent
the book-lined office of David Levin, a historian of Colonial
American literature, who was also on leave that year. I had
been assigned the status of associate professor of English, un-
tenured, at my own request. I had come to Virginia from a
Negro college in Baltimore. I had accepted Virginia's offer
for professional and personal reasons: I wanted to teach bet-
ter-motivated students and, on a spiritual level, I wanted to
go home.

If I recall correctly, 1976 was a year of extraordinary hope
in American politics. James Earl Carter, a southerner, was
running for the presidency, and people in all parts of the
country, black and white, were looking to that region with a
certain optimism. Carter had inspired in a great many people
the belief that *this* New South was the long-promised one.
And there were many of us who had followed the ancestral
imperative, seeking a better life in the North and in the
West, who silently hoped that the promises made during
Reconstruction were finally going to be kept. While in the
"white" American community Jimmy Carter's candidacy
provoked an interest in the nuances of southern speech and
in the ingredients of southern cooking, in the "black" American community the visibility of Carter—his speaking in a
black Baptist church, his walking the streets of Harlem and
Detroit—seemed to symbolize the emergence of a southern
culture, of which they had long been a part, into the broader
American imagination. The emergence of Carter suggested a

kind of reconciliation between two peoples shaped by this common culture. His appearance was a signal to refugees from the South—settled somewhat comfortably in other regions—that we were now being encouraged to reoccupy native ground. There were many of us who turned our imaginations toward the ancestral home.

I had left the South at twenty-one, a product of its segregated schools and degrading institutions, and had managed to make a career for myself in the North. Growing up in the South during those twenty-one years, I had never had a white friend. And although in later years I had known many white southerners in the North and in the West, these relationships had been compromised by the subtle fact that a southerner, outside the South, is often viewed as outside his proper context, and is sometimes as much of an outsider as a black American.

Friendships grounded in mutual alienation and self-consciously geared to the perceptions of others are seldom truly tested. They lack an organic relationship to a common landscape, a common or "normal" basis for the evolution of trust and mutual interest. Mutual self-interest—the need of the white southerner to appear "right" in the eyes of sometimes condescending northerners (the South being the traditional scapegoat on all matters racial) and the need of the black southerner for access to somewhat commonly held memories of the South and of southern culture—is the basis for political alliances rather than friendships. To achieve this true friendship, it is necessary for the two southerners to meet on southern soil. And if growing up in the South never presented this opportunity, and if one is still interested in "understanding" that part of oneself that the "other" possesses, it becomes necessary to return to the South. Ironically, while the candidacy of Jimmy Carter represented a political alliance between white and black southerners, the real meaning of the alliance, in 1976 at least, resided in the quality of the personal relationships between these two separate but same peoples on their home ground, in the homeplace. Perhaps this is what I was looking for in the fall of 1976, at Thomas Jefferson's University of Virginia.

I remember two incidents from those first days at Virginia, while I sat in David Levin's book-lined office. An over-refined and affected young man from Texas came in to inquire about my courses, and as I rose from my chair to greet him, he raised his hand in a gesture that affirmed the Old South tradition of noblesse oblige. He said, "Oh, no, no, no, no! You don't have to get up."

The second incident was the sound of a voice, and came several days later. It was in the hall outside my office door and it was saying, "I'm Jimmy Carter and I'm running for President, I'm Jimmy Carter and I'm running for President." The pitch and rhythms of the voice conveyed the necessary messages: the rhythm and intonation were southern, lower-middle-class or lower-class-southern, the kind that instantly calls to mind the word *cracker.* Its loudness, in the genteel buzz and hum of Wilson Hall, suggested either extreme arrogance or a certain insecurity. Why the voice repeated Carter's campaign slogan was obvious to anyone: the expectations of the South, especially of the lower-class and middle-class South, were with Carter. He was one of them. His campaign promised to redefine the image of those people whom William Faulkner had found distasteful, those who were replacing a decadent and impotent aristocracy. These were the people whose moral code, beyond a periodically expressed contempt for black Americans, had remained largely undefined in the years since Faulkner.

The bearer of this voice, when he appeared in my doorway, conformed to the herald that had preceded him. He was wiry and tall, just a little over six feet, with very direct, deepseeing brown eyes. His straw-blond hair lacked softness. In his face was that kind of half-smile/half-grimace that says, "I've seen it all and I still say, 'So what?' " He wore a checkered flannel shirt, faded blue-jeans, and a round brass U.S. Army–issue belt buckle over a slight beer belly. I think he also wore boots. He stood in the doorway, looking into the handsomely appointed office, and said, "Buddy, I want to work with you."

His name, after I had asked it again, was still Breece Pancake.

There was something stiff and military in his bearing. I immediately stereotyped him as of German ancestry (in the South, during its many periods of intolerance, German names have been known to metamorphose into metaphorical Anglo-Saxon ones, Gaspennys and perhaps Pancakes included). He had read some of my work, he said, and wanted to show me some of his. His directness made me wary of him. While I sat at a desk (in academia, a symbol of power), he seemed determined to know me, the person, apart from the desk. In an environment reeking with condescension, he was inviting me to abandon my very small area of protection.

He asked if I drank beer, if I played pinball, if I owned a

gun, if I hunted or fished. When these important *cultural* points had been settled, he asked, almost as an afterthought, if he could sign up to do independent study with me. When we had reached agreement, he strolled back out into the hall and resumed shouting, "I'm Jimmy Carter and I'm running for President! I'm Jimmy Carter and I'm running for President!" I recall now that there was also in his voice a certain boastful tone. It matched and complemented that half-smile of his that said, "So what?" Breece Pancake was a West Virginian, that peculiar kind of mountain-bred southerner, or part-southerner, who was just as alienated as I was in the hushed gentility of Wilson Hall.

The University of Virginia, during that time at least, was as fragmented as the nation. There were subtle currents that moved people in certain directions, toward certain constituency groups, and I soon learned that it was predictable that Breece Pancake should come to my office seeking something more than academic instruction. The university, always a state-supported school, had until very recently functioned as a kind of finishing school for the sons of the southern upper class. About a generation before, it had opened its doors to the sons of the middle class. And during the 1960s it had opened them farther to admit women and black students. In an attempt to make the institution a nationally recognized university, an effort was made to attract more students from the affluent suburbs of Washington and from the Northeast. More than this, an extraordinarily ambitious effort was made to upgrade all the departments within the university. Scholars had been recruited from Harvard and Princeton and Standford and Berkeley and Yale. The institution claimed intellectuals from all parts of the world. The faculty became and remains among the best in the nation.

But these rapid changes, far from modifying the basic identity of the institution, caused a kind of cultural dislocation, a period of stasis in the attempted redefinition of the basic institutional identity. In many respects, it was like a redecoration of the interior of a goldfish bowl. Many of the sons of the southern gentry, seeking the more traditional identity, began attending Vanderbilt, Tulane, Chapel Hill, and Washington and Lee. And while the basic identity of the school remained southern, very few southerners were visible. One result was the erosion of the values that had once given the institution an identity. Another was stratification by class and color considerations. Preppies banded together. So did women. So did the few black students. So did, in their fraternities and clubs, the remnants of the old gentry.

Ironically, the people who seemed most isolated and insecure were the sons and daughters of the southern lower and middle classes. They had come to the place their ancestors must have dreamed about—Charlottesville is to the South what Cambridge is to the rest of the nation—and for various reasons found themselves spiritually far from home. Some of them expressed their frustrations by attacking the traditional scapegoats—black teachers and students. Others began to parody themselves, accentuating and then assuming the stereotyped persona of the hillbilly, in an attempt to achieve a comfortable identity. Still others, the constitutional nonconformists like Breece Pancake, became extremely isolated and sought out the company of other outsiders.

A writer, no matter what the context, is made an outsider

by the demands of his vocation, and there was never any doubt in my mind that Breece Pancake was a writer. His style derived in large part from Hemingway, his themes from people and places he had known in West Virginia. His craftsmanship was exact, direct, unsentimental. His favorite comment was "Bull*shit!*" He wasted no words and rewrote ceaselessly for the precise effect he intended to convey. But constitutionally, Breece Pancake was a lonely and melancholy man. And his position at the university—as a Hoyns Fellow, as a teaching assistant, and as a man from a small town in the hills of West Virginia—contributed some to the cynicism and bitterness that was already in him. While his vocation as a writer made him part of a very small group, his middle-class West Virginia origins tended to isolate him from the much more sophisticated and worldly middle-class students from the suburbs of Washington and the Northeast, as well as from the upper-class students of southern background. From him I learned something of the contempt that many upper-class southerners have for the lower- and middle-class southerners, and from him I learned something about the abiding need these people have to be held in the high esteem of their upper-class co-regionalists. While I was offered the opportunity to be invited into certain homes as an affirmation of a certain tradition of noblesse oblige, this option was rarely available to Breece (an upper-class southerner once told me: "I like the blacks. They're a lot like European peasants, and they're *cleaner* than the poor whites"). Yet he was always trying to make friends, on any level available to him. He was in the habit of giving gifts, and once he complained to me that he had been reprimanded by a family for not bringing to them as many fish as he had promised to catch. To make up this deficiency, he had purchased with his own money additional fish, but not enough to meet the quota he had promised. When he was teased about this, he commented to me, "They acted as if they wanted me to tug at my forelock."

> You may keep the books or anything Breece gave you—he loved to give but never learned to receive. He never felt worthy of a gift—being tough on himself. His code of living was taught to him by his parents— be it Greek, Roman or whatever, it's just plain old honesty. God called him home because he saw too much dishonesty and evil in this world and he couldn't cope.
>
> Letter from Mrs. Helen Pancake, February 5, 1981

And I won't be running from the rain, when I'm gone
And I can't even suffer from the pain, when I'm gone
There's nothing I can lose or I can gain, when I'm gone
So I guess I'll have to do it while I'm here.

And I won't be laughing at the lies, when I'm gone
And I can't question how or when or why, when I'm gone
Can't live proud enough to die, when I'm gone
So I guess I'll have to do it while I'm here.

"When I'm Gone," Phil Ochs

Breece Pancake seemed driven to improve himself. His ambition was not primarily literary: he was struggling to define for himself an entire way of life, an all-embracing code of values that would allow him to live outside his home valley in Milton, West Virginia. The kind of books he gave me may suggest the scope of his search: a biography of Jack London, Eugene O'Neill's plays about the sea—works that concern the perceptions of men who looked at nature in the raw. In his mid-twenties Breece joined the Catholic Church and became active in church affairs. But I did not understand the focus of his life until I had driven through his home state, along those winding mountain roads, where at every turn one looks down at houses nestled in hollows. In those hollows, near those houses, there are abandoned cars and stoves and refrigerators. Nothing is thrown away by people in that region; some use is found for even the smallest evidence of affluence. And eyes, in that region, are trained to look either up or down: from the hollows up toward the sky or from the encircling hills down into the hollows. Horizontal vision, in that area, is rare. The sky there is circumscribed by insistent hillsides thrusting upward. It is an environment crafted by nature for the dreamer and for the resigned.

Breece once told me about his relationship with radio when he was growing up, about the range of stations available to him. Driving through those mountains, I could imagine the many directions in which his imagination was pulled. Like many West Virginians, he had been lured to Detroit by the nighttime radio stations. But he was also conscious of the many other parts of the country, especially those states that touched the borders of his own region. Once, I asked him how many people there were in the entire state of West Virginia. He estimated about two or three million, with about a hundred thousand people in Huntington, then the state's largest city. It was a casual question, one with no real purpose behind it. But several days later I received in my mailbox a note from him: "Jim, I was wrong, but proportionally correct (Huntington, W.VR. has 46,000 people). To the west, Ohio has approximately 9 million. To the east, Virginia has approx. 4 million. To the south, Kentucky has approximately 3 million. To the north, Pa. has approx. 11 million. West Virginia—1,800,000—a million more than Rhode Island. P.S. See you at lunch tomorrow?" It need not be emphasized that he was very self-conscious about the poverty of his state, and about its image in certain books. He told me he did not think much of Harry Caudill's *Night Comes to the Cumberlands.* He thought it presented an inaccurate image of his native ground, and his ambition, as a writer, was to improve on it.

This determination to improve himself dictated that Breece should be a wanderer and an adventurer. He had attended several small colleges in West Virginia, had traveled around the country. He had lived for a while on an Indian reservation in the West. He had taught himself German. He taught for a while at a military academy in Staunton, Virginia, the same one attended by his hero, Phil Ochs. He had great admiration for this songwriter, and encouraged me to listen closely to the lyrics of what he considered Ochs's best song, "Jim Dean of Indiana." Breece took his own writing just as seriously, placing all his hopes on its success. He seemed to be under self-imposed pressures to "make it" as a writer. He told me once: "All I have to sell is my experience. If things get really bad, they'll put you and me in the same ditch. They'll pay *me* a little more, but I'll still be in the ditch." He liked to impress people with tall tales he had made up, and he liked to impress them in self-destructive ways. He would get into fights in lower-class bars on the outskirts of Charlottesville, then return to the city to show off his scars. "These are stories," he would say.

He liked people who exhibited class. He spoke contemptuously of upper-class women with whom he had slept on a first date, but was full of praise for a woman who had allowed him to kiss her on the cheek only after several dates. "She's a lady," he bragged to me. I think that redefining himself in terms of his *idea* of Charlottesville society was very important to Breece, even if that idea had no basis in the reality of the place. Yet there was also an antagonistic strain in him, a contempt for the conformity imposed on people there. We once attended a movie together, and during the intermission, when people crowded together in the small lobby, he felt closed in and shouted, "Move away! Make room! Let people through!" The crowd, mostly students, immediately scattered. Then Breece turned to me and laughed. "They're clones!" he said. "They're *clones!*"

He loved the outdoors—hunting and fishing and hiking in the Blue Ridge Mountains. Several times he took me hiking with him. During these outings he gave me good advice: if ever I felt closed in by the insularity of Charlottesville, I should drive up to the Blue Ridge and walk around, and that would clear my head. He viewed this communion with nature as an absolute necessity, and during those trips into the mountains he seemed to be at peace.

He also loved to play pinball and pool and to drink beer. He was very competitive in these recreations. He almost always outdrank me, and when he was drunk he would be strangely silent. He sat stiff and erect during these times, his eyes focused on my face, his mind and imagination else-where. Sometimes he talked about old girlfriends in Milton who had hurt him. He related once his sorrow over the obli-gation imposed upon him—by a librarian in Milton—to burn and bury hundreds of old books. He liked old things. He talked about hunting in a relative's attic for certain items that once belonged to his father. He recollected letters his fa-ther had written, to his mother and to him, in the years be-fore his death.

Breece Pancake drank a great deal, and when he drank his imagination always returned to this same place. Within that private room, I think now, were stored all his old hurts and all his fantasies. When his imagination entered there, he be-came a melancholy man in great need of contact with other people. But because he was usually silent during these peri-ods, his presence tended often to make other people nervous. "Breece always hangs around," a mutual friend once said to me. He almost never asked for anything, and at the slightest show of someone else's discomfort, Breece would excuse himself and compensate—within a few hours or the next day—with a gift. I don't think there was anyone, in Char-lottesville at least, who knew just what, if anything, Breece expected in return. This had the effect of making people feel inadequate and guilty.

Jim, "Bullshit" was one of B's choice sayings—in fact he used to say he wanted his short stories entitled "Bullshit Artist." Love his heart!

Letter from Mrs. Helen Pancake, February 5, 1981

The mad director knows that freedom will not make
   you free,
And what's this got to do with me?
I declare the war is over. It's over. It's over.

"The War Is Over," Phil Ochs

In the winter of 1977 I went to Boston and mentioned the
work of several of my students, Breece included, to Phoebe-
Lou Adams of the *Atlantic*. She asked to be sent some of his
stories. I encouraged Breece to correspond with her, and very
soon afterward several of his stories were purchased by the
magazine. The day the letter of acceptance and check arrived,
Breece came to my office and invited me to dinner. We went
to Tiffany's, our favorite seafood restaurant. Far from being
pleased by his success, he seemed morose and nervous. He
said he had wired flowers to his mother that day but had not
yet heard from her. He drank a great deal. After dinner he
said that he had a gift for me and that I would have to go
home with him in order to claim it.

He lived in a small room on an estate just on the outskirts
of Charlottesville. It was more a workroom than a house, and
his work in progress was neatly laid out along a square of
plywood that served as his desk. He went immediately to a
closet and opened it. Inside were guns—rifles, shotguns,
handguns—of every possible kind. He selected a twelve-
gauge shotgun from one of the racks and gave it to me. He
also gave me the bill of sale for it—purchased in West Virginia—and two shells. He then invited me to go squirrel
hunting with him. I promised that I would. But since I had

never owned a gun or wanted one, I asked a friend who lived on a farm to hold on to it for me.

Several months later, I found another gift from Breece in my campus mailbox. It was a trilobite, a fossil once highly valued by the Indians of Breece's region. One of the stories he had sold the *Atlantic* had "Trilobites" as its title.

There was a mystery about Breece Pancake that I will not claim to have penetrated. This mystery is not racial; it had to do with that small room into which his imagination retreated from time to time. I always thought that the gifts he gave were a way of keeping people away from this very personal area, of focusing their attention on the persona he had created out of the raw materials of his best traits. I have very little evidence, beyond one small incident, to support this conclusion, but that one incident has caused me to believe it all the more.

The incident occurred one night during the summer of 1977. We had been seeing the films of Lina Wertmuller, and that evening *Seven Beauties* was being shown at a local theater. I telephoned Breece to see if he wanted to go. There was no answer. When I called later I let the telephone ring a number of times. Finally, a man answered and asked what I wanted. I asked for Breece. He said I had the wrong number, that Breece did not live there anymore. There was in the tone of his voice the abrupt authority of a policeman. He then held the line for a moment, and in the background I could hear quick and muffled conversation between Breece and several other people. Then the man came on the line again and asked my name and number. He said that Breece would call me back. But then Breece himself took the telephone and asked what it was I wanted. I mentioned the movie. He said he could not see it because he was going to West Virginia that same evening, but that be would get in touch with me when he returned. I left town myself soon after that, and did not see Breece again until early September. That was when he gave me the trilobite, and shortly afterward he made me promise that I would never tell anyone about the night I called him the summer before.

In the early summer of 1978 I left Charlottesville for New Haven, Connecticut. Carter was still President, but my ideas about the South had changed dramatically. I hoped that, with luck, I would never have to return to Charlottesville. I began making plans to resume my old lifestyle as a refugee from the South. But if life has any definition at all, it is the things that happen to us while we are making plans. In the early fall of that year I found out that I would be a father before spring arrived. Around that same time, a package from Breece, mailed from Charlottesville, arrived at my apartment in New Haven. I did not open it. I knew there would be a gift inside, but I also knew that renewing my connection with Breece would take my memories back to Charlottesville, and I wanted to be completely free of the place. The package from Breece remained unopened until the late evening of April 9, 1979.

On the evening of April 8 I had a dream that included Breece. I was trapped in a room by some menacing and sinister people and they were forcing me to eat things I did not want to eat. Breece was there, but I cannot remember the part he played in the drama. I woke up before dawn to find that my wife's contractions had begun. The rest of the day was spent in the delivery room of the Yale–New Haven Hospital. In the late afternoon I went to the Yale campus and taught a class, which earned me one hundred dollars. Then I walked home, happy with the new direction my life had taken as the hardworking father of Rachel Alice McPherson. At my apartment, however, there was a telegram from John Casey, sent from Charlottesville. It informed me that on the previous night Breece Pancake had killed himself.

I called Charlottesville immediately and was told certain facts by Jane Casey, John's wife. Breece had been drinking. He had, for some reason, gone into the home of a family near his little house and had sat there, in the dark, until they returned. When he made a noise, either by getting up or by saying something, they became frightened and thought he was a burglar. Breece ran from the house to his own place. There, for some reason, he took one of his shotguns, put the barrel in his mouth, and blew his head off.

I have never believed this story.

I speculate that Breece had his own reasons for hiding in a neighbor's house. They may have had to do with personal problems, or they may have had to do with emotional needs. Whatever their source, I am sure his reasons were extraordinary ones. As a writer, if I am to believe anything about Breece's "suicide," extract any lesson from it, that lesson has to do with the kind of life he led. I believe that Breece had had a few drinks and found himself locked inside that secret room he carried around with him. I believe that he had scattered so many gifts around Charlottesville, had given signals to so many people, that he felt it would be all right to ask someone

to help him during what must have been a very hard night. I
believe that he was so inarticulate about his own feelings, so
frightened that he would be rejected, that he panicked when
the couple came home. Whatever the cause of his desperation, he could not express it from within the persona he had
created. How does one say he expects things from people after
having cultivated the persona of the Provider? How does one
explain the contents of a secret room to people who, though
physically close, still remain strangers? How does one recon-
cile a lifetime of indiscriminate giving with the need for a
gesture as simple as a kind word, an instant of basic human
understanding? And what if this need is so bathed in bitterness and disappointment that the attempt itself, at a very
critical time, seems hopeless except through the written
word? In such a situation, a man might look at his typewriter,
and then at the rest of the world, and just give up the struggle. Phil Ochs hanged himself. Breece Pancake shot himself.
The rest of us, if we are lucky enough to be incapable of imagining such extreme acts of defiance, manage to endure.

Very late in the evening of the day I got the news, I opened
the package that Breece had sent me the previous fall. It contained some old photographs of railroad workers, some poetry, and a letter. The first line of the letter told the entire
story: "You are under no obligation to answer this." But he
had hoped anyway that I would. The pictures were from his
family collection, given to him in trust by his aunt Julia, who
was soon to die. He wanted to give them away rather than sell
them. The poetry represented an extension of this same impulse. "Also enclosed are some poems you might find interesting—again, I'm not asking for response, just sharing

news. I went to Staunton Correctional Institution (the pen) and stumbled onto this guy [an inmate]. Not knowing anything about poetry, I gave [his poems] to [the poet] Greg Orr. . . . He liked them and is doing what he can to help find the proper market thru CODA. Anyway, what was that Latin phrase about the Obligation of Nobility? If it's what I think it means—helping folks—it isn't bad as a duty or a calling. We'd both better get back to work."

Looked at in purely sociological terms, Breece Pancake's work was helping people, giving to people. I think that part of him, the part of West Virginia that borders on Virginia, wanted to affirm those old, aristocratic, eighteenth-century values that no longer had a context, especially in Charlottesville. He was working toward becoming an aristocrat in blue jeans. But he was from the southern lower-middle class, his accent had certain associations, he could find no conventional way to express his own needs, and while he was alive there were many of us who could not understand who or what he was.

Several weeks later, I sent the fossil he had given me, the trilobite, to the girl who had allowed him to kiss her cheek after several dates. She had left Charlottesville, and was then working in New York.

Grant Hall

Oikoumene

When I first settled into Iowa City, Iowa, which is approximately one hundred miles from the midpoints between the two coasts, athletics were of absolutely no interest to me. My chief concern was making a home for myself and getting on with my career as a teacher, which would, in turn, support my writing. For most of my life I had been on the move. I had spent my first seventeen years in Savannah, Georgia; then two more years in Atlanta; then one year in Baltimore; then another year in Atlanta; then three years in Cambridge; then one year in Iowa City; then two years in Santa Cruz; then one year in Berkeley, part of which was spent commuting to Chicago; then one year in Cranston, Rhode Island; then two years in San Francisco; then another year in Baltimore; then two years in Charlottesville, Virginia; then one year in New Haven; then two more years in Charlottesville. Then, in 1981, I returned to Iowa.

Back in 1969, before I left Iowa City for Santa Cruz, I had lived for one year in an apartment on Brown Street. In June of 1981, when I returned to Iowa City, I rented an apartment on Gilbert Street, just around the corner from the Brown Street apartment. I considered this juxtaposition an act of

Fate, a sign that perhaps I was *meant* to be in Iowa City; or, again perhaps, there had been something I missed when I first lived here. I tried my best to settle in. During all those years on the road, I had believed that I had been building some *oikoumene* thing in the Greek sense of the *oikoumene,* the places where there are homes. But friends of mine had been observing my movements in another light. One of them said, "Ever since we met you, Jim, you've been *running.* Why don't you settle in someplace and get some work done?" I have now lived in Iowa City for seventeen years, about as long as I lived in Savannah, Georgia. I have circled Home.

When I lived in Iowa in 1968–69, I had never really been there. Officially, I was enrolled in the M.F.A. program in the Writers' Workshop, but unofficially I was already a writer. I took the required courses, taught undergraduates in the Rhetoric program, might have attended some of the readings and a few of the parties; but each Friday afternoon, without fail, I would take the bus into Chicago to spend the weekend with a Chicago street gang named, then, the Blackstone Rangers. I was writing a series of articles on this gang for the *Atlantic.* I returned to Iowa City Sunday evenings, or well after midnight, and if there was too much snow, or if it was too late to walk from the bus station to my apartment on Brown Street, I would go to my office in the old Rhetoric Building and sleep on the floor. I always kept a toothbrush and a washcloth there, so I could be presentable for my Rhetoric class early on Monday mornings. I lived then, for some reason, a very spartan kind of life. During that year, I learned very little about Iowa City, about the life of the campus and the communal life beyond it. Someplace, in the distant background of my memories of that time, there are the sounds of cheering fans, images of colorful floats parading through the downtown area, details of stories about athletes in the student paper. The woman whom I would eventually date, Maxine Thomas, was selected as the Homecoming Queen for 1968. I remember a picture of her, smiling benevolently and holding roses and waving, seated atop the rear seat of a convertible in a Homecoming Parade. The first black Homecoming Queen was also a first-year law student, and a mutual interest in the law became one of the bases of our bond. He appeal had absolutely nothing to do with her tenuous connection with athletics. It would be accurate to say that, at the time, I harbored a profound distaste for athletes and their world. Since my early college years, I had ignored athletic games. I never attended them, never cared to watch them on television. I had never consciously established a friendship with a known athlete.

But in the fall of 1981, when I had a desperate need to fit into the community, a friend gave me some sage advice. "Now Mac," he told me, "you are living in a Teutonic community, and sports are a great part of this community's life. You should take an active interest in them." My friend was right. Beginning in late August, the mind of the entire community turned to football. Symbols of the Iowa Hawkeyes appeared everywhere. Sorority girls paraded before their sorority houses shaking black-and-gold pom-poms. And beginning in September, almost every Saturday, thousands of cars would sweep into Iowa City, from all the small towns, for the games in Kinnick Stadium. Long processions of people, most of them wearing black and gold, would walk almost the entire length of Burlington Street to crowd into the stadium. The Episcopal priest of the church I joined was also an announcer for the football games. He always gave me the soul handshake in the greeting line after his sermons.

A book that appeared during this time, *The Courting of Marcus Dupree,* by Willie Morris, provided me with a telling insight. "In the East," Morris wrote, "college football is a cultural exercise. On the West Coast, it is a tourist attraction. In the Midwest, it is cannibalism. But in the South, it is a religion." I have kept this insight in mind for many years because I believe there is some truth in it. But the truth, I think, goes far deeper than football itself. Instead, on its deeper levels, Willie Morris's insight may say something profound about the differences between the *styles* of the various regions.

Iowa City was intentionally planned to be a polis. Its model was Philadelphia, but also the style of Athens. According to one of the city's historians, Laurence Lafore, Iowa City was planned as an exemplar of the decisive and pervasive influence of Greek and Roman ideals in American life, and in a way that would have been intelligible to people in the seventeenth century as the opposite of the word *gothic.* Doric, Ionian, and Corinthian columns are still visible in university buildings and in some of the older houses. The Athens inhabited by Socrates and Aristotle and Plato was a polis in which everyone knew everyone else. It was a village with a cosmopolitan sense. Iowa City is such a village. It is not the antidemocratic polis of Socrates, who believed that everyone was good at some *one* thing and should be restricted to that one labor. It is a polis in which the president of a bank can be a former athlete, where the Episcopal priest sees no conflict between sermons and sports announcing. It is a city in which bus drivers and garbage men and clerks and postal workers almost always have advanced degrees. People delight in living here. Neighbors will shovel the snow off your sidewalk simply because they shovel in a straight line. Iowa City began as an attempt to reproduce the civil perfection of Athens in the American wilderness. Its subscription to democratic principles encouraged the same cosmopolitan sense that was in Athens, especially with respect to tolerance. Churches of every denomination have always co-existed in Iowa City. The only African Methodist Episcopal church, Bethel A.M.E. Church at 411 S. Governor Street, was built in 1868. Many of the homes in Iowa City were once stations on the Underground Railway. Runaway slaves were hidden in coal cellars and attics of homes I have visited. Someone has said that civilization rests on two very fragile bases—high culture and good topsoil. Both are in Iowa City in abundance. But there is also a feeling of Greek civic virtue combined with Roman cosmopolitanism.

This was the thing I had returned to Iowa City to learn.

Polis

The first order of business, then, was for me to renew my severed connection with the world of sports. The most important connection emerged from within the unusual blending of culture and democracy of which I have already written. A white male student from my first writing class here, in the summer of 1981, approached me that same fall for a favor. He explained that he was helping a black former athlete named Tyrone Dye (also known, from his days as a fullback on the Iowa team, as Rodan) to write his life story. He wanted me to meet Tyrone Dye and help them with the book. I agreed to this meeting out of a somewhat paternalistic sense that I might be able to do something for a poor athlete. We met for lunch at Hamburger Inn No. 2, my favorite restaurant in Iowa City. The former student entered with a very tall and very huge black man whose appearance immediately frightened me. He reminded me of something from which I had been running for most of my adult life. Like my return to Iowa City to live one-half block away from my old apartment, the image of Tyrone Dye took my memories back to my own college years in Atlanta, and to another huge black athlete named Tank. I had feared him.

But this present version of Tank was a gentle giant. There was something of a shy little boy in this eight-foot-tall, three-hundred-or-more-pound black man. Sitting, he filled the entire side of the table. His eyes moved quickly. He remained silent while the young writer told Tyrone Dye's story. He was born in Gary, Indiana, sometime during the 1950s to a mother who did not want him. Because she did not want him, or because of his size, she locked him in the basement most of the time when he was a child. He knew very little about his father, and the other children teased him and called him Rodan. He claimed to be related to the family of Michael Jackson. A high school football coach took an interest in him, and he was trained to be a gladiator, what the ancient Romans called *bustuarii*. His *lanista,* or his coach, must have trained him for the specific purpose of being recruited by some college. Indeed, he was recruited, by Iowa, during the early 1970s. He quickly became a star, Saturday's Hero, and he learned that his job was to be ferocious on the playing field. His legend as a star began here. I saw pictures of him in football gear, in the sacred black and gold. He seemed to be straining to look ferocious. Because he was a star, a man of importance to the Iowa team, he was passed along in his classes. Things were made easy for him, as they were for other stars on the team. The goal of the team seemed to be winning, and to the extent that Tyrone Dye's presence guaranteed many wins, he remained a star, and was also cannibalized academically.

During his senior year he was recruited by the Washington Redskins. After graduation from Iowa, without being able to read or write, Tyrone reported to the Redskins training camp in northern Virginia. His expectations were high, and he trained with enthusiasm. But during summer practice he broke a leg. The *lanistas* of that team, trying to get rid of him, insisted that he should still report for farm team practice. Tyrone, a true spartan partisan of *agoge,* got up early each morning to walk with crutches to the farm camp. One morning he was given a ride by an elderly white couple. When they saw his situation, they invited him to live in their home. They were deeply religious people, and Tyrone began calling them Mom and Dad. They wanted him to withdraw from the Washington Redskins training camp, but Tyrone refused. Tyrone says that one day, in the office of a Redskin *lanista,* a gun was pulled on him and he was ordered to sign a release. I never learned whether or not he signed the release, but soon after this incident Tyrone Dye returned to Iowa City. By this time his fame had faded, his time as a star had passed. Tyrone slept on the streets of Iowa City, even during the winter months. A family of poor whites finally took him in. He began to do odd jobs. He could get no higher work because, according to test results, even with a college degree he was illiterate.

Then a very beautiful thing, which involves the Athenian nature of Iowa City, took place. An old white woman named Miss Mary met Tyrone Dye in the Iowa Student Union, where he was sitting at a table trying to read a book. The two of them soon became a local legend. People began talking about the frail, elderly white woman and the huge black athlete meeting each morning at a table by the window in the dining room of the Iowa Student Union. They began with grade-school books, and then moved up, grade level by grade level. Tyrone Dye began to read. A little white female had passed on to him, against the sage advice of Socrates, the belief that he could do something more than be a killer fullback on the football field. Tyrone began reading his way into a better understanding of the world around him. Also, he began to make contact with his mother's family in Arkansas. He began to visit his Big Momma, his mother's mother. He began to visit his family back in Gary. He began to take religion seriously. He became a Hawkeye again, and he began giving pep talks to the team. He was invited to travel with the team for games in other parts of the country. But just to ensure people that he was still the Rodan of playing field fame, when some white policemen in Coralville, the next town from Iowa City, harassed him one night, Tyrone picked up one of them and threw him over the police car. But beyond this, he was still essentially a caring, gentle giant.

Now he wanted to write his story.

My heart went out to him, and I began to help him as best I could.

I began, then, to struggle with this new reality, to try to see deeper into the world that had produced Tyrone Dye. I met a track coach named Ted Wheeler, who had once won a gold medal at an Olympic event. He lived just around the corner from me, was from Georgia himself, and often invited me to his home for dinner. He grew collard greens in his backyard, and enjoyed cooking a pot of them for his friends and for the men on his team. Ted Wheeler is more than six feet tall, dresses elegantly, and is known to be a perfect gentleman. He also began to remind me of someone I had known before. There was an aristocratic manner about Ted Wheeler. He insisted that his runners excel in their academic work; he commanded them to violate Socrates' edict. He was always in deep trouble about this, but he always held his ground. Once, when an athlete was accused of raping a white female student in her dorm room, after everyone else had been convinced of the athlete's guilt, it was Ted Wheeler who put up his own home to support the athlete's bail and his legal fees. The rape had occurred back during the mid-1970s, but the athlete was not cleared of the charges until the middle-1980s. I began to admire Ted Wheeler.

I quickly learned that, since Iowa had always been a haven for black athletes, it was going to be assumed that I was also an athlete. There was at Iowa, during the early 1980s, a basketball coach named George Raveling. He seemed to be an eccentric, and his team began to lose games. In Hamburger Inn, during those years, I was almost certain to run into el-

derly people, coming into Iowa City from the country towns
to attend games. They would be polite with me, even sitting
at a table with me and sharing their newspapers. When the
proper degree of neighboring had been established, one of
them might look directly at me and whisper, "What's wrong
with George?" My own strategy became, of course, one of
passing as the most enthusiastic of fans. My password, especially during the Saturday Religious Ritual, when greeting
someone on the street, was the incantation "How 'Bout
Them Hawks?!!!" If I had to go into Seaton's Meat Market on
a sports day, I was sure to find all the butchers watching a
game on television. They had already assumed that I was an
athlete because all the black males they noticed were athletes. I did not disappoint them. If I had to go into Seaton's
on a Saturday, I always took my hammer along with me. I
would look soberly at the game in progress on the television
just to the right of the meat counter, and I would wave my
hammer and shout "Kill!!! Kill!!!" Such gestures eased my
transition into the heart of the community.

But in those days I was only acting.

Homoioi and Helots

The stereotypical images behind the images of Tyrone Dye
and Ted Wheeler came back to me in the summer of 1996 as
I watched the opening ceremonies of the Atlanta Olympics.
I saw Muhammad Ali, with a stern dignity imposed by
Parkinson's disease, bearing in a quivering hand the torch
that would light the fire, which in turn would signal the official opening of the Games. Muhammad Ali seemed much
larger than life at that moment, and I dwelt on the irony of

the moment. Peisistratids, a tyrant in late-fifth-century Athens, had established the first Pan-Atheniac procession in which all the people of Athens marched in a great procession to the Temple of Venus. This same Peisistratids the tyrant also sponsored the first written versions of the *Iliad* and the *Odyssey*. And he laid the basis for what, under Kleisthenes, his successor, would become the concept of *isonomia*—equality before the law—which, these many centuries later, would result in Muhammad Ali leading the Great Processional in Atlanta, a formerly segregated southern town. There was an abundance of significant history in this event, and as I watched some of the sporting events, for the first time in my life, I began to remember the athletes of my own day in Atlanta, and I began to put them into context, inspired by the insight in Willie Morris's observation that in the South football is a religion.

Willie Morris was talking about the style of ancient Sparta.

One requirement for all freshmen men at Morris Brown College, which I attended for three years, was that they live with the athletes in Grant Hall. The first image these country boys saw, when they arrived by bus or by train or by car from the small towns of Georgia, Alabama, and South Carolina, was the image of an athlete. His nickname was Tank, and he seemed much, much larger than his honorific. He was deep, dark, purple black, with gaps between his front teeth. He sat naked on the steps of Grant Hall, wearing only a red head rag, weighing a thick paddle in his right hand, testing its heft against the palm of his left hand. There was the stuff of ritual here. Morris Brown College, a private, working-class institution founded and supported by the African American Episcopal Church, was in continual struggle to prove itself equal to the much more affluent Morehouse (called "the whorehouse") and Spelman. While the two elite colleges were supported by white philanthropy, Morris Brown was mostly supported by the collection plates of ministers in the small towns of Georgia, Alabama, and South Carolina. Legend has it that the endowment of the college, in 1887, came from black washerwomen in the small towns who collected Octagon Soap wrappers, for their coupons, and who traded many thousands of them to the Octagon Soap Company for a certain amount of cash. On Founders Day, while white northern philanthropists visited the campuses of Morehouse and Spelman, gruff-speaking black ministers in shiny gabardine suits strolled across the Morris Brown campus, reaffirming its lower-class origins. Morris Brown made little pretense to academic excellence. The chosen path to fame was through the number of athletes trained there who would graduate into the starting lines of professional teams; or the number of accountants or teachers who would go back into the small towns, settle in them, have children, and send more poor students back to the college. The college song promised as much:

> Alma Mater, Pride of Earth
> Gavest to me another birth,
> Haven for all hungry souls,
> Feeding them shall be our goal. . . .

Tank's ritual purpose was to initiate the freshmen into this complex and ambiguous reality. While he had a sense of *his*

role, the freshmen did not have a sense of their *own*. This is
why they had to be instructed.

As in the Spartan martial utopia, athletes like Tank were of
the *homoioi*—the peers. They had already proved their worth
on football fields and basketball courts. Rough-and-tumble
country boys themselves, they came to Morris Brown College
already schooled in the norms of the *agoge,* the rough upbringing of the Spartan way of life. Perhaps the Latin word
bustuarii, gladiators, could be applied to them. If so, then perhaps the Greek word *helots*—serfs bound to the land, belonging to the entire Spartan state—could be applied to the
freshman boys. "Tank," "Bull" Thomas, Ivory Jones—these
bustuarii dominated Grant Hall. The football coach, the resident *lanista,* a man named Coach Thomas, was the master of
the dorm, lived in an apartment there with his family, and he
gave the athletes general license. It seemed to be their ritual
obligation, to a structure much larger than themselves, to
initiate the freshmen into the ways of the *homoioi* through
random beatings. They had access to all the room keys in
Grant Hall, and they used them religiously. Further proof of
their power was their connection with a patron—a very rich
black man, a homosexual—who lived close to the campus.
They called him Pal. They were his clients in the Roman
sense, his adopted sons. They told stories about visiting him
in his home and watching television with him. Whenever a
woman's face appeared on the screen, Pal would order, "Get
that bitch off!" They laughed a great deal over the power of
this refrain. They were served special meals in the cafeteria.
Their brothers dominated all the fraternities. Their temples
were the football field and the Joe Louis Gymnasium.

My roommate, a boy named Freddy Thomas, from a place called Eufala, Alabama, was a very sensitive and gentle soul. He and I quickly formed a bond. To avoid the company of the athletes in the communal shower, Freddy and I would get up each morning just before dawn. I can still hear his voice saying "Let's go down, Room." Freddy helped me with math while I helped him with English. Through some luck, Freddy had an easy relationship with Tank. He liked Freddy. On those ritual occasions when the Peers, with their communal keys, raided the rooms of the *helots,* Freddy and I sometimes had luck. While we pushed against the pressure of the door pushing in on us, Freddy would shout "Tank, Tank, *Tank!!!"* Once in a while, Tank's voice might be heard out in the hall. *"Y' all let Freddy alone!"* Freddy seemed to know the human side of Tank much better than I did.

Now, I remember back to those days because, besides the resemblance in size between Tank and Tyrone Dye, I can see more clearly the outline of a certain code coming into focus. Grant Hall *was* a rough approximation of a Spartan village. The freshmen boys *were* rough approximations of *helots.* The athletes *were bustuarii.* A group of country boys, some of them with intellectual ambitions, had been thrown into an institutional arrangement that had already settled on the athletes as elites. Their job became one of democratic leveling, one of forcing the freshman boys into accepting the pre-existing arrangement. In Sparta the *homoioi* often arranged "sacred missions" to kill *helots* who were too ambitious or too energetic, or who were getting too big for their settled status. Even the more enlightened Athenians, to protect their version of democracy, used secret ballots to ostracize, or to shun, those among them who had too much influence. Each year the people used broken pots to choose their victims. Those chosen were sent into exile for years, and would be recalled only under special circumstances. This process of leveling down, with roots in the very origins of democracy, made the athletes of Grant Hall the enforcers of *isonomia*—the code of complete equality—much more than they could ever imagine. They taught a life lesson that should have prepared anyone for the same rituals in the world outside Grant Hall.

They also made me into a kind of Spartan.

But I did not know this *then*. I did not know that such rituals helped to justify the expression of something deep in *human* nature. Even while I was tested and toughened and trained, I felt deep anger toward the athletes of Grant Hall. I could not appreciate the gift they were giving me, and I just did not understand the more perverse aspects of the *isonomia*.

My uncle, Thomas McPherson, was the chaplain of Morris Brown College. A recent graduate, Thomas had enrolled as a graduate student at the Interdenominational Theological Seminary just next door to the college. He was chaplain of the college during both my years in Grant Hall. His first order of business was to make attendance at vespers compulsory. Since many students, among them athletes, had other uses for the vespers hour, they cut it with an impunity that was religious. But Thomas retaliated by working with the dean to penalize this. A certain number of grade points were deducted if a certain number of vespers were missed. This enraged the athletes. They referred to him, privately, as Un-

cle Tom, among other things. Thomas had a habit of sitting
on the vespers platform with his left knee crossed over his
right leg at a distinctive angle. He became for the athletes
just as potent an image as Tank, seated naked on the steps of
Grant Hall, had become for me. One night the athletes came
to my room and took me away from any help that Freddy
might have given me. They blindfolded me and took me to a
room in another dormitory. They also brought another freshman named Jerome Tudas. He was a very bright man who
had already declared a major in physics. He was a mulatto,
was from New Jersey, and was extremely self-confident, if
not cocky, depending on one's point of view. Both Tudas and
I had been selected by the *homoioi* for one of their "sacred
missions."

"Is McPherson your uncle?" they asked me. I admitted to
this fact. They made me sit on a chair and ordered me to
cross my left knee over my right leg. It took a few tries and
some help from the athletes before my left leg was positioned
at just the angle they considered right. Then they ordered
me to hit Jerome Tudas. I refused. Then they ordered Jerome
Tudas to hit me. Tudas complied. Then they asked me to hit
Tudas. I refused. Then they asked Tudas to hit me. Tudas
complied. This exchange went on until, in either anger or in
frustration, Tudas, when his turn came around, hit me with
such force that I lost consciousness. When I recovered, most
of the athletes were gone. But Tudas was still there. He was
deeply sorry, and could not understand why I had kept refusing to hit him.

I know now that my only athletic skill, back then, was
running. In high school I had avoided athletics, in addition

to most other group activities. I had arrived at college unable even to dance. But I could run with great speed, and I moved across the campus with such swiftness that my best friend, Edward Halman, began calling me "The Flash." No one could see that I was juggling a great number of obligations. Besides the work required for my courses, I worked as a banquet waiter at the old Dinkler Plaza Hotel on Peachtree Street in downtown Atlanta. I could easily get to the Dinkler Plaza in fifteen minutes by running across the Hunter Street Bridge. I worked as a waiter at the Piedmount Driving Club in the Atlanta suburbs, and at Christmas break I worked as an extra in the post office. I worked part-time in the Morris Brown Library. And I worked as a janitor in Grant Hall. I also worked as an assistant to Dean Robinson, the dean of men. It seems that I was always running, and this continued to be my only athletic skill. But to complete the required course in gym, I purchased a jock strap and a sweat suit, and I reported to the Joe Louis Gymnasium on schedule each week, and went through the required training of an athlete. I was always missing baskets, could not dribble worth a damn, and could not manage headstands. Still, I was enthusiastic in my efforts. The basketball coach, a tall mulatto man, was both patient and kind. He was always encouraging, no matter how badly I performed.

When I was an assistant to Dean Robinson, one of my jobs was to sit at night in his office in Grant Hall and handle any small matters that might come up. Another responsibility was to clean the bathrooms of Grant Hall with Mr. Murchison, the school janitor. In this way I came to know the personal habits of pampered athletes. Dean Robinson always went home at the end of the day, and responsibility for Grant Hall then resided in Mr. Thomas, the resident *lanista,* the football coach, who lived with his family in a private apartment just behind Dean Robinson's office. My immediate supervisor was an older man, a graduate student at ITC. He was a former athlete, muscled narcissistically, and a member of Alpha Phi Alpha fraternity. I wanted very badly to pledge Alpha, but Dean Robinson, a cigar-chewing Phi Beta Sigma, had already hinted heavily that he expected me to pledge Sigma. The Alpha men were considered the intellectual and physical elites ("O when an Alpha Man walks down the street, he looks one-hundred per from head to feet. . . ."). Edward Halman, my best friend, had already pledged Alpha, and he was trying to bring me into the club. The older man in Dean Robinson's office, then, was my potential Big Brother. When I finally did buck Dean Robinson and pledged Alpha instead of Phi Beta Sigma, I delivered my soul into the small hands of this Big Brother.

I was soon required to take over his office hours, for which time he still collected pay. I was required to make a run, at any time of night he named, down Hunter Street to Pascal's to get him a fried chicken sandwich. I became his private *helot.* I was required to write love letters to girls on campus who had attracted his attention. Whenever I objected or refused, his reply was always "Then I'll see you in the Pledge Club meeting!" They beat you at Pledge Club meetings. Big Brothers from all the colleges in the Atlanta University Center, many of them former athletes, would turn up at these meetings in multitudes. They were smug, wore the Alpha colors, caressed thick, carefully polished wooden paddles,

66

also showing the Alpha colors. The pledges were required to "give up some skin" to any Big Brother who asked for it. The required technique was to bend over, holding one's balls with one hand and bracing oneself on the floor with the other. Then the Big Brothers would go to work. I never cried. Some of them were particularly hard on me because of their memories of compulsory vespers. Others suspected that I was a homosexual because I had never had a date or had even been seen with a girl. I can still remember this interrogation:

"Pledge McPherson, are you a punk?"

"No, Big Brother."

"When was the last time you had you some pussy?"

"Last week, Big Brother."

"On campus?"

"No, Big Brother. She lives in the city."

"What's her name and address?"

I gave the only Atlanta address I knew. It was my grandmother's address, my father's mother, who lived over a funeral parlor on a street many, many miles away from campus.

"Pledge McPherson, you better get yourself some pussy!"

I could take the beatings. But I could not take the constant orders, which I knew were calculated to degrade me. This was why I had refused to hit Jerome Tudas. One evening, during the pledge season, the Big Brother in Dean Robinson's office ordered me to make a run down Hunter Street to Pascal's to get him a fried chicken sandwich. Something in me had had enough. I said, "No. Get it yourself!" I even said, "No, *motherfucker!*" This was the first time, I think, that I had ever used this word in anger. Some nights later, at a basketball game in the Joe Louis Gym, this same Big Brother shouted to me from his bench on the other side of the basketball court, "Pledge McPherson, run down to Pascal's and get a fried chicken sandwich for my girlfriend!" I ignored him. He shouted again above the noise of the crowd: "You go and get that chicken sandwich or I'll burn your ass at Pledge Club meeting!"

Then I shouted back: "I'm not *going* to any more Pledge Club meetings. I *quit* the frat!"

Now, here in Iowa, these many years later, I still wonder what mysteries might have lain on the other side of true brotherhood *inside* the frat. I have read that those who survived the Spartan *Agoge,* the rough upbringing, moved into eating clubs, and from these a select few were elevated to the *homoioi*—the peers—who enjoyed complete equality and who had complete dedication to the Spartan State. Restriction was the key to all of Spartan life. At the height of Sparta's power, I have learned, there were only one thousand Spartans with pure citizenship. The others—the *parthenai* (the bastards), the *helots*—though they far outnumbered the *homoioi,* had no such rights. I know now that restrictive access is the key to *all* elite groupings. But the athletes in Grant Hall were the first to raise for me a certain question. What if the quality of the *agoge*—sleeping on beds made of bullrushes, taking cold baths, wearing a single garment, eating gruel made of pig's blood, hiding foxes under one's garment, and remaining stoical while the famished fox eats away at your own famished intestines—is *deficient* in compar-

ison with the quality of the tests you have set for *yourself?*
What if what resides *within* the mystery of full acceptance by
the Peers proves to be not worth the price that has already
been paid?

Over every stage of my life since Grant Hall, in areas far,
far removed from black American life, the voice of the Big
Brother in the Joe Louis Gymnasium has come back to me,
again and again and again. It always begins with your own
eagerness to commit to something, to pledge the frat. One
moves as far as one can with pure enthusiasm. Then a point is
always reached when something is asked which, if done,
would betray some part of oneself. This, I know now, is the
way of the world, the way of all greedy institutions. Even
street gangs, those now sophisticated enough to imitate the
rituals and norms of the higher levels of society, require their
pledges to take drugs, to vandalize cars, to prostitute themselves, even to kill other people. This has *always* been the
way of the world. Some infection of the soul diseased enough
to breed a degree of amorality that becomes normative, but
most especially an unwavering and fixed *loyalty,* must be the
price of admission to almost all elite groups, whether *homoioi*
or the athletes of Grant Hall. These rough-and-tumble men
taught me something essential, something that I have kept
in mind ever since. There is a point, which *always* comes,
when a certain trade-off is required for continued advance-
ment. One must watch carefully for this point, with the
practiced eye of a quarterback. One must *not* look for the ball
being thrown but rather for *any* patch of clear blue or green
space. Then one must *run* toward it, and *away* from catching
the ball and scoring the winning point and riding on the

shoulders, briefly, of one's peers. One must run like a *helot* from Grant Hall toward the Hunter Street Bridge and Peachtree Street. One must run like the wind, and not look back, no matter *what* it is that one is leaving behind. A certain amount of *self*-esteem resides in the quality of such a run. One must run like a fox, like an Athenian Greek, in one's own private Olympiad.

Deme

The Spartans were said to be like hedgehogs because they were slow, cautious, austere. They knew only one trick, but they knew it well. The Athenians, in contrast, were said to be like foxes. They were adaptable, clever, able to suffer defeats and then regroup and reverse those defeats. Socrates believed that, at least in his view of democracy, a person was good for only one thing. He might have been describing the Spartans rather than his fellow Athenians. Or he might have been describing the athletes of Grant Hall. I remember that late one night, during my second year in Grant Hall, a white policeman holding a gun brought one of the athletes into the lobby. He stood behind the athlete just outside Dean Robinson's office. The athlete had been arrested for either buying stolen property or receiving stolen property. He looked humble and afraid. The handcuffs on him, I believe now, had been calculated by the policeman to send a certain message to the other athletes. The handcuffs symbolized the prerogatives of the structure of white supremacy to invade, and even to dominate, the stronghold of the *homoioi*. An awareness of this prerogative was in the cold face and manner of the officer. The cuffed athlete had implicated others of his peers in the crime, the policeman said, and he was there to search the rooms of all the men named by this one humbled athlete. He had not bothered to get an official search warrant. I felt unequal to this problem, so I woke up Coach Thomas in his apartment behind Dean Robinson's office. Coach Thomas was a big man, a huge man, but he seemed to swell even larger when he confronted the smirking white policeman. But after he had listened to the allegations, he kept his attention, and his rage, focused on the athlete in handcuffs. "Did you receive stolen property?" he shouted at the athlete. The athlete began to moan and whine and whimper, like one of Richard Pryor's characters. "Aw, man, I didn't do nothin' . . ." "Did you receive any stolen property, and did you sell or give any to anybody here?" his *lanista* shouted. By this time all the athletes had come out of their rooms, as had the freshman boys, their *helots,* and had crowded into the lobby of Grant Hall. The white policeman, with his gun, seemed to be dominating all of us, except Coach Thomas. The athlete finally admitted to Coach Thomas that he had received some stolen property and had sold some of it to some of the other athletes. The coach required him to name all the men in the presence of the policeman. Then Coach Thomas shouted with absolute rage in his voice to all the assembled athletes, "I want you to go to your rooms and get every item that you got. I want you to bring it all down here." The athletes scattered, while the *lanista* looked at the policeman with a silent, studied fury. When the athletes had returned with their booty, Coach Thomas ordered them to give every item to the officer. Then he said to the policeman, "There it all is. You can take it. Now, don't you ever, ever,

ever, *ever* come into this dorm again without a search warrant! *Do you hear me?* Don't you *ever* try to raid this dorm again on a *bullshit tip!*" The coach was towering over the officer, almost unable to keep himself from attacking the little man in the blue uniform. In that moment I, and all the other *helots,* saw the deep country-boy fear drain out of the faces of the athletes, and we saw their renewed confidence, or manliness, returning. The *lanista* was leading his team again, and now they seemed ready to charge. The policeman saw it, too. There is a kind of self-hypnotic gaze that comes into the eyes of white people when they know they have power over black people. The sleepy, glazed eyes say that they have faded out of their individual selves and have merged with something much larger than themselves. This knowledge seems to be beneath the shallowness of their smiles. They seem unconsciously engaged with some mentoring voice suggesting *"Exterminate all the brutes!"* This same unconscious sense of self had been behind the policeman's power-smile from the moment he had entered Grant Hall. But after the words by Coach Thomas, the race-glaze faded into only the pale face of one individual white man facing a football team under the discipline of their coach. He gathered up the stolen items and hurried out the door of Grant Hall. "Now," Coach Thomas said, "I want all of you to go to your rooms and don't come out again!" They shuffled away like the hedgehogs they were, moaning and whining.

This was my sophomore year, and I began to respect Coach Thomas as a different kind of person than his athletes. When I worked at night in Dean Robinson's office, I would share my papers with him. Coach Thomas was a private, kindly man, one who was just trying to do his job and take care of his family. To the Romans, he would be a *lanista*—a member of the caste of men who bought and trained gladiators for the arena. But to me he became a role model of something larger than the Spartan code, the *agoge*, of Grant Hall. I did a paper on the life and death of Sir Walter Raleigh for a literature class and asked him to read it. He liked it, but could not understand why I chose to end the paper with Sir Walter's noble words when he was on the scaffold and about to die. I think that Coach Thomas was much more interested in the practical matter of winning one's way through life than he was in noble statements at the point of death. Football must have meant almost everything to him, but he still maintained the urbanity to endure the impracticalities of this world. I liked him.

During this time the Atlanta Public Library had just been integrated, and on Saturdays I would dress in my one suit and walk across the Hunter Street Bridge to Peachtree Street. I would turn left onto Peachtree and walk past Rich's, past the railroad station, past the Dinkler Plaza Hotel, and walk on to a place named Five Points. In this place five streets came together. On one corner there was an old Loew's theater featuring a permanent display of scenes from *Gone With the Wind.* On the Peachtree Street corner was the majestic Atlanta Public Library. I had never had any unrestricted social access to white people, and so I thought it proper to be at my best. This is why I wore my suit to the library. I just did not know the white customs of the country. Very few black people went into that library in those days immediately after its official desegration, but I was almost always there on Saturday mornings. The library allowed people to check out books, records, and paintings. I always borrowed as many as my library card allowed. The attendants were always gracious to me. I always returned the borrowed items on time.

During one trip away from the library, in my suit and with some borrowed paintings under my arm, a white man came up behind me on Peachtree Street. He moved quickly to my side, and with his right elbow he knocked me in the side as hard as he could. He said, *"Get on the other side of the street, goddamn nigger!"* Then he hurried on down Peachtree Street in his business suit. I gathered up the paintings, much more angry than hurt. Then I remembered Coach Thomas facing down the arrogant white policeman in the lobby of Grant Hall, and decided that I would not take this insult. I followed the man all the way down Peachtree Street, until we reached the area of the train station. Then he crossed the street and went into a bar. I followed him as far as the door, looked in, and saw him seated on a stool at the bar in a crowd of white men. A black woman was at the end of the bar washing glasses. I crossed Peachtree Street again and went up to a white policeman, who was directing traffic at the station. I said to him, "I want to report someone for assault and battery. He's now in that bar across the street." The policeman said he could not leave his post but would put in a call for someone else to hear my complaint. I crossed Peachtree Street again and waited outside the bar. I waited for almost an hour. Finally, a squad car pulled up, driven by a young white officer. I told him that the man I was charging with assault and battery was inside the bar. The officer looked intently at me, but he did walk with me to the bar door. I pointed to the white man in the business suit. The young officer looked puzzled, but he did go into the bar, from which I was happily segregated, and brought out the man. He was drunk, and must have been drunk when he elbowed me. I repeated my facts to the officer and to him. "Did you hit him and call him a nigger?" the young officer asked. The middle-aged man denied it. "Why," he said, "I happen to *love* nigras." He went back into the bar and soon came back out with the black woman, the dishwasher. "She knows me," he told the officer. "Tell him how much I like the culluds," he ordered the black woman. "Yassuh," she replied. "I know him," she said to the officer. "He likes the culluds. *Yassuh.*" The young officer called me aside. "If you complain," he told me, "you'll have to go downtown to sign some papers." "Let's go," I told him. He went back to the man in the suit and the black dishwasher. *"Yassuh,"* she kept insisting. "I knows him and he likes the culluds." The officer said that the three of us would have to go in his car to the police station. Then he took us to his car, and then we sat there, the officer behind the wheel and the drunk white man and I in the back seat. We sat there, equally arrested.

All of my life I had been passive. I was quiet and withdrawn. I did what my family expected of me. I seldom talked. I tried only to protect those few things that were of great importance to me. People called me shy, strange, a doormat, stoical, a person who could take it. I was all of these things, but I thought of myself as something more. In my private view, some things were of greater importance than others: not hitting Jerome Tudas at the order of someone else; refusing to return to the Pledge Club because this action would turn my life back over to the athletes who would become my tormentors again. I had already seen through the athletes. I had seen that they were Socrates' ideal citizens with a single skill. They were hedgehogs with only one way to exhibit their prowess. I did not want to be a hedgehog. Nor was it a matter of civil rights, which was then the new religion in the air. There were always group activities, based on theatrical demonstrations calculated to attract the attention of the media. I wanted to do something for *myself,* outside of any group involvement, something private but also *right* according to my own scale of values. And so we continued sitting in that police car, across Peachtree Street from the train station, while the Old Atlanta and the Becoming Atlanta—the white middle-aged man in the business suit and the young white policeman—silently anguished over the issue of what Atlanta would become.

The officer would not start the police car. He seemed intent on lecturing me on the byzantine procedures that awaited me once I filed my complaint. I would need a lawyer, bonds, fees, witnesses, court dates. The list went on and on. Most likely, he viewed me as an agitator, or as someone linked to a protest group who had set up this incident for purposes of publicity. He was torn between his legal duty to help me and his fear that he was being drawn into something beyond his own powers to even perceive or control. As for my assailant, he was then proving himself an unworthy antagonist, and even an unworthy white man. He put his hand on my shoulder, he patted me, he moaned. He straightened my tie, he apologized, he offered up a lifetime of heartfelt acts toward the cullud. The young white officer hated him—this was reflected by his face in the rearview mirror. While his sympathies were with his white compatriot and with the structure of white supremacy they shared, he was being forced, more and more, to sympathize with what was becoming for him a tragic distortion of what was supposed to be the best genetic expression of the human race. *Never allow a white man to cry in front of you. Afterwards he will hate you for seeing this show of weakness and will seek to do you harm.*

And so we sat there—the young officer listing the legal difficulties ahead of me, the drunk man fawning, and I torn between the two—while the car did not move. And then it came to me that I was degrading this drunk white man in the same way that he and his ancestors had degraded me and my ancestors, the way the athletes in Grant Hall had tried to degrade me. It came to me—not then, but afterwards—that the institution of racism was itself a kind of *homoioi,* that individuals were advanced from one level to another in the mind-set, simultaneously giving up the most human parts of themselves, until they reached the level of peers. This level was the point at which nothing else mattered except complete dedication to the race, or to the frat, or to the team. This was the only *good* left to contemplate.

I never knew whether or not the young officer ever understood the nature of the *human* issues his parked car raised; but his manner told me that, for an instant, he hated our fawning white companion much more than he hated me. As for me, I saw, for the first time in my life, the *fear* of a white man, and it made him *human,* not superior. I began to understand, then, that I should never get into the habit of oppressing anyone, because I could easily become like this empty, fawning white man.

I got out of the stalled police car and allowed the officer to have the victory he had tried so hard to plan. He could not see that my own victory, under such circumstances, would have been a Pyrrhic one. I walked away. When I got back to Grant Hall with my paintings and my story, Coach Thomas told me that I still had grounds for a civil rights suit against both the drunk white man and the police officer. I told Coach Thomas that I did not have the time and the energy and the money to follow through with the complaint. But privately, I did not want to become a hedgehog, knowing only one way to fight.

I wanted to get out of Grant Hall, and out of Atlanta. I wanted to find something worthy of defending by myself. I think I wanted to learn to improvise, to become an Athenian Fox, instead of a race-bound Spartan Hedgehog. I wanted to become anti-Socratesian in my actions, and work against the fate of a fixed purpose settled by single-mindedness. I wanted to run like the wind, toward something new and fresh and green.

Oikoumene

Ted Wheeler, the Iowa track coach, reminds me of the basketball coach at Morris Brown, a kindly man who gave me an *A* in Gym. I now find myself imposing on this nameless man an ethic that Ted Wheeler once explained to me: "Winning is not everything. When you win, somebody else loses, and you must feel human sympathy for that person." Ted Wheeler is an Athenian *lanista,* as was the Morris Brown *lanista* who gave me an *A* for mere effort.

It happened in this way: During the examination period of my first year at Morris Brown, I was still juggling responsibilities. I was still working with Mr. Murchinson, doing janitorial duties in and around Grant Hall. The morning of my final examination in Gym, during which I was expected to perform all the tumbles and headstands that had been practiced for a full year, I made my usual rounds of the bathrooms and staircases of Grant Hall. I scrubbed my usual toilets and collected the usual trash. Then I took the rubbish out of Grant Hall to a garbage collection unit. While I was dumping the trash, I misstepped and my left leg went between the gratings covering an underground sewer. The leg went through the grating all the way to my left kneecap, where my fall was stopped abruptly and where my left kneecap took the full weight of the stop. The kneecap was badly damaged in this way. I washed and bandaged the wound as best I could before putting on my jockstrap and my shorts and heading to the Joe Louis Gymnasium for my final exam. There I stood in line while the others demonstrated their mastery of the techniques. I remember that a man named Maddox was exceptionally good. When it was my turn I tumbled as best I could, did backrolls as best I could, did the assigned headstands. I did them no better and no worse than I had ever done them, except that the blood began seeping through the bandages on my left knee and I was in tremendous pain. The basketball coach, who was scoring our performances, watched me favor my left leg and saw the bloody bandage. He advised me to go immediately to the infirmary.

The *A* that came in the mail that summer taught something about the old Athenian idea of athletics. It taught that the discipline imposed on the body was intended to discipline the mind and the *spirit*.

Except for my grade in English, this was the most prized grade in my freshman year at Morris Brown.

A grade much higher than this one was awarded three years later, the day of my graduation from Morris Brown College. It happened in this way: During my three years at Morris Brown, I had never had a girlfriend. There were some girls that I liked, and one that I loved, but none of them ever responded to me. I had spent my junior year at Morgan State College, in Baltimore, and I fell in love with a girl there; but after my year at Morgan was over, I had to go back to Morris Brown, and the girl in Baltimore withdrew from me. From my freshman year on at Morris Brown, I had held on to a fantasy of sitting on a certain cement bench located under some trees on the lawn of the campus. For three years of running back and forth across the campus, I had envied the men who sat with their girlfriends on that bench. I believe that this slab of broken concrete represented for me the height of romantic love. It was superior to all my desires for sex and for love-tinged telephone calls in the night. I had had none of these things during my years at Morris Brown, but there was always the visible promise represented by the concrete bench.

There was a girl I had come to like, a warm, mature, older girl who had already graduated from Spelman College and who had ambitions to become a professional singer. But she was the girlfriend of Jerome Tudas. It happened that, during my senior year, I became editor of the yearbook as well as co-editor of the school newspaper. My office was on the ground-floor room on the left side of Grant Hall. Jerome Tudas, who was then a teaching assistant in the Physics Department, had an office just across the courtyard from me. His girlfriend, Jean Wayner, used to cook food for him in her sister's home and take it to him in the evenings. She often stopped by my office, on her way back home, to talk with me. She was a very pretty, very warm and refined young woman. She was always smiling. She listened to what I had to say, and she made me feel that I did indeed have something to say.

Near graduation, the day before the ceremony, Jerome Tudas and I had dinner at Pascal's. He bragged about the hot date he had for graduation night. He mentioned that a certain girl had had her hand under his black robe during graduation practice. He was confident in his belief that the next night his passion would be consummated. I asked Tudas if he would be taking out Jean Waymer after the graduation ceremonies. Tudas said that he had no plans for her. I then excused myself, went straight to a telephone, and called up Jean Waymer. I told her that Tudas had said that they would not be going out together after graduation. I asked if she would be willing to have dinner with me. Jean said yes.

After dinner at Pascal's on graduation night, I walked with Jean Waymer up Hunter Street and back to the Morris Brown campus. We walked slowly in the sweet, warm early June Atlanta evening. Jean Waymer always giggled at the slightest thing. She always smiled. We walked back to the almost deserted campus, and when we were on its lawn I asked Jean if she would do a favor for me before I took her back to her sister's house. I pointed out the concrete bench to her, under the trees on the lawn almost across from Grant Hall. I asked if she would sit on it with me. She laughed. But then she did walk with me across the lawn and sat with me on that bench, that love seat. We sat there for a long time in the birdsong-filled, sweet-leaves-smelling Atlanta evening. We sat there. Looking forward from that bench you could see Fountain Hall, the main teaching building. To the left of Fountain Hall was the other teaching building, Grant Hall. Most of its windows were dark. The freshman boys had already left and the only people in were Coach Thomas and his family and those athletes who had no place to go. I remembered back to the Christmas vacation of my own freshman year, when I worked as an extra in the Atlanta post office, and also as a waiter at the Dinkler Plaza Hotel. In the late evening hours I would walk across the Hunter Street Bridge and back to my room in a dark Grant Hall. Besides a few athletes who had no place to go, the place was dark and quiet and foreboding, the way it looked from the perspective of the concrete bench.

I tried to kiss Jean Waymer, but knew nothing about seduction. I had never thought beyond getting someone to sit with me on the bench. Jean Waymer giggled. Then she laughed. Then she kissed me. She kissed me for all of the days I had spent learning to be Spartan inside Grant Hall.

El Camino Real

Each day, from early morning until the evening hours, at the exit of the Town and Country Mall on El Camino Real in affluent Palo Alto, California, a middle-aged white man in a weathered gray down jacket and a brown touring cap stands, looking downward, always downward, while holding a cardboard sign. The sign reads: "I am a Christian man." This man is a professional beggar. Begging, it seems, has become his job, and he has established a prescriptive easement, if not a spiritual fee simple, in his space just at the exit of the affluent mall. The security guards never chase him away. Whenever someone, driving away from that consortium of upscale shops, stops and hands money to him, the solitary man becomes animated. He smiles, showing decayed teeth, and looks intently at the face beyond the hand reaching out of the car window. He smiles with the glow of communal connection. He says, always. "God bless you."

This broad commercial roadway, El Camino Real (Route 82), runs northward as far as San Francisco and as far southward, I have been told, through a great number of identical but differently incorporated communities, as Los Angeles and the

Pacific Coast. The Spanish conquistadores who first cut this highway named it "the Royal Road." It was aptly named. The rising affluence of this area of northern California, buoyed by the Silicon Valley to the south, has accelerated the number of standardized malls in each of the small communities along this road, featuring Blockbuster Video, Safeway, Carl's Jr., Bank of America, Starbucks Coffee. Even the ethnic restaurants—Chinese, Spanish, Japanese, Korean, Ethiopian, Indian, Caribbean, Greek, Italian—are standardized in their sad lack of exoticism. This is so because there are just too many of them on each block. Within the banks and commercial outlets, clerks and salespersons—Hindu, Ethiopian, Spanish, Korean, Chinese, Southeast Asian, and, yes, even black and white—testify by their presence that a demographic revolution has already taken place here, has already been standardized in commercial terms. Each morning, all along El Camino Real, there are groups of Spanish men, clustered on both sides of the highway, waiting to be picked up for day labor. And, of course, there are the homeless people, some riding bicycles, some pushing shopping carts loaded with their material possessions, peddling and pushing, clothed in a pathetic individualism, among the cars and human traffic. The tragic arch of this highway grows out of the fact that the high-tech munificence of San Jose and the Silicon Valley and the human muscle of the barrios are locked in an extremely unfair competition. Two radically different worlds, or economic worldviews, are in contention here, and there is really no doubt which world will lose. But still, the descendants of the conquistadores and the root races native to this region stand, defiantly, each morning, waiting to connect with work.

Last September, when I first observed the man at the Town and Country Mall, I gave money to him. I promised myself, then, that I would always stop and give money to such people. I made an easy moral-dandy judgment that it was *shameful* that the state of California, sitting on the ninth largest economy in the world, could not do more to help such people. I promised myself that I would remain an outsider to this casual indifference, and maintain my own moral integrity, only as long as I continued to give money to beggars. But after several months I slowly began to end this practice. There were just too many people—black, white, male, female—begging at stoplights and at street corners up and down that road. To my own credit, I will add that this withdrawal of moral effort and energy was a gradual and unconscious process. The efficiency of my daily commutes up and down that road required that I conform to the flow of traffic. The average speed on El Camino is thirty-five to fifty miles per hour. Beyond this, I live in a town house inside a gated community of town houses, one with its own private road. People inside the gate love the private road (for residents and their guests), the elegant swimming pool, the sauna, the clubhouse, our own Spanish maintenance men, as well as the privacy and the quiet. When I turn my car right, off the busy El Camino Real, onto our private road, I abruptly enter into another world, an *inside* one, a gated one. This is a world in which the other holders of fee simple are hardly ever seen; a world in which the Spanish maintenance men are always busy watering plots of grass or vacuuming fallen leaves. But, slowly and much more consciously than I would like to think, these men *inside* the gate had become, like the groups of Spanish men along El Camino Real, and like the middle-aged white man standing by the exit of the Town and Country Mall, no more than abstractions. I had accepted them as only part of the landscape.

Then, several months ago, one rainy afternoon, the flow of *outside* human traffic intruded into this haven. A knock on my door, something that had grown unfamiliar to me, brought me back to consciousness. The uninvited visitor was a middle-aged overweight white female, one dressed almost in rags. She had already begun to run away when I opened the door. "I'm hungry," she explained. "I was knocking on doors asking for money for food." I speculated that she was just as surprised to see me, a black male in such an affluent context, as I was to see her. I know I was surprised, if not shaken, to see a person looking like her *inside* our gated community. I reached into my pockets for some change, and it was then that I remembered the pledge I had made to myself back in the early fall. I located my wallet and gave her ten dollars, most of it for the man outside the Town and Country Mall, whom I had begun to ignore. I realized, after this encounter, that both of them must have had stories to tell and that I, as a writer, should have been interested in imagining the failures or the tragedies or the betrayals, or even the comic confidencings, that had led both of them, two white people within a mostly white community of great affluence, to go begging. But something had grown dull, or coarse, *inside of me,* and had prevented me from placing value on their stories. I realized, then, that the gated community in which I live and make my reality had taken up an existence inside of me.

Since that rainy winter day I have kept careful watch for the middle-aged white beggar at the exit to the Town and Country Mall. I have looked for him each time I go into the mall or drive past it. Why does he always stand at the exit and not at the entrance? It would seem that more people would be taking extra money into the mall than out of it. Why does he wear the same costume day after day? Why does he seem to stand at perpetual attention? Why does he choose to stand in the rain? What does he do with the money? Most important of all, I have tried to imagine the essentials of his story. If I can avoid being cynical and dismissing him as just another hustler who, like a great number of people in California, have made a lucrative profession out of begging, and if I can employ the full powers of my imagination, I can see coming into focus something brilliantly simple in its complexity. I can see a story: This man, who is only masquerading as a beggar, is in reality a philosopher and a teacher. His real job is to remind the affluent shoppers, only when they *leave* the Town and Country Mall, of their moral obligations to all the other beggars to the north and south along El Camino Real. The philosopher wearing a worn down jacket is really conducting a semi-secular *church* at the exit of the Town and Country Mall.

Consider the existential undercurrents of his sermon:

The written words on his cardboard sign proclaim to the outside world: "I am a Christian man." And his oral response to any gesture of human kindness ("God bless you") is in perfect balance. The two taken together, the flowing between the outside and what is inside, recall to mind the expression "Let the words of my mouth and the meditation of my heart be acceptable in Thy sight." Inside his disguise, this philosopher is quietly announcing a solution to one of the most fundamental problems in the Western tradition—the proper relation between the outer and the inner, the outside and the inside of the self. He is suggesting a principle of alternation. Also, perhaps, he is offering insights into the reasons for the rise of autobiographical forms of writing—the memoir and the personal essay—that has engendered distaste, if not contempt, among the watchdogs of the cultural establishment. Such clues to the importance of the relation of what is inside the self to what is outside the self may well reside in many such refugees from middle-class society. This beggar/philosopher, then, is only reminding the affluent shoppers, *even if they do not stop to give to him,* to remember his message and to act kindly toward the other beggars *outside* the Town and Country Mall, along the Royal Road.

It was St. Augustine who advised that "memory is the belly of the soul." This is the place which, in recent years, has begun to challenge the supremacy of the novel as the finest portrait of the culture. There is an increasing inwardness in narrative expressions, whether in memoir or in autobiographical essays. The university at which I teach, the University of Iowa, has two nationally noted writing programs: the Writers' Workshop, and a new Non-Fiction Writing Workshop. As many students flock to get into the former as into the latter. And each summer, the university sponsors Summer Writing Institutes for elderly people, who come from all parts of the country to spend two to six weeks committing their memories to paper. Even in this gated community, with its quiet and its remove from the flow of life along El Camino Real, there is an inward turn. Each Thursday afternoon, at 3:00 P.M., a group of the residents meet to share their memories with one another. One elderly man, a former officer in the O.S.S., is writing an autobiographical novel about his exploits in France and in North Africa. An elderly woman, from Texas, is recapturing her family-centered youth in a small Texas town. Another woman, from Kansas City, is reconstructing the texture of the Midwest out of which Harry Truman and Kansas City jazz came. And still another woman, crippled since birth, and childless, is fingering the wounds left by her childhood. There is a growing inwardness in most of our expressions. But whether this withdrawal has been caused by the bent toward a thin entertainment culture in the world outside our own, or whether it is a retreat from the fragmentation and uncertainty of the larger world, has yet to be decided. Whatever the cause, this turning inward, beyond its narcissism, may be the expression of a private yet communal effort to relocate some human essentials that have been obscured, if not lost altogether.

It was the Greek philosopher Plato whose teaching about eternal forms, or ideas, laid the basis in the Western tradition for the division between the inner and the outer. His idea of the human soul as akin to the "intelligible" world but having fallen into the "sensible" world is the first barricade between the inside and the outside. Plotinus later built on

Plato's Allegory of the Cave by connecting the intelligible, inside world with the Divine Mind. When the soul looks inward, according to Plotinus, it sees a Divine Mind and an inner world that is radically different from the sensible world. Augustine took up this same problem in the tenth book of his *Confessions.* Because he was laying the theological foundations for Christianity, Augustine modified his old doctrine of predestination—the doctrine spelled out in his earlier *On Grace and Free Will,* that God has an eternal plan to give grace to some people and not to others—and posits that Plato's idea of the "fall" is in reality original sin in the sense suggested in the Book of Genesis. The inner world, then—memory—is like the courtyard of an inner palace, open at the roof, from which the soul looks up to God.

Augustine writes:

You are always there above me, and I rise toward you in my mind. I shall go beyond even this force which is in me, this force which we call memory, longing to reach out to you by the only possible means and to cling to you in the only way it is possible to cling to you. . . . So I must go beyond memory, too, if I am to reach the God who made me different from the beasts that walk on the earth and wiser than the birds that fly in the air. I must pass *beyond memory* [my italics] to find you, my true God, my sure sweetness. But where will the search lead me? Where am I to find you? If I find you beyond my memory, it means that I have no memory of you. How, then, am I to find you, if I have no memory of you?

El Camino Real

This is the *other* El Camino Real, the real "Royal Road," toward which St. Augustine directs his readers. But it is a road pointing ever inward and upward, away from the concrete conditions of the sensible world. It is a road laid for mystics and for saints, but not for human beings who must, of necessity, live in this sensate and wayward world. It seems to be safe to say that the current writers of memoirs are not really following the Royal Road provided with inner road signs by St. Augustine. They are not looking *up* from inside the courtyard of a sacred palace of memory. Instead, they are contemplating their own navels, or else their spiritual bellies, in search of something as secular as it is sacred, as inside themselves as it is *outside.* They seem to be seeking the synthesis, the alternation suggested by the beggar at the Town and Country Mall.

It is Kathryn Harrison's *The Kiss* that is most often cited as the most daring, and perhaps the most inner-directed, of the new memoirs. This "confession," written in the form of a novella, dramatizes the sexual affair Ms. Harrison had with her father during her college years. The book was endorsed by the noted child psychiatrist Robert Coles for its emotional honesty, but some critics condemned the book for its portrait of the father, still a practicing minister, and for its potential impact on Ms. Harrison's two young children. I took a personal interest in this book when it appeared because I had worked with both Ms. Harrison and her husband, Colin, when they were students in the Writers' Workshop at the University of Iowa. As a matter of fact, the two of them met in my classes. They became a very loving couple, and they both seemed to have remarkable moral senses. Colin

Harrison, as I recall, was still a practicing Quaker. He wrote, in some of his stories, about the retarded children with whom he once worked. I had many conversations with him about contemporary affairs. I recall that one day, when we were discussing the reelection of Ronald Reagan by a tremendous landslide (in 1984), Colin suddenly said, "I'm tired of feeling guilty!" It was only then that I recognized just how much of a moral burden had been placed on the remnant of the "liberal" element in American society. Reagan's reelection, by such a huge margin, has allowed them to disengage from other people's problems and to consider their own individual problems. Kathryn Harrison, on the other hand, wrote very quiet stories about family life in Los Angeles. I remember that during a concert at the university auditorium, which I attended with my daughter, Colin and Kathryn passed down, from a great number of rows behind me, their own opera glasses for my daughter to use.

I receive, every Christmas, a card from them, always with a picture of their happy-seeming two children building snowmen.

I took my time in reading Kathryn's *The Kiss.*

Jill Ker Conway, in her recent consideration of the memoir form, *When Memory Speaks,* is ambivalent about the intentions behind Ms. Harrison's disclosures. "Stories of incest victims usually receive favorable treatment," she observed, "because the child is presented as the innocent object of someone else's illicit desires. It is Harrison's acknowledgment of mutuality that has shocked her critics and has made

The Kiss a riveting story, albeit one which leaves many issues of the author's identity and the familial relationships unresolved. The reader wonders whether she will ever be able to like other women, and thus like herself in later life, or whether she'll remain as exclusively focused on bonds with men as she was in her twenties."

It is of interest to note that in 1994, several years before publication of *The Kiss,* Ms. Harrison contributed an essay to a book called *A Tremor of Bliss: Contemporary Writers on the Saints.* Here again, Robert Coles was enthusiastic in his introduction. Once again, Ms. Harrison wrote about deeply personal matters. In her essay, "Catherine Means Pure," about St. Catherine of Siena, Ms. Harrison confronts her own complex religious background—Jewish, Christian Scientist, Catholic—as well as the meaning of her own name. In this essay are some of the same themes that are given greater dramatization in *The Kiss:* a spiritually transcendent experience with a practitioner of Christian Science whose laying on of hands caused "the top of my skull . . . to be opened by a sudden, revelatory blow." And: "Mysteriously, unexpectedly, this stranger had ushered me into an experience of something I cannot help but call rapture. I felt myself separated from flesh, and from all earthly things. I felt myself no more corporeal than the tremble in the air over a fire. . . ." Finally, there are the comparisons between Ms. Harrison and St. Catherine of Siena, who share the same name: "She wanted to do all her suffering on earth so that she would be spared purgatory. *This will make you pure,* I used to think when I made myself throw up." And again:

93

No one believed more firmly in Catherine's debasement than did Catherine. Determined that she be the least among mortals, so also by the topsy-turvy logic of Christian salvation—she would be assured of being the greatest. In her vision of Christ, it is Catherine alone who stands beside Him as His bride. To earn that place was exhausting beyond mortal ability. Catherine would guide me to the salvation I sought. Inhumanly, she had triumphed over mortal imitations, over hunger, fatigue and despair. She had seen demons and fought them off. And I would use her to fashion my solitary and sinful faith. Sin. A term long ago borrowed from archery: to miss the mark.

Such spiritual longings are at the basis of Ms. Harrison's *The Kiss.* Simply put, like St. Augustine, and like St. Catherine, Ms. Harrison has gone deep into her memories of her own debasement in order to connect with what Augustine called the place "beyond memory" in order to reach a transcendent level. And Ms. Harrison does manage to reach this level, even in so secular and sociological a memoir as *The Kiss.* By exploring into such a deeply hidden part of her memory, she seems to have found something transcendent that she has brought into the outside world, in full view of her children. Once again, like the beggar at the exit of the Town and Country Mall, there is suggested the principle of *alternation,* of *integration* between the inner and the outer. Ms. Harrison's critics tend to ignore the mystical threads that parallel the sexual theme of the book. Besides the experience with the Christian Scientist, at the end of the book there is a dream about the writer's dead mother, who had caused her daughter so much pain:

> Yet she doesn't disappear, she is luminously real. With the split consciousness that sometimes characterizes a dream I remark to my sleeping self that perhaps my mother's spirit is really with me, that I can't have fabricated a presence so convincing simply by virtue of longing. . . . We look into each other's eyes more deeply than we ever did in life, and for much longer. Our eyes don't move or blink, they are no more than a few inches apart. As we look, all that we have ever felt but have never said is manifest. Her youth and selfishness and misery, my youth and selfishness and misery. Our loneliness. The ways we betrayed each other. In this dream I feel that at last she knows me, and I her. I feel us stop hoping for a different daughter and a different mother.

Both women, here, seem to have located, in one integrated memory, the ultimate source of love.

How beautiful my mother and I are.

In *When Memory Speaks,* Jill Ker Conway attempts to offer insights into the entrenched cultural patterns that seem to be beneath the rise of the memoir form. She sees the sources of it in the rise of feminism over the past three decades and its formal patterns moving outside the self and into the public world. She reminds us that whether we are aware of it or not, our culture gives us an inner script by which we live our lives. The main acts for the play come from the way our world understands human development; the scenes and the characters from our families and socialization, which provide the pattern for investing others with emotional significance; and the dynamics of the script come from whatever our world defines as success or achievement.

Ms. Conway sees different patterns for men and women. "For men," she says, "the overarching pattern for life comes from adaptations of the story of the epic hero in classical antiquity." That is, the quester-hero must accomplish, through use of his own will, a feat of purposeful endurance or of victory over some adversary. Women, in contrast, have been traditionally assigned to writing narratives about their relation to God or to their households. "The secular forms of women's narratives emerge," according to Ms. Conway, "in the bourgeois preoccupation with romantic love, marriage, family and property." But over the past three decades, it seems there has been an erosion, or else a merging, of these two separate domains. Thus Kathryn Harrison can write an essay about St. Catherine of Siena, and then follow this with a memoir about her own sexual adventures with her father, a quest-novel about the road to parental love. But while Ms. Conway's paradigm may have once had authenticity in the world as it once *was,* an even more radical argument can be made for the kind of world, both inside and outside, that exists *now.* Perhaps it is only the beggar/philosopher, who stands at the exit to the Town and Country Mall, who can open up insights into this new world for us. Or, perhaps, it is time for his black brother to instruct us in this mystery.

One recent winter, a seventy-one-year-old homeless black

man named Arthur Bell was found nearly frozen on the streets of Brooklyn, New York. He kept maintaining, to a social worker named Maria Mackin, that he had once been a celebrated ballet dancer in New York and in Paris. The social worker, who was initially doubtful of his story, began checking the facts suggested to her. Bell's story was picked up by the Associated Press, reaching a much wider audience, and a black minister in Florida, who knew Bell's sister, contacted her and other members of the homeless man's family. *Jet* magazine later reported that Bell was subsequently reunited with his brother, a successful businessman in suburban New Rochelle, and with his five sisters in Florida. He had not seen them for forty years. Then the deeper story came out. Fifty-seven years before, the young Arthur Bell had fled his Florida home to follow his dream to become a ballet dancer. He had run away because his restrictive fundamentalist family in Tampa, Florida, made it difficult for him to achieve his secular dream. In 1950, Bell had premiered in *Illuminations* with the New York City Ballet. He danced, later, with the Ballet de la Tour Eiffel in Paris and achieved some fame. But, apparently, between the late 1950s and 1997, while the civil rights movement had brought prosperity to a great number of black people with comparable dreams, Bell's life became increasingly desperate. He had been homeless for several decades, sustained only by his memories of what he had been. His retreat into the *inside* of himself, where he kept his memories alive, resulted from the prolonged uncertainty of the *outside* world. But what he had preserved inside himself soon became, through the ministrations of the mass media, a portrait of the millions of other nameless and homeless men and women who also function as abstractions in the outside world.

Bell's true brother, the man at the exit to the Town and Country Mall, would know this instinctively. He knows that in the famous Silicon Valley, south on El Camino Real, among the rising number of technocrats and entrepreneurs, there is a similar sense of fragmentation. This new elite finds that it has more in common with its peers, worldwide, who use the same technocratic vocabulary, fly on the same airplanes, shop in the same airport malls, use the same hotels in New York, Chicago, Paris, Tokyo, Berlin, London, than they have in common with the people along the road to the north and south of them. A man wearing the usual business suit has his shoes shined by an Asian man in the lobby of an airport while he uses a cellular telephone to cement a business deal. He has no reason to even look at the Asian man shining his shoes until the job is done. The women in this elite are guarded from the haphazard intrusions of Eros by the growing number of company sexual-harassment codes. There is a growing tribe of affluent people, called "Eagles," who employ the new technology to enhance their mobility. Once connected to the workplace by the Internet, such people can make very comfortable homes for themselves, away from the cities, in the small towns of Vermont, New Hampshire, Maine, or else in Iowa, Illinois, or even Kansas. They tend to live among, but *above,* the old-time residents of these small towns. The suburbs are now being abandoned for the exurbs, and the locals feel displaced by their much better educated and much more affluent neighbors. There are the beginnings of tensions between the generations, as medical science allows older people to live longer, healthier lives, and collect more Social Security, at the expense of much younger people whose labor will pay for these benefits. Prosperity has been polarized, with great wealth concentrated in fewer and fewer hands. The institution of the nation-state is rapidly being replaced by global corporate ties under invisible managements. The middle class is frightened. The poor no longer exist as human beings. Europe is becoming one federated nation, while the demographics of the United States are changing relentlessly. Information is everywhere, but there is less and less of it with any substance. Private events that used to have tragic implications—the O.J. Simpson saga, the Atlanta Olympics bombing, the death of Princess Diana, the murder of Jon-Benet Ramsey, the moral hollowness of Bill Clinton—are now treated as farce. Frank Sinatra is dead, and Seinfeld is going off the air. On a more personal level, a radically new type of human being is appearing—one who employs language only as a means to the negotiation of self-interested ends, with no regard for either truth or the consequences of his untruths because the language that is used is no longer grounded in a consistent sense of *self.* We say only what we *have* to say to get through each day.

Confronted on all sides by such radical trends, it is only predictable that the remnants of the individual self would need to take refuge within personal memories, within St. Augstine's "belly of the soul." Arthur Bell, the Town and Country Mall man's brother, was himself a very wise man. He held fiercely onto the hidden high point of his life, even while he remained homeless in the world outside himself.

. . .

At each stop along El Camino Real are narratives that have been stored in memory, narratives eager to be told, almost to any pedestrian. An Arab American who runs a flower shop has become an expert in observing the cynical, "romantic" manipulations employed by his customers. If you give him time, he will detail the many ploys they impose on the fragile red and pink blossoms he sells. If you give him even more time, he will draw his own experiences into the narrative ("My wife left me three times, and she came back three times. I took her back three times, but I put my property in my mother's name. My wife can't get shit! She's American and she's *crazy*. This is a garbage culture, man! A *garbage* culture!"). Such stories, living at almost each stop along the Royal Road, are being forged by newly arrived immigrants —Koreans, Ethiopians, Hindu, Caribs, Chinese, Spanish. At an automobile-repair shop, south on that road toward San Jose, a Chinese customer sits politely while complaining and complaining to a white male clerk about the shoddy repairs that have been made on his car. The reserved middle-aged clerk periodically breaks into the monologue with an offer to correct a specific mistake for free. The Chinese man ignores him. Intent on saving face, and knowing that the clerk has already conceded error, the Chinese man sits passively. He alternates, instead, between stoical silence and the refrain of complaints. North of them, at the checkout counter of a huge state-of-the-art copy center, an elderly black woman slowly inspects the pile of old black-and-white photographs that have just been copied. She holds her place at the usually efficient counter, against all the other customers behind her, to offer stories to the patient clerk about the children and the grandchildren in the pictures, as well as stories about their ancestors in the South. Farther north of this place, at a bus stop, two people waiting for a bus give directions to a driver who is lost. One of the two is a black man, with the badge of a city bus driver on his coat, who directs the lost driver through a complicated network of turns, so as to place the driver just at the door he is seeking. His fixation is on the "style" of the arrival. But the woman, a Chinese, points out a much more practical route to the destination. Two ethnic ethics are in competition, both for the benefit of the lost driver. Farther south, inside another flower shop, a middle-aged white female, also a clerk, fantasizes about a lost love who has the same name as the man who is buying flowers. She swears that she once loved this black man, truly loved him, and will love him forever. She keeps vowing to seek out his relatives, and track him down one day, over in San Francisco. She keeps insisting that true love lasts forever.

What prevents such stories from having a wider audience? Why do they remain imprisoned in private memories?

A few years ago, a Green Bay Packer star named Reggie White destroyed his career, and lost a job with CBS Sports, by making what was called a "racist speech" to the Wisconsin State Assembly in Madison. His condemnation of homosexuals was the least offensive part of the speech. Even more controversial was his assessment of the "talents" given by God to each race. Black people were gifted at worship and celebration, the ordained minister told the legislators. "If you go to a black church, you see people jumping up and down because they really get into it. White people are good at organizing," he said. "You guys do a good job of building businesses, and you know how to tap into money." "Hispanics," he went on, "are gifted in family structure, and you can see a Hispanic person, and they can put twenty, thirty people in one house. Asians are gifted inventors and can turn a television into a watch. Indians are gifted in spirituality," he added. "When you put all of that together, guess what it makes? It forms a complete image of God."

While Mr. White will not be working for CBS Sports in the near future, his blunt remarks do raise a certain issue that touches the trend under consideration here. While the ideology of equality is a benevolent construct, and while considerations of "political correctness" may help alleviate certain ethnic/sexual tensions, it may be helpful to abandon both concepts and attempt to view human experience from what has been roundly condemned as a "racist" perspective. It may well be that the *ideology* of equality, with its rhetorical insistence on "sameness," tends to obscure some fundamental *differences,* the examination of which may provide a badly needed perspective on this present moment in the culture.

The one "sameness" that applies to each member of the human race is the fact of death, man's fate, as a given, as the fundamental end of life. Death is the great equalizer. But what is not equal is the range of responses to the ethical problem of *what should survive death.* This issue is ethical in the deepest possible sense because attempts at solving it are the basis of all great literature (from the *Upanishads* of the ancient Hindus to the *Epic of Gilgamesh* of the ancient Babylonians to the story of the Flood in the Book of Genesis), and of all great religions. Each society, if it is to achieve personality, and if it is to provide a philosophical or a religious orientation for its members, must wrestle with the fact of death, and with what should survive it, in order to project an ethical system, a *meaning,* that will survive death, whether in this world or in some other.

Among the Hindus, for example, *being* is to survive by stripping all the moral qualities from the self; death is to be attained by removing that which lives. The idea of reincarnation as other forms of life evolved out of this core belief. Among the Chinese, the family survives death, linking the ancestors in the world of the spirit with living members on the earth. The Japanese have adapted this ethical system to their own needs, except that among them the *ki,* the life force itself, is what survives death. The ancient Egyptians invested the *ka,* the mystic double of a person, with the capacity to survive among the spirits, while in this world the cult of the kingdom of Egypt lived on. Among the ancient Greeks, the myth of the exemplary person survived death. This idea was adapted by the Romans, and centuries later found an echo in Hegel's philosophy of history. Among the Muslims, the inhabitants of the ancient Levantine world (from which Augustine of Hippo emerged), the consensus of the Faithful survived, the unity of those who have received the same spirit, in the Kingdom of Heaven. In sharp contrast to all these ethical systems, Western peoples view the personal will, the "inner script" described by Jill Ker Conway, as the agent of survival. From this point of view, a person's will becomes the causative agent of one's spiritual fate. This is an ethic based on actions in this world, the creation of cognitive institutions—businesses, churches, family lines, fortunes, foundations—that will impose one's will on the future.

These may be some of the archetypal ethical patterns beneath Reggie White's cloudy stereotypes. It is apparent to me that these diverse ethical systems are now coming into proximity, if not into conflict, along El Camino Real. This recent shrinkage of the world into a single Royal Road is one of the sources, I believe, of the fear leading to the massive retreat from the public square and into the gated community of the self. There is a growing fear of the unknown along that Great Road. It needs to be emphasized that El Camino Real, following the changing demographic patterns of the nation, has become a veritable supermarket of free-floating ethical systems, some of them degraded now beyond easy recognition. People have retreated deep into themselves, trying desperately to connect with the fading, familiar forms of "home." This in itself is a noteworthy expression of *one* side of the principle of alternation, but the completion of the principle, the return to the *outside* of the self, is not an easy thing to do, especially without the recognition that the habits of mind beneath all such efforts are *different.* They are invisible. But still they exist, as do the stories that can be filtered through them. They can only be drawn into greater focus through personal encounters that take place outside the gated community of the self.

But this is the great risk that many of us are unwilling to chance now, in those dangerous places outside of ourselves, along the Royal Road.

Several years ago, when the new Hindu government of

India began testing nuclear weapons, I had been reading the works of Mohandas Gandhi for several months, and after the tests started I began reading him much more carefully. The appropriation of Western physics by India seemed to make meaningless much of what Gandhi taught. "Strength lies in the absence of fear, not in the quality of flesh and muscle we have on our bodies. . . . The Gujarati equivalent for civilization means 'good conduct.' India has nothing to learn from anybody else. . . . To arm India on a large scale is to Europeanize it. Then her condition will be just as pitiable as that of Europe. This means, in short, that India must accept European civilization. . . ."

These quotations are from Gandhi's first book, *Hind Swaraj,* published in 1908. In this book he outlined a tactic that, he predicted, would drive out the English and their civilization and liberate modern India. Things seem now not to have worked out as Gandhi had planned. Still, the vitality of his core conviction, Swaraj (self-rule), drawn by him from the Hindu *Upanishads* of 600–300 B.C. and the *Bhagavad Gita,* had the power to influence the many millions of occupied India and activists like Martin Luther King. The concept, which preceded the meditations on freedom by Plato and Aristotle, offered a solution to the division between the outside and the inside that has since been wrestled with by Plotinus, St. Augustine, and even John Locke. It suggested the same principle of alternation conveyed by the beggar/philosopher stationed by the exit at the Town and Country Mall: "Let the words of my mouth and the meditation of my heart be acceptable in Thy sight," as the Episcopalians would say.

Gandhi explained his interpretation of Swaraj in a dual sense, one physical and one spiritual, working together to achieve the same end. To rule over territory or even to rule over people, one must first rule over one's self, over one's own soul. One must, first, free oneself psychologically of all illusions and fears. The highest level of consciousness comes when our individual being is *one* with all being. The freest person, then, is the one who sees all being in himself and himself in all being. The engagement with this Royal Road, which leads to self-knowledge and to unity-in-diversity, Gandhi argued in his *Hind Swaraj,* was the only practical road to Indian independence. He repeated this lesson all his life. In speaking against the practice of untouchability he said, once again reemphasizing Swaraj:

Hinduism has sinned in giving sanction to untouchability. It has degraded us, made us the pariahs of the [British] Empire. . . . What crimes for which we condemn the [British] government as satanic, have not we been guilty of toward our untouchable brethern? . . . It is ideal to talk of Swaraj so long as we do not protect the weak and the helpless or so long as it is possible for a simple Swarajist to injure the feelings of any individual. Swaraj means not a single Hindu or Muslim shall for a moment arrogantly think that he can crush with impunity meek Hindus or Muslims. Unless this condition is fulfilled we will gain Swaraj only to lose it the next moment. We are not better than the brute until we have purged ourselves of the sins we have committed against our weaker brothers. . . . I do not want to attain Moksha [Salvation, merger with God]. I do not want to be re-born. But if I have to be re-born, I should be born as an untouchable so that I may share their sorrows, suffering and the affronts leveled at them in order that I may endeavor to free myself and them from that miserable condition.

Since the practice of Swaraj is an individual discipline, Gandhi resolved the *inward* problem for himself by creating a new designation, Harijans ("Children of God"), that would remove the stigma of untouchability. And then, as an *outward* expression of the freedom that resulted, he adopted an untouchable girl, Lakshmi, into his own family at the Satyagraha Ashram.

It remains to be seen just how much of this ancient and muscular ethic remains after the explosion of nuclear bombs derived from Western physics. But it seems to me that if India has turned to nuclear force in order to calm its fears of its neighbors, some other people will need to return to Gandhi's advocacy of the uses of soul force. As he demonstrated, this is the work of solitary individuals. And since writers are the most solitary and self-aware of people, it seems to be our responsibility to use this period of inward-turning, of reidentification with our own ethical systems, the grain in our own wood, as a preparation for moving *out* of ourselves, having conquered our own fears of the rope that resembles a snake, or the beggar who threatens, to see what else in the outside world can be reclaimed. This is only a return to the principle of alternation suggested by Gandhi and by Martin Luther King, as well as by the beggar/philosopher who stands at the exit to the Town and Country Mall. Gloria Steinem, an early leader of the feminist movement, called it "a revolution from within." The pre-nuclear Hindi called it simply Swaraj.

There is, finally, one very important aesthetic consideration that should not be overlooked. It may well be that the conventional literary forms—the short story, the novel, and even the memoir—are unsuited to deal adequately with the new realities (global, demographic, economic, interpersonal) evolving just outside our gated communities. It should be recalled that these old forms grew out of specific cultural changes, primarily in Europe—the rise of a middle class, the consolidation of the nation-state, the invention of the printing press, the focus on the individual as worthy of emotional exploration, the exploration by Europeans of other parts of the world; but most important of all, *settled habits of mind that formed a psychological consensus in favor of specific forms.* Now, the concrete conditions of the outside world are changing at an increasingly accelerated rate of speed. Perhaps the old forms will not suffice to capture the new habits of mind, the new fears we are obliged to confront every day. If this is truly the case, for my own part I still draw inspiration from a speech made by Ralph Ellison in 1953 when he was given the National Book Award for his novel *Invisible Man.* Ellison said:

We who struggle with form and with America should remember Eidothea's advice to Menelaus when in the *Odyssey* he and his friends are seeking their way home. She tells him to seize her father, Proteus, and to hold him fast, "however he may struggle and fight. He will turn into all sorts of shapes to try you," she says, "into all the creatures that live and move upon the earth, into water, into blazing fire; but you must hold him fast and press him all the harder. When he is himself, and questions you in the same shape that he was when you saw him in his bed, let the old man go; and then, sir, ask which god it is who is angry, and how you shall make your way homewards over the fish-giving sea?"

I think it is time for me to go outside and look for another story, a new one, along the Royal Road.

Gravitas

Suddenly from behind us a dark old fellow wearing a black Cordoba hat, a blue denim jacket and a scarf of fuchsia silk wrapped around his throat moved stiffly past on a black seven-gaited mare. Small and dry, he sat her with the stylized and momentary dignity of an equestrian statue and in the sun slant the street became quite dreamlike. His leathery hands held the gathered reins upon the polished horn of a gleaming cowboy saddle and his black, high-heeled boots, topped by the neat, deep cuff of short tan cowboy riding chaps, rested easy and spurless in the stirrups as he moved slowly past as in meditation, his narrow eyes bright glints in the shadow of his hard-brimmed hat. . . . a little boy in blue overalls exploded from between two small houses across the street and ran after the horseman, propelled by an explosion of joy. *Hi, there, Mister Love,* he yelled. *Make her dance, Mister Love. I'll sing the music. Will you, Mister Love? Won't you please, Mr. Love? Please, please, Mister Love?*

—Juneteenth

With the publication in June of 1999 of *Juneteenth,* his second novel, a kind of cottage industry has grown up around Ralph Ellison's name. I can imagine Ralph's ironic laughter at the mythic allusions that have been imposed on his forty

or so years of wanderings in the desert of the American literary imagination. One motif is what has been left to "that
vanishing tribe, the American Negro" during the forty years
the leader spent gathering his sacred text. Charles Johnson,
in the *New York Times Magazine,* lamented the lateness of the
text's arrival. "He was engaging in an examination of America and race that would have been so valuable to have in the
'60s and '70s and '80s," Johnson said. "If we could have just
had this integrated into the discourse of race in America. But
we didn't see any of this until now." Another is the mysterious fire by night that destroyed Ralph's summer cottage as
well as a huge section of the original manuscript. Another
motif, this one offered by the critic John Leonard in *The Nation,* is Ellison's inability to spend less time conversing
amidst the tempting ambience of New York's elite Century
Club. "In the early seventies," Leonard wrote, "I was an appalled witness at a literary cocktail party when Alfred Kazin
told him he should spend less time at the Century Club and
more at the typewriter, followed by a scuffle on the wet
street, from which an equally appalled cabbie roared away
without a fare, like the locomotive of history." And another
motif is Ralph's stubborn dedication to a radically new, perfected form of literary art. Wandering in the desert, fire by
night, the fatted calf, absolute dedication to a perfect form of
Jehovah. These allusions have attached themselves to Ralph
as easily as they once attached themselves to Moses. Like the
media-inspired marathon mourning of John F. Kennedy,
Jr., these allusions speak not to either man, both of whom
were flesh-and-blood human beings, but to our own deep

hunger for community, for intellectual and spiritual leadership.

I recognize, now, that I have also contributed to this mythologizing of a human being. Several years ago, I participated in a tribute to Ralph sponsored by the 92nd Street Y in New York. John F. Callahan, Ellison's executor, had been urged by the staff of the 92nd Street Y to keep the comments by all the participants brief. When my turn to read came, I just could not resist my own impulse to mythologize. I read a passage from Suetonius's *The Twelve Ceasars,* a passage touching the life of Julius Caesar:

> He was fifty-five years old when he died, and his immediate deification, formally decreed, was more than an official decree since it reflected public conviction: if only because, on the first day of the Games given by his successor Augustus in honor of this apotheosis, a comet appeared about an hour before sunset and shone for seven days running. This was held to be the soul of Caesar, elevated to Heaven; hence the star, now placed above the forehead of his divine image.

Now, two years later, I recognize the human truth of the matter. Ralph Ellison was a human being, a brilliant and generous and deeply dedicated *human* human being. He was also my friend.

Since the publication of *Juneteenth,* I have read a wide range of reviews of Ralph's last novel, from Jonathan Yardley's disinclination to review it in the *Washington Post Book World,* to

Gregory Feeley's very cautious appraisal in the *New York Times Magazine*. It struck me that almost all the East Coast reviews focused on the mythology of Ralph Ellison, while papers such as the *Washington Times,* the *Denver Rocky Mountain News,* the *Oregonian,* and the *Seattle Weekly* focused mostly, and very kindly, on the novel itself. It was interesting to note that the musical idiom of the novel was better appreciated by those reviewers who were able to disengage the content of the novel from the myth of Ralph Ellison, The most "knowing" cultivator of the myth, John Leonard in *The Nation,* lamented that he was once bothered that Ellison "so seldom reviewed and never encouraged any of the other black American writers of his time, which was a long one." Leonard went on to speculate that this father-son tension was almost fatal to the development of black American literature. "He seemed almost to have felt that encouraging the children who cherished his example and struggled with his shadow would cost him some body heat. So he hibernated for the long winter and sucked like Ahab the paws of his gloom."

After reading this review I imagined Ralph laughing. And then I could *remember* him laughing. This last laugh took place in early April of 1984, the last time I saw Ralph alive. We were seated around a luncheon table at City College, after a ceremonial honoring Ralph. Michael Harper had stood and had displayed a wrapped gift for Ralph. He said, as he proposed a toast, "Ralph, this is a gift from your sons!" Ralph had laughed, but then had said to Mike, "Then you'd better open it yourself, because it might explode!" Ralph knew very well the burden that Freud had placed on friendships between older men and the younger men they mentored. I believe that Ralph never wanted to have children, daughters or sons. But he was a genuine and good friend to those people he nurtured.

It was Aristotle who thought the most deeply about friendship as a moral virtue. He distinguished between friendships grounded in pleasure and utility, which friendships last as long as pleasure and usefulness last. These two grounds of friendship are common. For Aristotle, the best of all grounds for friendship was what he termed "perfected friendship." This degree of friendship obtains when one person wants for the other what is good for him simply because it is good for him. He believed that only people with comparable virtues could sustain this kind of friendship. Aristotle did not mean equality of virtue; he meant proportionate virtue. He meant that each is prepared to render to the other what the other deserved. Ellison himself explored this quality of friendship with Richard Wright, his early mentor. From reading through their exchange of letters during Wright's years of exile, I can see that it was Ralph who was the more gracious and giving of the two. Ralph had this same quality of friendship with Albert Murray, with R.B.W. Lewis, with Robert Penn Warren, with Richard Wilbur, and with William Styron. He also passed along this model of perfected friendship to another generation: John Callahan, Michael Harper, Stanley Crouch, Horace Porter, Charles Johnson, and to me. Simply put, Ralph was generous to a fault. I think now that John Callahan was expecting too much from people who were captivated by the myth of Ralph Ellison, people who failed to see that invisible qualities, quite beyond literary chitchat, can still exist as expressions of friendship.

*This is awkward. You call me Ralph and I'll call you
Jim. . . .*

After Ralph's death, in April of 1994, Stanley Crouch told
me that he did not believe that Fanny would last through the
winter. Six years later, John Callahan told me "those sonsof-
bitches who used to eat at Ralph's table won't even call up
Fanny now, so I am glad now that I began then to do what I
could for Fanny." I had already learned something about the
sterile nature of literary friendships, so I began to do what I
could for Fanny. John Callahan and I decided to get her a
VCR, and then I began to send her videotapes, the kind of
classics that Ralph loved, and batches of roses. I went from
Iowa to New York to see about her, and once my daughter
and I took her to the theater and then to dinner. Once I went
to check on the VCR and took her to lunch at one of her favorite restaurants on St. Nicholas Avenue. Walking with her
back to the apartment on Riverside Drive, I remembered
walking with Ralph along those same streets in the late
evenings, after our talks, when he took Tucka-Tarby, their
dog, for his evening walk. Fanny seemed very frail and sad
and I worried about her health. The apartment was cluttered
with books and boxes of papers, but it still felt empty without Ralph's presence, his gentle voice, his ironic chuckle.
Fanny was living from one day to the next within this empti-
ness, so I enlisted Mary, my sister, in a plan to help Fanny out
of her grief and depression. Mary lives in Stamford, Connecticut, so it was easy for her to drive from her home to
Fanny's apartment on Riverside Drive. Mary began taking
food to Fanny, meals that she cooked in her home—a turkey

dinner at Thanksgiving, special treats at Christmas. Mary would call each week to see if Fanny needed anything. Mary offered to take her to church, for a drive, anything that Fanny might want to do. Fanny accepted the food for a while, but said that she and Ralph had never attended church. Mary kept going to see her. During one visit, as she was leaving, Mary pointed to the great piles of scattered papers, books, and boxes and offered to help Fanny sort and store them and then clean the apartment. Fanny got mad, Mary told me, and shouted, "These are *Ralph's* things. I have to do it myself, *and I'm going to take my goddamn time!* Then Fanny began to cry. She hugged Mary while she cried. Mary could not see that Fanny was acting out of a perfected friendship with Ralph.

> Even good king Ancus looked his last at the light and was a far, far better man than you, you scoundrel! And many other kings and potentates have died . . . Scipio, thunderbolt of war and terror of Carthage, gave his bones to the earth the same as the meanest slave. Add to these the discoverers of knowledge and beauty, add the companions of the Muses, Homer among them, their only king—yes, even he was laid to rest.
>
> Lucretius, *De Rerum Natura*

Several years ago, Avon Kirkland, a film producer in Berkeley, allowed me to view a hidden treasure. Through some miracle, he had obtained a film of an interview with Ralph, the last one ever made, by a producer who had been making a biographical film about Richard Wright. Avon had all the scenes with Ellison that had been edited out of the finished production. I saw Ralph again, sitting in his favorite arm-chair and at his desk. There were many takes of him, some blocked momentarily by the director's chart. Ralph seemed to be trying to come to life again, his vitality breaking through all those many frames and poses. I heard his Okla-homa drawl, his ironic humor, his absolute brilliance. He talked mostly about his experiences with Wright, who be-came his mentor when he moved from Tuskeegee to New York. The one word Ralph kept repeating was "envy": how much Wright's fellow black Communists envied Wright's talents and his intellectual ambitions. Ralph always laughed after he had used this word. It came to me, then, that Ralph was still confronting, toward the end of his life, the same hu-man problem that Wright has confronted all his life. It made me very sober, in a very frightening way, that black men who had joined the Communist Party, ostensibly to win "free-dom" for their fellows, still remained so small-minded, at least toward Richard Wright, that a flea could very easily perch on the bridge of their noses and kick all their eyeballs out. Wright had been wounded by his own people the same way that Ellison had been wounded. I recalled, then, the fa-mous episode at Grinnell College in 1967, as recounted by Willie Morris in his *new york days,* when Ellison cried on the shoulder of a student after having been denounced as an Un-cle Tom by a motorcycle-riding black nationalist. "I'm not a Tom," Ellison kept insisting to the student, Henry Wingate. "I'm not a Tom!" Morris attributed this incident to the ideo-logical battles of the 1960's. But now I think he might have missed something, something very important and helpful in understanding the anti-intellectualism of the group itself, especially as it affects those, like Wright and Ellison, who attempt to think beyond, and to go beyond, what has already been accepted as reality.

If one begins to think of white supremacy as a structure, instead of as simply bad manners, one might then begin to explore into just what a system, an organic system, does in order to perpetuate itself. Central to this structuring of institutionalized inequality is the cooperation of some segment of the marginalized population who act, almost unconsciously, as watchdogs over those others who challenge, in whatever way, the status quo. Such people do the dirty work of the system—to keep violators in their place, whether in school, in the workplace, or in public forums. In other words, what precedes Willie Morris's account of the attack on Ellison is a narrative about how the motorcycle-riding nationalist from Chicago had first expressed disdain toward other guests at the party: S. I. Hayakawa, Fred Friendly, Marshall McLuhan, and Morris himself. The party was full of intellectuals, Ellison the only black one. To any envious or self-hating black person, whether nationalist or Communist, Ellison would be the safest target to degrade. Envy can be creative in some of its aspects, as the ancients taught. It is far more constructive for the envious man to follow the example of the neighbor who prepares his fields for future planting very early in the season, rather than to not follow his example and then, in the spring, destroy what the neighbor's industry has brought into being.

Ellison talked about the Grinnell incident when I first interviewed him in 1969. He said then, "Some of these people can be as vicious as the Negro Communists were." He had been deeply wounded. I remember from that time telling a young black woman, at a party in Albany, California, that I was writing an essay about Ellison. She stiffened and then said, "I hate that man!" But later in the evening she approached me and said with great sadness, "You know, I don't really know why I hate him." Since that time, I have had occasion to wonder whether open-admissions programs, black studies programs, and, yes, affirmative-action programs have been manipulated by Machiavellians to encourage an anti-intellectual "third force" made up of envious, narrow, academic hustlers whose only real job is to sabotage those intellectually ambitious black people who just might compete with whites for the good things of the society.

I do know that their experiences with Communists, black and white, scarred both Wright and Ellison. In Wright's last speech, given a few days before he died, he spoke of meeting James Baldwin and a white American female at a sidewalk café in Paris. Baldwin said to Wright, "Dick, I'm going to destroy you!" And Wright answered, "Why, Jimmy?" Then the white female said, *"He's telling you for me!"* Wright's letters to Ellison are full of taunts directed at the Communists: "Won't the Reds howl then!" he wrote Ellison in 1945. In another letter he said, "We ought to be a kind of continuous conscience for the Negro people. They'll [Communists] hate us for it, but they hate us anyhow." I was recently shown a State Department document that strongly suggests that Wright, while he was in the Gold Coast in 1953, informed on Kwame Nkrumah and the Communists around him. If Richard Wright managed to locate an ideological jurispru-

dence in rabid anticommunism, Ellison seemed to have located his own sense of transcendence in the passionate embrace of two seemingly conflicting claims: Negro tradition
and modernism as aesthetic resources for his art. His celebration of the Negro idiom so impressed me that, years ago, after I had written what I took to be a good letter, I began
using the closing "Negroly." As for modernism, Ellison
claimed as his mentors T. S. Eliot, James Joyce, William
Faulkner. Richard Wilbur told Avon Kirkland in an interview,

> He wanted to be more than a race spokesman, I think.
> He was so deeply a spokesman for modern literature
> and art that sometimes he would have been talking for
> an hour and he would suddenly rather unconsciously
> come up with such a phrase as "but to return to your
> first question." He did this very often, you know, and
> you'd have thought you were just sitting having a talk
> with Ralph but this revealed that, in some deep sense,
> even with his close friends, he was a modern writer be-
> ing interviewed.

I have no clear definition of what modernism is, but I
know it was created by outlanders from the settled literary
traditions of Europe—James Joyce from Ireland, T. S. Eliot
from the American Midwest, Ezra Pound also from the Midwest, D. H. Lawrence, Henry James, W. H. Auden from
England and Greenwich Village—who came to believe that
European culture had lost its vitality. These outlanders were
shaped by landscapes in which myths were still being cre-

ated out of rich oral traditions (the myth of the American West is mostly a product of the late nineteenth century as filtered through twentieth-century technology). They were also nurtured by the study of the classical traditions of Greece and Rome. Many were inspired by two nineteenth-century intellectuals who wrote about a return to the aesthetic of the classical ages for the resources to reintegrate aesthetic disciplines: Jakob Burckhardt, in his *The Civilization of the Renaissance in Italy* (1860), and the various writings of Friedrich Nietzsche. The notion of rebirth (*nostoi* is the Greek word for "return") was said by Burckhardt to have revitalized Italian society, and so the look back by Eliot, Joyce, Pound, and others was intended to revitalize the decaying minds of middle-class people in Europe and in America. In brief, the movement was about relocating the myths and rituals that would inspire the fusion of opposing aesthetic categories—realism, romanticism, symbolism—into a new wholeness, something that, according to Nietzsche, had been missing since Plato in his philosophical speculations inspired such divisions. Friedrich Nietzsche, in the nineteenth century, had predicted that the cycle of history would eventually return (once again *nostoi*) the divided narrative categories to a sense of wholeness.

According to Ellison's own account, his first encounter with the modernist world took place within the segregated world that Tuskeegee Institute was when Ellison was a student there. This initial encounter took place in the Tuskeegee Library, where Ellison read T. S. Eliot for the first time. Albert Murray has told me that he first met Ralph in this same library through his name on the cards of the many books he had checked out. An avid reader himself, Al once showed me a picture of himself and his very young daughter as they posed against a very tall bookcase packed with books. But Ellison had an advantage not available to Albert Murray. As he recalls in the essay "The Little Man at Chehaw Station," as a music major he was able to work with Hazel Harrison, a concert pianist. He tells us that Miss Harrison had been one of Ferruccio Busoni's prize students and had lived in his home in Berlin before the Nazis came to power and she had to leave. She had met in Busoni's home such accomplished composers as Egon Petri, Percy Grainger, and Sergei Prokofiev. It was her encouragement that led him deeper into music. It is interesting to note that Prokofiev was a close friend of the Russian symbolist novelist Andrei Bely, whose *Petersburg,* I want to suggest, may have had a lasting influence on Ralph. It is also of interest to note that Miss Harrison had in her office manuscripts of Prokofiev's compositions, which she often played for Ralph. As modernists, then, Ralph Ellison and Albert Murray had another advantage over their fellow writers with modernist sensibilities. They both were on deeply familiar terms with what they both called "the blues idiom." So far as I know, Ellison was the first to define the idiom as an art form. He did this in his own very generous way in his review of Richard Wright's *Black Boy:*

> The blues is an impulse to keep the painful details and episodes of a brutal experience alive in one's aching consciousness, to finger its jagged grain, and to transcend it, not by the consolation of philosophy but by the squeezing from it a near tragic–near comic lyri-

cism. As a form, the blues is an autobiographical chronicle of personal catastrophe expressed lyrically.

It is interesting to note, by reading the exchange between
Wright and Ellison after he published this review in the
Summer 1945 *Antioch Review*, that Wright seemed to have
no idea of what Ellison was talking about. "The *Antioch* came
and I read the article," Wright wrote to Ellison. "I think I
mentioned over the phone that I did not see the blues concept: I do see it, but only very slightly. And surely not
enough to play such an important role as you assigned it. I'm
not trying to carp over the fact that it was a Negro expression
form. I simply do not see it."

But Ralph Ellison saw. He saw that the American vernacular tradition, mightily contributed to by the vitality and the
resilience of "Negro Americans," had thrown up an art form
that was comparable, in some ways, to what the Greek
dramatists in fifth-century Athens had done. Strife, to them,
agon—agonistic conflict and competition as the basic driving
force in human life—in warfare and politics and drama, was a
norm of daily existence. So were tragedy and comedy. The
tragedies of Aeschylus, Sophocles, and Euripides depicted the
essential tragic facts of human life—incest, patricide, state
law conflicting with moral law. To the ancient Greeks, life
was tragic, full of *agon*. But to them it was also comic. And
the two dramatic categories were linked. Tragedies performed during the day, usually during a religious festival,
were followed each night by comedies grounded in absurdi-
ties. The two together, working to achieve some kind of bal-

ance, some sense of earthy well-being, provided what Ralph has called "antagonist cooperation."

The exploration of the range of the blues idiom became a passion for Ralph. The uses of the idiom for literary purposes seemed to be his contribution to the modernist quest for reintegration of opposing opposites. He had already read the "high" modernists, those who have been called paleomodernists. His ambition seems to have been to add something that was uniquely his own to the aesthetic conversation. *Invisible Man* was his first attempt at this reintegration. But what is at the basis of *Juneteenth* is Ellison's dramatization of the jazz musician as hero. In this novel Alonzo Hickman practices a kind of improvisational heroism in his nurturing and mentoring of Bliss. More than this, the novel merges the idiom of the folk preacher with the style of a jazzman. Ellison had great reverence for the individualized styles of such men. His old friend Charlie Davison, owner of the Andover Shop in Cambridge, told me four years ago that he and Ralph used to attend the Jazz Festivals at Newport. Ellison always tried to get a motel or hotel room next to one of the featured players, so he could listen to them practice before they went onstage. Ralph was deeply skilled in keeping his eye "peeled." He wanted to learn if the sense of style displayed onstage, before an audience, partook of the style that could be overheard during rehearsal. Charlie Davison told me that Ralph once brought the blues "shouter" Jimmy Rushing into the Andover Shop so he could purchase a tie. Rushing, a burly man, chose the thickest tie. He put it around his neck and then rolled it up from the bottom and used a safety pin to secure it to his shirt. Charlie Davison had objected to this display of country manners within the exclusive Andover Shop, very close to the center of Harvard Square. But then Ralph told him, "Look. Jimmy is the leader of a territorial bank back in Oklahoma. The people out there expect him to create his *own* style." It was this same sense of the importance of style, I think, that led Ralph to make Alonzo Hickman, a former jazz musician and a minister, the hero of his novel. I think he wanted, like any good modernist, to fuse the two different styles.

I thought about Ralph this summer when I saw a widely syndicated picture of people running from the mass shooting in Buckhead, the Atlanta suburb. The original picture showed a white man in the lead and a black male and then a white female, all running from the gunfire. Earlier in the picture's circulation, all three runners were visible. But soon the white man was edited out of the frame, leaving the black man and the white female to run together. The picture was apparently intended to dramatize the impression of panic. The white female's dress is running up her leg, exposing her thighs. But the black man is running with his thumbs up. It is as if his dedication to style is greater than his panic at that moment. I know that Ralph would have loved this picture.

"Craft to me is an aspect of personal morality . . ."

Like Henry James, one of his modernist heroes, Ralph Ellison had a mind so fine that no ideology could violate it. The most radical stance he took, given his own racial background, was his refusal to view basic human experience exclusively through the narrow prism of race. This steadfast refusal was the source of many of his problems, and not with just those black people who viewed him as a "Tom." Even the most educated of whites could view him with suspicion. I once attended a seminar at Berkeley taught by Henry Nash Smith, the Mark Twain scholar. When one of the graduate students mentioned an insight she had gained from reading Ellison's work, Mr. Smith said, "Ah, Ellison, he thinks he's white!" Mr. Smith later apologized to me for this outburst. Of course Ralph knew he was not white, but he remained steadfast in his refusal to be limited in intellectual and human range because of race. He saw himself as simply an American, a product of the complex history of black Americans in this society. He knew that race, and thus racism, was the great obstacle in the emotional and intellectual paths of all black people, but he consistently refused to allow it to overcome him. Both his life and his art were deeply grounded, of necessity, in *agon.* Ralph Ellison was a blues hero.

The stands he took were principled ones. When I met him, back during the late 1960s, when antiwar protest was at its peak, his reputation had been damaged because of the rumor that he was *for* the war policies of Lyndon Johnson. The reality, as I found out, was very different. Johnson, as part of his Great Society ambition, wanted to do something to help the arts. Ellison had agreed to serve on a planning panel, along with Robert Lowell, Paul Engle, and other prominent artists, for what later became the National Endowment for the Arts. But soon the antiwar spirit of the times caused Lowell and others to boycott the panel. Ellison and Engle, in contrast, remained steadfast in their dedication to the project. Ellison told me, years later, that ever since his work with the New York Writers Project of the WPA, back during the late 1930s, he had been interested in the role that government could play in the cultivation of the arts. While the New York Writers Project began as an effort to provide employment for writers during the Depression, Ellison believed that Lyndon Johnson's attempt to revive some aspect of the idea, during a time of great prosperity, was a very valuable thing. Museums and symphony orchestras, he told me, had no trouble getting private funding, while writers had to struggle. To him the antiwar protest was one thing, while planning for the Endowment was another. Ellison chose to help lay the foundations for the Endowment while others protested. He told me, "My politics are my *own!*" He paid a great price for holding to this stance, but the war in Vietnam is history now, while the National Endowment is still here helping writers. Ellison's sense of *agon* was unlike that of Ezra Pound, who also believed that government had a role to play in the encouragement of the arts. But Pound took the radical step of joining the Fascists. He did it, he told Benito Mussolini, "for my poem."

The path that Ellison chose was grounded in something more than a selfish dedication to his own ambition. If one reads through the interviews he made during the years when he supported himself by working for the Federal Writers Program, one can see how deeply embedded these exchanges with black peasants, many of them recent migrants from the South, remained in Ellison's memories. One interview, with a man named Lloyd Green, contains some of the seeds of what would eventually become *Invisible Man*. Another interview, with a deeply religious man named Eli Luster, contains some preview of the sermonizing voice of Reverend Alonzo Hickman in *Juneteenth*.

During the great IQ debates of the early 1970s, Ellison's true, finely balanced temperament became visible to me again. Because of a deeply wounding experience with the initial wave of this racial backlash, I had grown somewhat cynical and wary. I became detached enough to see that a racial reaction was being organized, or orchestrated, from the highest levels of the society. I saw the mythologizing of race as linked to a ritual that I named "the Uncle Biff and the Aunt Bop." Stated simply, racially motivated academics, Uncle Biffs, advanced the argument that black Americans were, genetically, inferior to white Americans. And then the Aunt Bops, sentimental liberals, argued that black Americans were inferior because of our environment backgrounds. No matter what position was more prominent, the debate itself caused the deadly premise to be carried forward. The real question remained as to why this debate, which had the effect of reversing much of the progress that was being made, was taking place at all.

The fallout from this debate affected everyone, Ralph Ellison included. There was a great need, particularly at this time, for some clarity of thinking. Ellison and Albert Murray, his best friend and intellectual partner, were estranged at this time. But when some black Harvard students created the Alain Locke Symposium and invited both men to participate, the two old friends came together. They joined other black intellectuals—Harold Cruse, Nathan Huggins, Hollie

West—in a wide-ranging discussion of the errors that had been made, politically as well as aesthetically, during the past decade. Ellison was especially eloquent on this occasion, speaking to students who, before, might have viewed him with suspicion. In a brilliant speech, he sketched for them the place of black Americans as co-creators of American culture from the very beginnings of the American experiment. He said:

> And speaking of language, whenever anyone tells you you're outside the framework of American culture and when they deflect you into something called "black English," remember that the American version of the English language was born in rebellion against proper English usage, and that the music of the African voice and the imagery coming from the people who lived close to the soil under the condition of slavery added greatly to that language. And when you look for the spiritual context of that language you can be sure that some of the passion for the unfulfilled ideals of democracy comes from the voices of those black and unknown bards, as well as from my mama and papa and your mama and papa crying in church, protesting in pool halls, cussing in shine parlors, and celebrating Juneteenth (that's what we call emancipation). The language of the United States is part of black people's creation. . . . There is no imagery of the great nineteenth-century writers which ignores our existence as metaphor of the human con-

dition. There is no specifically American vernacular and language which has not been touched by us and our style.

I saw Ralph at his apartment in New York shortly after he had attended the Alain Locke Symposium. He told me, in strict confidence, that Derek Bok, the president of Harvard, had been so deeply embarrassed that the great IQ debate had been aided by Harvard faculty members that he had flown from Boston to New York, had met Ralph for a meal, and had offered him a professorship at Harvard. But Ralph was wary. He told me, "I don't want to get involved in any foolishness," and asked me to go to Cambridge and assess what was happening. I went to Cambridge and spoke with Walter Leonard, who was then Bok's vice president for affirmative action. Walter told me that he had done all he could do, that the Harvard faculty had become polarized, and that rather than stay on in a token job, he was about to resign. I conveyed this information to Ralph, and, perhaps for his own reasons, he never accepted the professorship. In later years, as identity politics began to be the new academic fashion, I found myself wondering what positive things Ralph might have contributed to the students, to *all* the students, if, during his final years he had taken that professorship at Harvard.

The last time I saw Ralph alive, as I have said, was at the Ninth Annual Langston Hughes Festival at City College in New York. It was a wonderful gathering of people and memory, one of the most beautiful and deeply personal gatherings I have ever attended. Of course Ralph and Fanny were there, and Mike Harper, and Robert Stepto, and Bernard Harlston, the president of City College, who gave a medal to Ralph and called him "teacher to us all." A group of students, named the Davis Carter Dancers, presented a dance based on five scenes in *Invisible Man*. Their jazz improvisations recalled the rhythm of words, the profound symbolism, that have gone into both *Invisible Man* and Bely's *Peterburg*. Ellison's mind was on *nostoi,* on return, I think now, because he recalled in his speech his loving and nurturing relationship with Langston Hughes. "I must confess," he told the audience, "I'm overwhelmed not only because I have been granted this honor but because the occasion imposes a certain amount of symmetry." He then recalled that Langston Hughes had lived only a few blocks away from the campus while Ralph himself, a young man struggling to become *something,* lived in poverty just across the street from the City College campus. In his speech he tried, once again, to lay out his sense of aesthetics to the students.

In our part of society, which is not always available to the more highly structured levels of social hierarchy, we *have* to depend on personal contacts. These *must not* be destroyed because they are our lifeblood. We communicate through language, through gesture, through inflection, the timbre of laugh, the cast of the eye, and expression. This is, in many ways, the lifeblood of Afro-American experience. It has not been codified—I tend to say "thank God"—but it is our task to codify it. This defining of what it means to be an American who is also black, and part Indian, part white, or whatever. It is at

the core of American experience. We are constantly attempting to define ourselves and then backing away
from some conclusions. . . . Now is the time and the
opportunity through which we can extend the consciousness of the entire American society. And in doing
so we will accomplish something that has escaped us.
That is, we will assist other groups in arriving at some
sort of vital connections between our ideals and our actions. We will make the dream, the ideals of society, a
living fact in the land. And then we can get on with
what is important. You're going to discover that race itself is of secondary importance. Ah, but *culture*—that is
what is important.

I am very, very happy, now, that I was asked to give my
own tribute to Ralph *before* he made this impromptu speech.
Our two speeches, like the published interview we "made"
together, in 1969 and 1970, are *linked,* one by copyright, the
other by sentiment. Of Ralph I said that day, among many
other things:

Rome, in Julius Caesar's time, was content with the
tradition of the city-state inherited from the Greeks.
Rome was said to be "blind" to the future because it
could not move forward without first looking back for
precedent. Caesar's genius led him to *imagine* that by
making the provinces equal with the city of Rome, authority would no longer have to flow outward from the
city square. The concept of the nation-state appeared
first in Caesar's imagination. The price he paid for this

imaginative leap was assassination. It was left to Augustus to impose, consciously, the psychological habits that made ideas and institutions, and not blood, the basis for membership in a community. Perry Miller has remarked that only two nations in the history of the world—Rome under Augustus and America under Jefferson—came consciously into existence. He also noted that black Americans and Indians were the only wild cards in the ethnic equation. The cultural factors imposed by these two groups were the only elements that kept this country from becoming a mere extension of Europe. Of these two, black Americans made up the only group that *could not* look back to a time before the very earliest colonial period, the only group on this continent which created itself, consciously, out of the raw materials indigenous to this country's basic tradition: European, African, and Indian. I admire Ralph Ellison because he had the courage, when it was not fashionable, to stick to his guns—to confirm the complexity of his ethnic and cultural background.

"Oh, yes, Yes, Yes. Yes. YESS,
Do you Love. AH Do you Love?"
'Dear Ralph',

During all the years since Ralph's death, I tried my best to remain loyal to Fanny and also to my best memories of him. I declined an invitation to speak at his funeral, but I did attend the ceremony for him at the American Academy in

1994. I sat in one of the back rows and videotaped the many
tributes to him. In about 1997, I was asked by R.W.B. Lewis
to participate in another tribute to him, this one at the Century Club in New York. Henry Louis Gates, a member of the
club, had arranged the event to help raise money for a portrait of Ralph to be placed on the wall of the Century Club. I
was very, very busy with my teaching, so I declined the invitation to appear. But I did send Skip Gates a copy of my tribute to Ralph, and Skip did read it at the assembly. Now,
trying to think as Ralph did in the modernist vein, I think it
may be useful to recall the words I used then in order to provide a backdrop for the words I am using now. I wrote:

> Just about one week ago I was having a good, soul-
> renewing visit with Stanley Crouch in Iowa City, Iowa,
> where I live. Stanley spoke to my literature class last
> Wednesday evening about the place of improvisation in
> American tradition. He recalled that during the 1980s,
> Ralph Ellison had encouraged him to watch for the per-
> sistence of this tradition in, of all places, a television se-
> ries named *The A Team,* starring a man named Mr. T.
> When Stanley dramatized the conversation between
> himself and Ralph, he imitated perfectly the under-
> stated eloquence of Ellison's voice. I sat with the stu-
> dents and listened to Stanley's re-articulation of
> Ellison's ideas, and I realized that I miss him, and still
> grieve for him, much more than I had cared to admit to
> myself. Ellison's voice had been an intellectual lifeline
> for me, as well as for a great number of people, during
> the Golden Age of this American century.

The hint from Stanley encouraged me to listen again to Ellison's voice. Ever since his death in April of 1994, I have been trying, and failing, to pull together my *thoughts and feelings* about this extraordinarily generous mentor and friend. By the time Stanley arrived in Iowa City, I had written more than two legal pads full of praises of Ellison's ideas. But all those pages were lifeless, I realized now, because until Stanley came, I had never dared to listen again to the tapes of Ellison's real voice, tapes I had collected in an interview with him in 1969 and 1970, and the tapes of a few of his lectures, which I had attended. Stanley helped me break this emotional impasse, and so last Wednesday night I went down to the basement and located those tapes and listened to them, and knew Ralph again as I had once known him: cautioning, suggesting, probing, ironic, laughing, humanly aware, unfailingly eloquent. I grew excited again, almost as excited as I had been when I first heard that voice in the summer of 1969. I copied for Stanley a tape of a speech by Ellison, at the University of Virginia, back in 1978. Then I copied a tape by Albert Murray speaking at Brown University during the early 1970s. I gave both tapes to Stanley, because these two men, their two mentoring voices, were, and still are, inseparable in my memories, as they probably are in Stanley's.

The essay that I am writing about Ralph Ellison I am calling "Gravitas." This word has been so bandied about in recent years by politicians and pundits that I was tempted, as an American Negro (in Ellison's phrase), to "steal" it and to make it my own in terms of meaning. I can imagine Ralph's ironic laughter when I use that old-fashioned description of black Americans. He knew the hidden joke. If, as he suggested, the American Negro was a new form of human expression created on this continent, he also knew Henry James's insistence that "form takes!" Secure in this ironic certainty, Ralph might even approve my efforts to link him to the ancient Latins, especially those of the *Res Publica Romana,* the Roman Thing.

Virgil, in his *Aeneid,* tells Augustus, and also tells us, that the Roman legacy is what Ralph Ellison once said was a hidden name and a complex fate. Both men spoke of the connection between history and destiny, of the relationship between past and future. If to Ellison the essential ritual gesture of American tradition was the signing of the Declaration of Independence and the drafting of the Constitution, to Virgil's Rome it was the circumstances surrounding the flight of Aeneas from burning Troy. Both writers, many centuries apart in time, counseled *piatas* as one cementing value in their societies. Aeneas leaves Troy bearing his father Anchises on his back (who in turn is bearing the Household Gods) and Aeneas is holding his son, Ascanius, by the hand and is leading a small community of people. This community of people will, centuries later, lay the foundation of the *communitas* named Rome. Virgil thus teaches Augustus that it is piety toward the ancestors, toward the gods, toward the family, and toward the community that has in the past, and will in the future, keep Rome vital. It is the self-negating of the individual will, Virgil taught, and the subscription to *religio,* to the binding forces, which result in *communitas,* that best describes *pias Aeneas.* When a man is in harmony with all these forces, he may have "weight," "consequence," that intrinsic quality named "gravitas."

During all of his writing life, Ralph Ellison insisted, sometimes to the extent of irritating some people, on the importance of *piatas* toward what the founding documents, and what the American *mos miorum* (the traditions of the greaters) pointed to as essential for the future. Ellison's insistence on this was almost religious in its intensity. I can still hear his voice saying, "Things were not *supposed* to be this way!" I had always been skeptical of his liberal use of the collective "we Americans" and "us" until I realized that this language always presupposed a community of people, whether or not they were conscious of it, relying in one way or another on the *mos miorum,* the traditions which grew out of the democratic principles and the aesthetics which Ellison so eloquently defined. I came to realize, slowly, that Ralph was speaking out of a sense of *religio,* one based on the promise of democracy, without which binding the entire American experiment would fail. The great irony is that he made these assertions as a black American, as a person in no way exempt from the slights and scars which derive from racism. He possessed the emotional strength to look beyond slights and rebuffs and attempt to envision an aesthetic approach to an evolving culture that would move us all beyond race as the beginning and end of all discussions. I have the highest possible admiration for him because he held to this high standard until the day he died. If Ralph Ellison did not possess what the Latins called *gravitas*, then the term has lost the content of its original meaning.

I have been told that the ritual occasion for this gathering of Ralph's friends is the unveiling of a portrait of him that will be hung in the halls of the Century Club. I have never been inside your club, but I can imagine Ralph being there, and I can also imagine the ambience he must have felt being an equal among his peers. I know that if Ralph were alive he would rise to this occasion with all of his eloquence. He liked ceremonies, and he was dogged in his pursuit of their ritual basis. I wonder what he would say now, looking at the unveiling of a likeness of himself. I think he would find some way to look back on the origins of the Century Club, to the *mos miorum* evolved by its past members, and he would not blush to say that, given the magic implicit in the movement of American democracy, it was only a matter of time before someone of his complexion and his background shared a place on the walls of the club, even as he had shared the ambience of the club during his lifetime. Ellison would see this ceremony within the context of something much larger than himself. I can see the self-deprecating modesty in his face, and I can hear him speaking about his own background in Oklahoma City, his riding freight trains to college at Tuskeegee, his various jobs, the things he learned in the most unexpected of places. No doubt he would flesh out his biography. But then he would add to it that he might never have become a novelist, or even have been invited to be a member of the Century Club, but for that one thing he loved, perhaps better than himself: the American experiment in democracy and the "rightness" of its proofs. Ralph would find some way to put that *Res Publica Americana*—the American Thing—at the basis of his own achievements and then far above them in importance. If this is not the *piatas* written about by Virgil, then the original meaning of that old Latin word has also been lost.

Even so, during his lifetime, Ralph Ellison personified this word, as well as many others. Among those others, perhaps it was *gravitas* that he personified with an illuminating persistence.

"Si monumentum requiris, circumspice."
"If you seek his monument, look around you."

Disneyland

Not long ago, as a kind of joke, I sent Rachel, my daughter, by E-mail, a line from an old song by Lambert, Hendricks, and Ross and Louis Armstrong:

> If you're king for only a day,
> How'd you go about having your way . . . ?

This is the answer that came back:

If I were king, people couldn't blast their bass players in their cars, and if they did they would be punished by listening to "All Things Considered" on NPR all day long. Except that (if I were king) NPR wouldn't have much to report on the radio. Only good news. And so they would fill up the airtime by playing songs backwards and giving $100 to listeners who can name the tune. Everyone would have to smile at least once a day! Band-Aids wouldn't hurt when you yanked them off sores; the walls in dentists' offices would be covered with Waterhouse and Rosetti murals instead of lame, symmetrical, diamond patterns; and no one would have to listen to elevator music while on hold—only Swing. If I were king oranges would grow prepeeled, and pens wouldn't leak, and no one would be named Gertrude. Parks would have giant tree houses with signs that read: People of Any Height May Climb! Anyone could order off a damn kiddy menu, and swivel chairs would be a requirement for every dinner table—so if conversation got really boring people could twirl around instead. Everyone would have their own ideas about religion and no judgments about anyone else's. . . . [Weddings:] At twilight everyone would wander around a giant park with spouting fountains and a double rainbow would streak the sky. A church chime would ring at 7:00 P.M. (you know, the one that sounds like our doorbell) and that would be the sign for everybody to make a circle (not caring or even wondering if you're standing next to a bum, a Ph.D., or a movie star) and do the hokeypokey. That's what it's all about.

I was amazed by the reach and vitality of Rachel's imagination as she attempted to reorder the world according to her own sense of happiness. I sent her another E-mail:

You have learned that God created the world in six days, and on the seventh day He rested. But this is not entirely true. I have heard it said that on the seventh day God was not yet pleased with His creations. So on that day He created another thing that would be able to celebrate all the work He had done on the first six days. On the seventh day God created IMAGINATION, and

he gave this thing dominion over all else He had created. The person who is blessed with this is able to
stand in his own place and at the same time project
himself into another person's place, see from the eyes of
that person, and understand the world from that
person's point of view. This gift is called "compassion,"
and it is a very, very rare thing.

Rachel, at eighteen, is doubly privileged. She has had
imaginative as well as emotional support, all that I could
give her from a great distance, for all her life. She seems to be
a very happy and self-directed young woman. She graduated
from high school in Charlottesville, Virginia, on June 5,
1997. She came to Iowa City for ten days, and then went off
to New York to enroll in the Alvin Ailey Summer Dance
Workshop. I supported her eight weeks in New York as a
kind of graduation gift to her. Other friends in New York—
Nancy Ramsey, Stanley Crouch, Albert Murray and his family, Faith Childs, Suketu and Sunita Mehta, Ana Debevoise,
Sherman Malone—supported her emotionally. Rachel has
benefited from being "closely held" by impromptu structures of dependability, which can be improvised around
friends in any other part of the United States, as well as in
England, Japan, and Australia. Both her life and my own
have been blessed by instances of kindly interference which,
while renewing our spirits, have taught me that the increase
in the range of their possibility depends on one's involvement in the lives of people outside of one's own group. This
is the Great Road that Rachel and I have traveled since she
was a baby. Now that she is eighteen, and enrolled in college,

I think and hope, and even pray, that she is secure and well adjusted and *whole* in the deepest human sense.

In a recent correspondence with a divorced writer, he expressed how extremely painful his isolation from his daughter was. He loved her a great deal; she lived with her mother in Atlanta, while he lived in Baltimore. In writing back to him about this modern condition of alienation between fathers and children, an alienation that results from divorce, I restrained an impulse to quote to him a line from a song in Walt Disney's *Peter Pan:* "You can fly, you can fly, you can fly."

I know the truth of this from my own experience.

I will not give in to the temptation to finger all the details of my own divorce except to say that it was extremely complicated and extremely bitter. All my efforts to negotiate a peaceful end to a very bad marriage failed, and this void was quickly filled by predatory lawyers. Since I had announced publicly that my only goal was to get appropriate time with my daughter and then get out of Charlottesville, Rachel, who was then not quite two years old, became a pawn in the manipulation of lawyers and other, hidden forces that were determined that I would remain "captive." She was withheld from me through a series of devices, even when visitation times had already been scheduled. When I responded in anger, my voice was recorded and used against me at another time. But it was here that an instance of what I have called "kindly interference" took place. I went to see Shirley Porter, a black woman who worked as a nanny for mothers in the Charlottesville community. Shirley was a wise and kindly woman, one who wanted to be fair. Since Rachel spent most of her nights at Shirley's home, while being withheld from me, I would go to Shirley's home in the early evenings, eat dinner with her and Rachel, and help Shirley give Rachel a bath. Then I would sleep on the floor next to Rachel's crib. The next morning, before the other "mommies" brought their children to Shirley's house, I would help Shirley give Rachel breakfast, and even share the meal with her. If any of the "mommies" showed up early, while I was still there, I would hide in Shirley's closet until they left. On those Sundays when Rachel was with me, I would take her to Shirley's church. The two of us would sit, Rachel between us, on the same bench. Shirley Porter risked her own economic well-being to help us in this way.

In the early spring of the following year, 1981, a second small miracle occurred. I had been trying my best to heed the advice of friends in other parts of the country: *"Get out of there!"* I saw two jobs being advertised—one at Tucson, by Vance Bourjaily, and another at Iowa, by Jack Leggett. Both men were understanding, but Jack Leggett was especially kind. On a Sunday morning, about one month later, he called me in Charlottesville and said, "Jim, the job is yours in the fall, if you are able to take it. In addition, we want you to teach summer school." Jack had a gentle laugh, an easy, patrician manner. I believe that he was incapable of kicking anyone who was down. It was simply a matter of breeding and habit.

But the most important incident of kindly interference, the one that set Rachel and me on the pathway leading to the Great Road, came in May of that same year. By this time I had secured, through the legal system, some visitation time with Rachel. We had one overnight every other weekend, plus one afternoon together on Wednesdays. One Saturday evening when I brought Rachel to my small apartment, I saw an Express Mail envelope taped to the door. I tore it down, believing it was another notice from one of the credit card companies to which, back then, I owed my future. Rachel and I had worked out certain rituals for her overnights with me: counting off the steps as we walked up them, playing games while she ate her dinner and while she took her bath. We had a plastic windup duck, and this toy would go into the bathtub of water. And then we would splash water, sing songs, and play until the antique clock next to her crib chimed 8:00 P.M. This hour was our sacred time: the eight chimes signaled that our play would be transported to Rachel's crib, where it would continue until she fell asleep. But that Saturday night our bath ritual was interrupted by a telephone call. When I answered a voice with great authority in it said, "Young man, I . . ." But I never allowed the voice to continue. I said, "Look, I'm giving my daughter a bath. Call me some other time." Then I hung up. After Rachel and I had finished *Goodnight Moon* and she had fallen asleep, I opened the Express Mail letter. It was from the MacArthur Foundation in Chicago. It informed me that I had been awarded a five-year grant of $192,000. Later that evening the telephone rang again. It was Roderick MacArthur, who had been personally calling up the winners of that very first round of awards. I had hung up on him. I apologized profusely. Then I spoke with Gerald Freund, who was then the director of the Prize Fellows Program. I thanked him, but asked if public news about my selection could be avoided. I tried to explain to him the personal complexities of a situation that must have been a world away from his understanding; what to a white person would be an honor can also be, to a black person, the sense that one is being made a target in a society devoted to white supremacy. Gerald Freund just could not understand why I did not want the news about my recent good fortune to be made public. But I could remember, very well, just why I had avoided all publicity after, less than three years before, I had won a Pulitzer Prize for fiction. I could remember the contempt of a white colleague, who sneered intentionally in my presence, "Somebody around here is getting *too much* attention!" But Gerald Freund said that the news about the awards had already been sent out for publication on Monday morning. He said I should be proud, having been the first choice on the first list of MacArthur Fellows.

On Monday morning, I said to the caller from National Public Radio, "The gods are playful."

Later that week, I told a reporter for the *Washington Post,* who had come to Charlottesville to interview me, "I'm going to give some of the money to my church, I'm going to take Mrs. Julia Smith to visit her relatives more often, and I'm going to be the best father I can be to Rachel."

Mrs. Julia Smith, an elderly black woman whom I had met a little over one year before, had been, in those days, my constant companion. As a matter of fact, part of the interview had taken place at Mrs. Smith's home in Barboursville. Rachel was with me. I was holding Rachel while I talked with the reporter. The reporter later wrote that Mrs. Julia Smith kept saying "Moo" to Rachel. Rachel herself kept repeating "Candy."

Rachel was in my arms holding a lollipop when she said this.

Rachel remembers very little about those early years, but she does retain some emotional clues. She remembers the plastic duck, she remembers the antique clock, and she remembers the crib next to it. She also remembers Mrs. Julia Smith. Some years ago, I asked her who, of all our friends, were the best people. She replied, "Mrs. Julia Smith, Joellen MacDougall, Ellie Simmons, and the man at the Coralville Fruit Stand" (where we buy our Christmas tree each year). A year or so ago, Rachel, in high school, located through a library computer a copy of the old interview in the *Washington Post*. She sent me a decorated picture of a much younger version of myself holding her while she licked a lollipop. Through some miracle, Rachel seems to have escaped the extreme pain of that period.

But I did not.

I completed my last classes at Virginia, adjusting my schedule to meet the very powerful legal pressures placed on me. One of them was a list of written interrogatories, one hundred or more, and the very first inquiry was an accounting of all my books by authors, titles, dates purchased, places purchased, prices paid. I hired a student named Edward Jones to help me with the list. We spent almost one week listing close to two thousand books. But I taught well that last semester. The student evaluations, which were turned in to the people in the English Department office, were glowing. I know this because, for some reason, they were never filed with the proper university or state officials. Although they were turned over to the English office when my classes ended in May, in the late fall of that same year, when I had begun teaching again, this time in Iowa, some kindly soul placed them in my departmental mailbox and Edward Jones retrieved them for me. The students said, "Excellent." "He is the best teacher here." "He knows too much." My heart grew full when I read, almost six months later, these student evaluations from my last semester in Charlottesville. And I will thank, for the rest of my life, the person who made this kindly interference on my behalf. This angel must have been familiar with the destructive strategy then at work: hamstring the suspect, and then gossip abroad that he is crazy.

But before this strategy could work its will, I was in Iowa.

Before I left, even before the custody hearings, I took some things I had purchased for Rachel to her mother's house. Some of my former colleagues were there. One of them said, "*Who* do you think you are? You've *fired* the University of Virginia?" We were standing in the front yard. Rachel was shouting "Jim . . . Jim?" in imitation of my outraged former colleagues. I picked Rachel up and I kissed her. I told my daughter, "I will always come for you. I will always come for you."

Then I drove, nonstop, to St. Louis. I rested there. And then I drove the rest of the way to Iowa.

I flew back three times for the custody hearings during the summer of 1981, while I was teaching two courses at Iowa. Each time I was pressured to return to the marriage and to Charlottesville. I finally asked the judge to get the issue settled. But when his final decree arrived at my apartment in Iowa City, in late July, I decided to not open the envelope until after my summer school classes were over. The envelope

lay on my desk for over three weeks. Finally, a friend from
New Haven, Sherman Malone, came by bus through Iowa
City on her way back from a camping trip with her family.
We had lunch, and Sherman pleaded with me to open the envelope. She went home with me and watched as I read the
judge's language: full custody to the mother, limited visitation rights, hefty alimony and child support, and lawyers'
fees. In addition, in response to the largesse of the Mac-
Arthur Foundation, my apartment in Charlottesville, without any formal inspection, was decreed "inferior" to the
home of the custodial parent.

Sherman Malone said that I got drunk and raged all night
in my bed. She told me that she lay awake all night, in her
sleeping bag in the living room, and listened to my ravings.
Sherman told me, when I took her the next day to the bus de-
pot, for her trip back to New Haven, that I never expressed
any anger toward her. Then she left. In the evening of that
same day, I went out to Lone Tree, Iowa, to keep a dinner ap-
pointment with Bob Shacochis and Catfish, Bob's companion. A number of young writers from my classes that summer
were also at Bob's home in Lone Tree. But I did not feel
teacherly that evening. Emotionally unequipped for small
talk, I excused myself and went up to Bob and Catfish's bedroom and lay in their bed. Later, Bob came up and asked what
was wrong. I disclosed a few facts to him. And it was then,
during that bleak evening, that another instance of kindly intervention occurred. Bob Shacochis insisted that I go for a
drive with him in his car. We drove slowly along the narrow,
dirt roads of Lone Tree, up hillocks and down dales, through
the dying summer light. Bob drove aimlessly past tall corn-

fields, past soybeans begging for harvest. We smelled farm-lands and animal manure in the moist breezes of sunset. The heavy smells seemed to be insisting that one form of life was *intended* to sustain another form of life. The bursting crops said that this was Nature's Way, and that all of life was, fi-nally, only an extension of this same blueprint in Nature's Plan. Kindly, cooking-loving Bob Shacochis drove me up and down those roads, desperate to find some way to help, until something renewing from Nature began flowing into me from those fields and I knew that I would not die. When we returned to Bob's house, well after dark, people wondered what had been wrong with me. Bob never said a word to any-one.

This was in mid-August of 1981, when I touched bottom and slowly began to rebuild.

I wrote to the judge, acknowledging his decree, and asked him, as chancellor, if the situation could still be moved to-ward arbitration instead of remaining in the legal system. He wrote back to me, saying that he was bound by law. He also suggested that I should return to Charlottesville, be-cause the noncustodial parent and the child "tend to lose a great deal." I wrote back that I could not return. I also wrote my resignation from the University of Virginia on the back of the judge's decree. And it was here that my priorities came into clear focus, and it was here that I began to make some firm decisions.

I had about $3,000 each month coming in from the MacArthur Foundation, plus about $29,000 per year com-ing from the University of Iowa, plus another $6,000 for each summer that I taught summer school. In addition, the

MacArthur Foundation awarded, in those days, an institutional grant of $15,000 for a period of five years to the institution with which I was connected. I had an apartment in Charlottesville, and another one in Iowa City, and friends in both places. Most important of all, I still had my imagination. I decided that I would not spend any of the MacArthur money on myself. The institutional grant, amounting to $75,000 over a period of five years, I gave to the University of Iowa Foundation for the support of young writers in the workshop. Jack Leggett and I agreed, over a handshake, that the money would be used to support any talented writer who, because of special circumstances, was not eligible for the usual areas of financial aid. I made a will, one leaving everything I owned to Rachel, and I named my older sister, Mary, Rachel's guardian, just in case something should happen to me. I tried as best I could to strip myself of everything that was a distraction to my focus. I began, then, in my *imagination*, to view the country as one big house. My bedroom was in Iowa City. Rachel's bedroom was in Charlottesville. Friends had guest rooms, for Rachel and for me, in Richmond, in Washington, D.C., in Stamford and in New Haven, in New York, in Boston, in Cambridge, in Chicago, in Oakland, and in Los Angeles. All Rachel and I had to do, with the MacArthur money, and with my own earnings after that largesse had run out, was to move from room to room in this huge house, bonding as we went with each other and with our friends.

It was then that I began to fly.

One weekend each month Rachel and I spent "quality time" together with Edward Jones, my former student, who

lived in my old apartment on Little High Street in Charlottesville.

I hired a therapist in Charlottesville, one who expressed
outrage over the terms of the judge's decree. He helped me
negotiate more time with Rachel. He suggested that, since
Rachel was older, she ought to be able to spend one weekend
each month, and then one full week each month, with me in
Iowa City.

Then Rachel and I began to fly.

The therapist suggested that, because Rachel was getting
older, she should spend two weeks, then three weeks, then
six weeks during the summers with me in Iowa City.

But, later, this same therapist declared that he could no
longer do any more for me. He advised me to return to Charlottesville.

In 1986, after a court hearing, the legal system of Charlottesville conceded to me the full summer. I also "won"
spring breaks, including Easter, every other Christmas, plus
one weekend each month from after Rachel's school on Friday afternoon until school time on Monday mornings. The
lawyer who secured this "boon" for me noted, with some theatrical relish, that the long weekend each month made room
for me to remain with my daughter until time for her school
on Monday morning. This, he said, was the best possible reason for me to return to Charlottesville for good. He told me,
with some hint of brotherly love, "Now, don't make yourself
such a stranger to Charlottesville."

I made myself a stranger.

Rachel and I met in Washington, D.C. We met in New
York. We met in Boston. The United Airlines people at

Dulles came to know Rachel through their escort service. She told me they always said, when she was connecting at Dulles for her flight into Chicago, "There goes Rachel again." The ticket agents and security people at the Cedar Rapids Airport also came to know me and our ritual. One of the security guards, a woman, would always say when she saw me, "There goes that father who loves his daughter." Rachel came to Cedar Rapids; I went to Dulles or to National. When she was still too young to travel unescorted, I *imagined* a pathway for us. I hired Opie Porter, Shirley Porter's son, to drive Rachel from Charlottesville to Dulles or to National. My usual pathway was through St. Louis. To reach St. Louis on the very first flight out of Cedar Rapids, I had to get up early enough to drive from Iowa City to the Cedar Rapids Airport to take the flight at 6:45 A.M. When I reached St. Louis, and was sure that I would be booked on the flight into National or Dulles, I would call up Opie Porter in Charlottesville and tell him to begin his drive. My own flight usually arrived at National at 11:30 A.M. The same flight back to St. Louis, and from there into Cedar Rapids, left National Airport at 12:30 P.M. During this hour, I would arrive at National, and Opie would arrive with Rachel in his car; she would be led to me, and then she and I would take the 12:30 P.M. flight back to St. Louis, then back to Cedar Rapids, arriving at 3:30 P.M. or so. Then we would drive in my car directly to my class at 4:30 P.M. Rachel would sit through the class with the grace of the innocent. And then, after class, we would go *home*.

Rachel passed through dangers. Once, during the Persian Gulf War, she told me by telephone that she could not fly anymore because Saddam Hussein had threatened to blow up the airplanes. She, like many other people, was very frightened of the Arabs. I asked her if she actually *knew* any Arabs. She said that she did not. I told her that I knew some Arabs, and that if she found the courage to fly from Charlottesville to Dulles, I would fly there to meet her. And then we would spend the weekend in Washington, D.C., and I would introduce her to an Arab. She consented. Then I called up Sam Hamod, an old friend, a Lebanese Arab with roots in Detroit, and asked if Rachel and I could meet him and Shirley, his girlfriend, in Washington. After Rachel and I arrived, and after Sam came to our hotel, I told Rachel, "This is Sam Hamod. He is a friend and an Arab." Rachel liked Sam because of his personality, but she especially liked Shirley. We spent a number of years, during many trips, exploring Washington with Sam and Shirley.

Just before Christmas, during a visitation period, Rachel called me from O'Hare Airport with quiet hysteria in her voice. A massive snow and ice storm had closed down the airport, and all flights in and out of O'Hare had been canceled. And since the cancellations had been due to the weather and not to any mechanical failures, United Airlines would not be responsible for meals and lodging for its stranded passengers. Rachel was then about ten years old. She had no money, and was being obliged to sleep in a chair or else on the floor of the airport with the other children of divorce, tagged like Christmas gifts, who were serving out their obligations to distant parents. I heard in my daughter's voice, that cold December evening, the quiet desperation of the many millions of young people who, through no fault of their own, had become casualties of two decades of gender warfare between selfish adults. In reality, the children had had to assume the responsibilities of adults, while the adults were content to dramatize their own fantasies. During that hard December night, I sat at my table and made telephone calls, like thousands of other anonymous parents, to every possible source of help. I called up Leon Forrest in Evanston. I called up Marshall and Irene Patner in Hyde Park. I called up a former student, Joe Hurka, who lived in a suburb closer to O'Hare than Evanston and Hyde Park. There is a kind of doom-filled desperation, if not hysteria, that comes when one realizes that almost every established structure of dependability—parenting, family, technology—can be rendered useless when the mysterious currents of life, or when the indifferences of Nature, decide to announce themselves. While the old structures still remain defined and intact and viable, the flow of life, which has moved beyond them, looks back at this impotency and laughs at the naïveté of those who once placed all their faith in inventions of the human mind. I learned that night, or perhaps I only *relearned,* that all such dead ends are under the control of the gods of life, and that one must depend on *them* for magic, for instances of kindly intervention.

All of the friends I called offered to drive to O'Hare and rescue Rachel. But Joe Hurka's father had a tractioned car, and his suburb was closest to O'Hare. Joe Hurka and his father went to Rachel, while I waited by the telephone ready to comfort her if, by some miracle, she was able to get through the crowd of hysterical children and use the telephone again. Well after midnight, Joe Hurka called me from his home. They had arrived safely and Rachel was in bed. Joe advised me to also go to bed. He said that Rachel was fine, that she had viewed the experience as an adventure, and that I was much more upset than she was. He said that before she went to bed, Rachel had gone out to have a snowball fight with his mother, and that the entire family had been struck by her calm, politeness, and good manners. Joe promised that he and his father would drive Rachel back to O'Hare in the morning and put her on the first flight into Cedar Rapids. He advised me to go out to the airport as early as possible so that, when Rachel arrived, mine would be the first face she saw.

I did not go to bed that night. I waited until dawn, and after Joe Hurka called to say that they were leaving for O'Hare, I drove, ahead of the snowplows and the salt spreaders, to the Cedar Rapids Airport. When the flight from O'Hare arrived and when Rachel came down the jetway, I thought my heart would break.

Rachel knows very little about my side of the story.

A belief in the possibility of magic, or of acts of kindly intervention, has been one of the sources of our bond during all these years. I did not want my own pain, my own bitterness, to affect Rachel, so I intentionally grounded our bond in instances of spiritual nurture as a way of calling her attention to the possibility of magic in life, or perhaps I did this in order to heal myself. I just do not know. I know that, like many black males, I had never had a loving bond with a father. The void that this loss left in me was, when I consider it, a kind of opportunity. I was "free" to imagine the kind of father-child bond I would have liked for myself. I knew, from my own experiences as a child, *what I must not do.* But I did not know exactly *what I should do.* I was thus forced to improvise. During all these years, Rachel has not wanted for anything of a material nature. I grew up in extreme poverty, and, as for all other children of poverty, the expatriation of this condition from the lives of our children is the first order of business, the first "Thou shalt not." But I wanted Rachel to exhaust her appetites for material comforts early on, and then I wanted her to look for something beyond the material world. I think I wanted, first of all, to open up a philosophical issue for her.

It is common knowledge that the human spirit has, for its illusion of stability, a sense of being totally encompassed, of being *held,* in a reality that has a structure of dependability. That is, all things *inside* the self and all things *outside* the self, ideally, must cohere, must seem to belong *together.* This is the gift of childhood, the gift of natural integrity that is basic to human equipment. I did not want Rachel to lose this gift, even as I flew with her over a corrupt and uncaring world. I wanted very badly to provide her with something she could hold on to, through childhood and adolescence, and as far into adulthood as she could carry the idea. Simply put, I wanted her to know that something *more* existed beyond the conventional structures of dependability. This thing had to do with, *has* to do with, the frightening vistas that come into focus when all things on which we once depended—family, status, settled orders—erode, and we are left to make a path for ourselves. During such times, when the gods of life seem to be laughing at our mind-based illusions, our only refuge must be in the realm of magic, or religion, or imagination, or in those instances of kindly interference that flow from the coveted goodness in the hearts of other people. This realm is beyond race, or class, or region, or all the other structures of social gradation. It ministers to life itself, to what is best in other people. I had come to learn this the hard way, and I wanted to pass it on, with my approval, to Rachel. *Something is always with us, in the darkness as well as in the light. And if this is true, then one must walk through the world, even in darkness, by the same light one saw when all was light.* Without really believing this, I tried my best to walk with Rachel through all the dark places as if I could guide us by my concentration on the light. This seems to me the footpath to the Great Road that would take my daughter toward some absolute meanings. As for myself, I could only approach that road by way of the footpath. Perhaps this was, finally, my destiny. But I wanted very badly for Rachel to leave the footpath I had trod for her and get on the Great Road that will lead, eventually, to transcendent meanings.

Perhaps, for this reason, we began at Disneyland.

The three great revolutions into which my daughter was born—the one called civil rights, the one called feminist, and the one called technological—had, as one of their consequences, eroded all accepted structures of dependability, structures which, in much of human history, had helped define what was meaningful in human life. A black person was *supposed* to be a servant, an inferior. A woman was *supposed* to be an appendage to a man. A technique was *supposed* to be something linked to ritual, and the ritual itself was *supposed* to be an affirmation of ancient, ancestral imperatives. Then, quite suddenly, all of this changed, and a new generation was left with the responsibility of walking its way through a broken world, one with no certainties and, much more crucial, one with no real purchase on the future. The fear and the anger and the defensivenesses that resulted from this massive breakdown has caused those who were supposed to be inno- cents, those who were supposed to be the saving remnants, the future generations, to retreat in fear from the world that has been made for them. They seem to not want the future, because they cannot yet see themselves at home in it. News- paper accounts, daily, provide stories about young people in all regions and groups and classes acting out this sense of spiritual impotence. Stories of killings in Iowa, in New Jer- sey, in New York, in Mississippi. And closer to home, my daughter recently told me that a young woman she knew, named Elizabeth, had hanged herself. She was a brilliant young woman, was about to graduate at the top of her class, had everything going for her. And yet she hanged herself, without telling any of her friends that she was in extreme pain. And it is here that I want to believe that some of what I have been trying to pass on to Rachel may have been effec- tive. Rachel tells me that, ever since Elizabeth's suicide, she has taken it upon herself to write letters to all her friends, letting them know that she will be there for them if they are ever in that kind of deep despair. Rachel, I want to believe, has learned about the magic that derives from instances of kindly intervention. She has learned this, I want to believe, from the sense of magic that has been cultivated between the two of us, over the past eighteen years. We have gone to Dis- neyland, a place where the established order of dependability soars up into fields of magic. Perhaps Rachel has seen, in that Magic Kingdom, the places at which the rational world, with all its assaults, and the irrational world, with all its potency, meet and dance in some kind of benign compromise about the hidden gods of life and their intentions. I do not know. I do know that I have tried, despite my own pain, to take my daughter along the footpath leading to this Great Road.

We went to Disneyland many times and in many different ways.

We began with fireflies. We began with sitting on the back steps, on the front steps, of our house in Iowa City, always at dusk, and watching motes of light scramble and blink in hurried conversation about their hidden secrets. My girlfriend helped deepen this mood. Her name was Vera. She was less than two feet tall, and she lived under my dining room table. She only came out at night, and even then she disclosed herself only to me. A magic tree soon grew up just outside Rachel's bedroom window. It was in secret communication with a magic rock we found by sheer luck. If one wished sincerely enough for something, while holding the magic rock, that thing wished for sometimes appeared, overnight, on the branches of or under the magic tree. We attended church. Almost every Christmas Eve, when Rachel was with me. Santa would call from some point on his journey to speak with us and to determine whether we were being good. We always wrote letters to him and to Mrs. Claus, wishing them well. Fresh food—carrots, eggnog, peanuts, candies—were left on the windowsill just behind our Fraser fir, our sweet-smelling Christmas tree. Santa and his crew always had a feast. They always left us many great gifts. The only time I was slighted was when I wrote my own letter to Santa in the braggadocio of rap lyrics. I have never, ever repeated this mistake. The Easter Bunny, too, came to our house each spring. He could be counted on to leave bounteous Easter baskets brimming with choice candies. The Iowa Tooth Fairy came, once in a while, usually disguised as a pig. When the accelerating technological revolution produced the VCR, we considered this artifact benign, but only if used for a good purpose. We secured tapes of Disney's *Dumbo, Bambi,* and *Jack and the Beanstalk.* We waited breathlessly for each new Disney release. Once, with this same streak of luck, we secured a copy of Disney's *Song of the South* in a London department store. In a mall in downtown Washington, D.C., we located a store dealing with items for magical acts. We always went there to study the demonstrations, and we secured a great many devices. We spent the winter months planning, by long-distance telephone, our plans for the summer and for vacation trips in late August. Our watch-word was, always, *"When the leaves come, we'll go to Iowa."* We flew, on magic carpets, to London, to Paris, to Madrid. We toured the Tower of London, walked the streets of Paris, took a train to the Disneyland in the suburbs of Paris. We took a bus tour from Madrid to Toledo.

But most of all, for at least six summers, we went to Disneyland. At first we went by train across the Rocky Mountains and the Cascades. We flew to Los Angeles from Seattle, and we drove a car from the city into Anaheim. We went to *Dis*-neyland, diz, diz, diz *Dis*-ney-land. Then we went by airplane directly into the John Wayne Airport. We took friends there with us. Sometimes we stayed for almost a full week. We took Jarilyn Woodard, Yarri Lutz, from Iowa City to the freeways of Los Angeles leading to Anaheim. Driving, I would say to my female passengers, "Let's go, *men!*" And they would answer, *"We're not men!"* We went to *Dis*-ney-land, to diz, diz, diz *Dis*neyland. We met friends from Los Angeles there: Cynthia Kadohata, Jeannette Miyamoto, Adrienna Woodard, Brenda Chadwick. Jarilyn Woodard, Rachel's best friend, always went with us; and her sister, Adrienna, always met us there. Once we went there with the entire Woodard family, Jarilyn's mother, Barbara, included. While the young people explored, Barbara and I would sit and talk about adult things.

The best thing about Disneyland is that the real world is left at the door. Nothing unhappy gets into that place. It is a controlled environment, one strolled and controlled by infectious illusions. Mickey, Goofy, Minnie, and Company are always visible in the crowds to remind people of the possibility of magic. I have a picture of Rachel, when she was four or five years old, trying to pull Arthur's sword from its stone. I have pictures of her hugging Mickey, Goofy, Tinkerbell, Peter Pan, Wendy, Captain Hook. We always stayed late enough to watch the Electric Lights Parade, one in which the entire product of Walt Disney's imagination, waving from lighted floats, would parade through the entire length of Disneyland. Thousands of people stay until closing time just to see this act. The adults among them, from almost every nation in the world, seem, at that special time, to forget that they are adults and glow with the magic of children. In that place, both imaginations and spirits are renewed. It is a place chock-full of kindly interferences. I have heard it said that Walt Disney was inspired by God. I do not know this for a fact, but I do know that we went many times to *Dis*ney-land, to diz, diz, diz, diz *Dis*-neyland, always looking for something.

Rachel liked the Peter Pan ride and also the Pirates of the Caribbean. I was partial to the Small World tour. It was an old ride, in boats, one that displayed in each carefully crafted exhibit comic hints of a number of cultures. I always considered this Small World tour an optimistic assertion of untested assumptions. The beauty of the ride resided in its stubborn insistence on something—all those nations singing in one accord "It's a small world after all"—that was steadily being called into question by reality. But reality, as I have said, had been banned from the park. Both Rachel and I liked that. We liked to be renewed by the old insistences.

A time of reckoning came, however. When Rachel entered high school, realities began to crowd in. Her peers began to challenge the authenticity of Santa Claus, of her magic rock, of all the good things she kept associating with Iowa. She got into a fight with one critic and was suspended from school for a day. After this she grew depressed. After Christmas of that year she told me that she wanted to come to Iowa to live with me. A month or so later she tried to do harm to herself. I tried, at first, to negotiate a way for her to get out. This effort failed, and so I had to mount a legal fight. I lost this battle. Now both Rachel and I were disillusioned. I was prepared to throw in the towel, to give up on all the flights and on the constant wear on my health and on my resources. I was prepared to let Rachel go. But then, in another instance of kindly intervention, at another point at which an established structure has asserted the dominance of its reality, a wise friend advised me that the currents of life are not, finally, under the control of *any* structure of dependability. She counseled me, in response to my desire to give up the struggle, "I would suggest just the opposite." So the flying continued, through all of Rachel's high school years. And so did the reliance on fields of magic. If *something* magical sensed that Rachel was frightened of the growing expectations and demands of adulthood, as all teenagers are, some magic beads and crystals might just appear on her magic tree outside her bedroom window. This was sent by the gods of life for purposes of reassurance. And so, during those high school years, with the steady optimism of childhood behind us, Rachel and I kept going to *Dis*neyland. We went to *diz* diz diz *Dis*-neyland.

I have no way of knowing, now, whether or not this cushion of unreality has helped or hurt my daughter. The world is an unrelenting enemy of all illusions. But, at the very same time, the world is always in great need of some guarantors of the future. It may well be that Elizabeth, the young woman who hanged herself, had no such guarantors. It may well be that Rachel did not harm *herself* because she, after being educated into the power of illusions, had something *more* to look forward to. I just do not know. But I do know that something was learned, by Rachel and by her best friend, Jarilyn Woodard, during all those excursions to see the Magic Kingdom.

It was Jarilyn Woodard who taught this thing to me.

We went, on our next-to-last trip to Disneyland, with Jarilyn Woodard and John, her brother, and with Barbara Woodard, their mother. Fred Woodard, Barbara's husband, did not go with us. But all of us had a wonderful time, as an extended family, during those five days. Rachel and Jarilyn had grown up together in Iowa City. Even when Jarilyn was two or three years old, Barbara would allow me to fly with her to O'Hare Airport to meet Rachel's plane coming in from Dulles. Jarilyn's heart would break each time Rachel left, and it pained me to have to inflict this loss on her so periodically. Both girls spent a great deal of time together in my house. We played "Big Bad Wolf" together; I cooked for them; I laughed when they imitated me at my table, mechanically turning pages in books, smoking cigarettes, and drinking beer. They used to write little tomes to me about the dangers of smoking ("STOP In The Name Of Health, Before You Kill Yourself!"), and many times I chased them down the block, in mock desperation, because they had taken my cigarettes. I loved Jarilyn Woodward as I loved my own daughter. Rachel and Jarilyn grew as close as sisters. They *were* sisters when we went to Disneyland during the 1980s. And they were still sisters when we went there with Barbara Woodard in August of 1988.

But four months later, on January 10, 1989, Barbara Woodard had a heart attack. Fred Woodard called me early that evening and said, "Would you come and get the children? I have to go to the hospital. I think that Barbara has just died." I drove out to their house and found Jarilyn in a state of shock. John was down in the basement, kicking at the wall. I took both children back to my house. I put John in a sofa bed. I put Jarilyn in Rachel's bed. Then I prayed with her until she fell asleep. I sat at my table then, and waited. Around 1:00 A.M., Fred came to the house from the hospital to say that Barbara was indeed dead. Then we sat until Barbara's family arrived from another town in Iowa. While we talked, Jarilyn woke up. She came out of Rachel's room and walked to her grandmother and sat on her lap. She never cried.

But for several years after that, whenever she spent time in our house, Jarilyn would, at the least expected time, burst into tears. This happened over and over. Then, one day, purely by accident, I discovered a roll of film that I had neglected to get developed. When the prints came back, I saw a collection of pictures that had been taken at Disneyland in August of 1988. There were many pictures of the children— Rachel and Jarilyn and John—and there was also one of Barbara Woodard, one taken at the Denver Airport just before we boarded our flight back to Cedar Rapids. Barbara looked tired, but she was smiling. Some weeks later, Jarilyn was in our home. I showed this picture to her. Jarilyn looked at her mother, and then she began to laugh. I want to believe that she laughed because, beneath the tragedy of her mother's death, lay an optimism still grounded in the happy time all of us had had the past summer at Disneyland. We went to *Dis*-neyland, to diz-diz-diz-diz-*Dis*-neyland.

Rachel will have to tell me, years from now, whether all the things I tried to do have made some difference in her life.

My daughter graduated, as I have said, on June 5 of 1997. I had vowed, years before, that I would not reenter Charlottesville. But the high school graduation date, as it approached, became a kind of emotional clock tick-tocking inside my heart. It was the old problem, the old deeply *hu-*

man problem. It was a commitment to the purity of an abstract commitment that had come to ignore the reality out of which the commitment first grew. It was in essence an emotional structure of dependability that had grown into something just as adamant and just as unyielding as the structure of white supremacy that had first caused me to leave Charlottesville. And it was here that *I* learned something.

The real tragedy of the history of black Americans is that we are shaped in part by the structures that constantly abuse us. We study the sources of those structures, their mental habits, and we learn from them. It is a truism that the prisoner always knows more about the prison keeper than the prison keeper knows about *him.* But the deeper human tragedy is that the prisoner, who knows so much about the prison keeper, runs the risk of *becoming like him.* There may be a certain degree of "equality" in this appropriation, but it is always *self-destructive.* And, ultimately, it is the prison keeper who wins because his onetime charge now generalizes his old guard's habits of mind farther into the future than the *life* of his former guard. This freezes the flow of human emotions into habits of mind that have already proved to be destructive. The gods of life must expect something *more* from the prescient prisoner. Perhaps this thing is only a refusal to impose on the future the smallnesses of mind that have been imposed on the past and on the present.

Perhaps another way of making this abstraction concrete is to say that I will do for love what no power on earth could make me do if I *did not* love.

Early on the morning of June 5 I drove to Cedar Rapids Airport and took a flight into Richmond, Virginia. I rented a car in Richmond and drove the sixty or so miles into Charlottesville. I located the building where Rachel's graduation would take place, and then I went to a shopping mall. I found a florist shop and I purchased one rose. Then I went back to the auditorium and watched Rachel's graduation ceremony. This was the first time I had ever seen any aspect of her life in that place. When all the seniors had been awarded their degrees and were marching out of the auditorium, I stood up in the balcony and walked as far down the steps as the railing overlooking the main floor. When I saw my daughter marching in line and approaching a place almost underneath the railing, I shouted "Rachel! Rachel!" She looked up just as I was throwing the rose to her.

Then I walked out to my car and drove straight back to the Richmond Airport.

I took the next flight into Chicago, and from there I returned to Iowa.

Rachel came to Iowa City, two weeks later. She brought the wilted rose with her.

Now that Rachel is growing secure in college, I still want to take her again out to Disneyland. We'll go to *Dis*-neyland, diz-diz-diz-*Dis*-neyland, just for a reminder of something very precious.

"It Is Good to Be Shifty
in a New Country"

Adventures of Huckleberry Finn:
the Restoration, by Mark Twain

While reading through the Introduction and the Foreword
to Justin Kaplan and Victor Doyno's masterful restoration of
Mark Twain's classic *Huckleberry Finn,* I kept looking for the
name of Henry Nash Smith, a Mark Twain scholar and my
old teacher at Berkeley. Mr. Smith was, at one time, in charge
of the Mark Twain Papers at the Bancroft Library at Berkeley. But he is not mentioned as one of the "Twainians" who
advised the editors of this extremely useful restoration. The
five sections cut by Twain from the version of *Huckleberry
Finn* published in England in 1884 and in America in 1885
have now been rewoven into the established version of the
book. Still, Mr. Smith's *Mark Twain: The Development of
a Writer* stands next to Mr. Kaplan's own *Mr. Clemens and
Mark Twain* on my bookshelf, as classics of Twain scholarship. I can imagine Mr. Smith's delight over the restoration
to the novel of some of the sections which, for either aesthetic
or commercial reasons, were edited by Twain from the original text.

The five sections now restored to the original text will be quite helpful to Twain scholars, and also to serious readers who want to see how a great novel can be cut and edited without losing its moral core. The general reader might find it constructive to study the mysterious ways in which those sections of great books, and films, once edited and discarded, are now being recovered to guide the reader deeper into an artist's real intention. Richard Wright's *Black Boy,* for example, published in 1944, had in reality been excerpted from a much longer manuscript named *American Hunger.* The second part of the book, an indictment of American materialism and shallowness of character, was not published until 1977. Recently, the *New Yorker* published two of six old stories written by Ralph Ellison, stories allegedly discovered in a cardboard box under Ellison's dining room table. In the present instance, the 665 manuscript pages of Twain's rejected sections of the novel have had an interesting underground life. In 1885, Twain gave the discarded sections of his just-published novel to James Fraser Gluck, a Buffalo, New York, lawyer and civic leader, who had solicited the manuscript pages for the collection of what would later become the Buffalo and Eric County Library. But the 665 pages were never delivered to the library. Gluck died ten years later, in 1897, and the manuscript pages were "lost" again, stored away in a trunk, until 1990, when Fraser's granddaughter, then living in California, found the lost manuscript pages in her grandfather's trunk. She and her sister sent the manuscript pages to Sotheby's auction house for public sale. But the news about the manuscript became public in 1991, and soon a complex legal case developed. The

Buffalo and Erie County Public Library claimed ownership of the pages as something like an "overdue book"; the descendants of James F. Gluck claimed ownership by rights of inheritance; and the Mark Twain Foundation claimed ownership as the trustee of all his property. After seventeen months of litigation, a settlement was reached. Random House agreed to publish this special comprehensive edition of the novel, giving all three parties in the litigation proceeds from its earnings. The restored novel has now arrived, with great fanfare, and one wants to imagine that, someplace, Mark Twain is laughing at the shifty way the drama of this contest has placed his novel after 116 years again at the center of public attention.

In a strictly sober view, nothing has been added to the novel that diminishes its old claim to greatness, to the status of a classic. The first new section, in Chapter 9, is a story told to Huck by Jim, in dialect, about the way a cadaver came alive in a dissecting room and attacked him. This passage confirms that, in Twain's initial conception, Jim was more or less a minstrel figure, a Mr. Bones to Huck's Mr. Tambourine. The reader will see the same kind of exchange between a straight man and an interlocutor as there is in Chapter 8. In these two chapters, Twain is still struggling with his love of the minstrel tradition and the growing necessity of Jim to the moral dimensions of his story. The second additional section of the novel is the "Raftsmen's Passage," which was apparently at one time part of the very important sixteenth chapter, when Huck first wrestles with his conscience over the "moral" necessity to turn Jim over to the slave catchers. This restored version is probably the best part of the new book because it explores Huck in a much more complex way. It should be noted that Twain added a much more restrained version of this same material to his *Life on the Mississippi,* but in the new and uncensored version, Huck confronts a company of raftsmen who display all the rough, homespun "manners" of the "ring-tailed roarer" of backwoods fame:

> They had a jug, and tin cups, and they kept the jug moving. One man was singing—roaring, you may say; and it wasn't a nice song—for a parlor, anyway. He roared through his nose, and strung out the last word of every song very long. When they was done they all fetched a kind of Injun war-woop, and then another one sung. . . .

Henry Nash Smith taught, and this restored section of the novel confirms, that Twain was drawing some of his portraits of frontier life from Johnson Jones Hooper's sketches of "Captain Simon Suggs," whose motto was "It is good to be shifty in a new country." These ring-tailed roarers, or braggarts, of popular frontier sketches used language and body movements as devices for self-definition and pseudo-aggression in much the same way that rap singers and break dancers use language and body movements today. But Twain's use of Huck's encounter with the belligerent raftsmen adds a kind of background for the troublesome moral dilemma with which Huck wrestles in this same chapter. He listens to a raftsman tell the story about the resurrection of a baby, killed by its father, from a barrel floating in the river. Afterwards,

Huck is discovered by the raftsmen, who threaten to kill him. To protect himself, Huck steps into another masquerade (he has already presented himself as Sarah Williams and then George Peters to Mrs. Judith Loftus in Chapter 11). Now he assumes the name of Charles William Allbright, the name of the supposedly dead child in the tale he has just heard from a raftsman. When confronted, Huck changes his name again, this time to Alex James Hopkins. The raftsmen show compassion for him and allow Huck to leave.

It is in this same chapter, when Huck returns to Jim waiting on the raft, that Huck battles his "conscience" over Jim. Henry Nash Smith has said in his study of Twain that the "conscience" that speaks to Huck during his debate over whether or not to betray Jim, a "conscience" that speaks in dialogue *outside* of Huck, is in reality the voice of a morally deformed community of which Huck is only a product. But the new additions to this chapter, incorporating Huck's encounter with the raftsmen, show that they are capable of belief in divine retribution, and are also capable of compassion. Possibly, *theirs is the voice with which Huck is debating the fate of Jim*—an extension of the communal voice of the raftsmen. Even though Huck eventually "saves" Jim, he does so while affirming the norms of white supremacy by telling the slave catchers that Jim is "white." Also, it is interesting to read Twain's first draft of Huck's resolution of the dilemma:

> From this out I mean to do everything as wrong as I can do it, and just go straight to the dogs and done with it. *I don't see why people's put here anyway.* . . . [Italics mine]

This is a very cynical resolution, but also ironic in the way Huck has come to equate what is morally "right" with what is conventionally "wrong." It is also of interest to see that the "I" employed in this restored section is an internalized "I" and not a communal conscience *outside* of Huck, much like the same "I" that Huck will confront again in Chapter 33, when he once again decides to help Jim go free.

The final two restored sections of the novel have to do with religion. In one of them, at the revival meeting in Pokeville, Twain describes the religious hypocrisy of the revivalists. They are willing to give money, and even kisses, to the King, who is masquerading as a Barbary pirate who has been converted by the revival, for the salvation of other wicked Barbary pirates who are at a distance from them; but like all moral dandies, who relish the affectation of a moral style over actual substance, they shun the black woman who would share their religious enthusiasm:

> One fat nigger woman about forty, was the worst. The white mourners couldn't fend her off, no way—fast as one would get loose, she'd tackle the next one, and *smother* him. Next, down she went in the straw, along with the rest, and wallowed around, chewing dirt and shouting glory hallelujah same as they did.

The second restored religious section involved the King coming back to the raft and expressing to Huck his expertise in "missionaring" moral dandies such as the ones in Polkville: "It warn't no use talking, heathens didn't amount to a dern, alongside of pirates, to work a camp meeting with."

. . .

The editors of this restored version seem to anticipate renewed moral outcry against *Huckleberry Finn* from the parti-
sans of "political correctness." Kaplan notes that there were
215 references to "niggers" in the old version, and the newly
restored sections will raise that number somewhat. Those ad-
dicted to symbolic protest are certain to have enough new
ammunition to fuel even more rage. Yet, as Kaplan reminds
us in his introduction, this epithet "has more preemptive
force today than it had in Mark Twain's day." This assessment may be hard to believe, given the self-righteous
"shock" on the parts of people repulsed, at least publicly, by
the recorded language of Officer Mark Fuhrman. And yet it
is a reality to be considered. Perhaps it would take a twenty-
first-century Mark Twain to appreciate the possibility that
Fuhrman's infamous taped interviews, in which "the N
word" resounded so freely, really sounded like an uptight
white man doing a poor imitation of Richard Pryor. Twain's
sense of irony would not miss the fact that the "Freemen"
who had a standoff with federal authorities in Montana
named their community "Justus," a word coined by Richard
Pryor, in one of his comic routines, about the treatment of
black men by the criminal justice system. Twain would have
appreciated the fact, with the novelist and critic Albert Murray, that even if the men in the Freemen group were white
supremacists out to remove "niggers" from American society, while they consolidated their plans, and if they want to
appease their teenage sons, they had better buy them Air-
Jordan tennis shoes.

Mark Twain would have known, as the historian Francis

Parkman observed in his account of the Oregon Territory, that in the frontier areas those whites who were below or *outside* the hierarchy of social mobility sometimes called *themselves* "niggers," in a self-affirming way. One can see and hear this epithet, the sense of self-congratulation added to their frontier brags, in films like *The Mountain Men* with Charlton Heston and Brian Keith. During the 1960s, there was a radical underground pamphlet named "The Student as Nigger." And there is Flannery O'Connor's ironic understanding of the uses made of the concept in her story "The Artificial Nigger." It may well be that some of the young people now being shut out of the job market by corporate downsizing will one day gain a deeper appreciation of the complexity of the concept. Mr. Kaplan is right. In Mark Twain's day the use of the word *nigger* sometimes had very complex implications. Melville saw this. So did Stephen Crane. But Ernest Hemingway, while a great booster of Twain, could not penetrate into the human complexity of his black characters. Mark Twain *always* saw the archetypal human experience that hid behind the stereotype.

I have someplace the copy of a Christmas card that Twain once sent to a prominent Eastern family about 1900. It is a picture of Mark Twain, with his trademark white suit and white hair, sitting with a black man who was his close companion. At Twain's home in Hartford, Connecticut, the tour guides like to show visitors the design of the writer's dining room. There is on display a large, well-polished table at which Twain liked to entertain his guests. In a corner, some distance from the table, there is a small pantry. Twain's house servants were ordered to stand in the pantry, between the kitchen and the living room, in complete silence, until they were called to serve the table. Twain delighted in telling comic stories to his guests. He kept telling story after story until one of the servants, the black companion who was his friend, would break the prohibition against any sound and laugh in defiance of his best instincts, against the settled rules of the house. Both Freud and Henri Bergson might have made much of this in their theories about the mysterious sources of laughter, but as a very practical matter, the black man was "approving" the comic value of stories that Twain would later tell on the lecture circuit. On this level of reality, the black companion, who masqueraded as Twain's "servant," was in fact Ralph Ellison's Lucius Brockway, who, in the sub-basement of the Liberty Paint Factory, added one drop of "black" to help create an "optic white."

For many reasons, in 1996, after so much celebrated "change," we seem unable to reach again the level of complexity and ironic understanding that was almost normative for Mark Twain. Something has happened—call it the arrival of political correctness, or else the substitution of ideology for the genuine feelings of the human heart—to erode the feeling tones essential for the understanding of basic *human* motivations. There now seems to be a growing awareness of some essential things that are missing from our lives. In supermarkets and in restaurants one can hear a desperate reaching back to the confident music of the 1950s and 1960s. Among scholars there is a movement of interest back to the nineteenth century for guidance into the twenty-first century. Recent years have seen the publication of biographies of Harriet Beecher Stowe, Richard Harding Davis, Ambrose Bierce. There has been a detailed study of the building of the B&O Railroad, an exploration of the foundations of the consumer culture and the advertising industry. And now there is Mark Twain's masterpiece, restored, for better or worse, to its original length. We all seem to be looking backwards for some moral essentials that have become obscured, if not lost altogether.

I remember my last classes with Henry Nash Smith, the Mark Twain scholar, in the spring of 1973, at Berkeley. It was during the time of the movement toward impeachment of Richard Nixon. Mr. Smith was teaching his last seminar at Berkeley, one on the long-forgotten female novelists of the mid-nineteenth century. Mr. Smith was providing his students with clues useful for the reading of American popular culture and its trends. He was a great scholar, and he took care to bring to class many rare books and magazines, as well as his notes. But as the news of Nixon's impending impeachment began to dominate all our imaginations, Mr. Smith, one day, put aside his index cards and notes, and said, "How could a man like Richard Nixon become President in the first place?" Then he began talking off the top of his head. He talked about the standardization of tastes (as Twain wrote about in much more subtle ways). He talked about the introduction of IQ tests to select elites for elevation, elites who were often bright but without any character. He talked about the introduction of television, and about the ways in which televised images were employed to distort or even to displace reality. One young woman, a budding academic, said, "But Mr. Smith, much of what you are saying now contradicts some of what you told us before!" Mr. Smith replied, "That was false consciousness," and he kept going. He said, "Those young people out there in Sproul Plaza are playing country music, passing it into the popular culture, without knowing that it could lead to a terrible fascism." After class, I approached Mr. Smith and said, "Mr. Smith, you were riffing." He said, "Like in jazz?"

There was something of Mark Twain's ironic humor in his voice.

Some days later I watched Nixon's resignation speech on television. And the next day I heard on the radio Nixon's farewell speech to his White House staff. Close to tears, Nixon was more human than I had ever seen him in public life. He spoke about his mother: "No one will ever write a book about my mother," he told his staff. "But she was a saint. She lost two boys and . . ." A deeply wounded human being, a profoundly sympathetic human being, suddenly came through the radio. But then he tried to compose himself and said, "Nevertheless, we must go forward to the future that is before us, and so I say to you, my friends, as T.R. once said . . ." It was only then that I understood what Mr. Smith, and Mark Twain through him, was trying to say. Nixon had become a human being whose entire emotional life had been standardized around political clichés. He did not even possess the emotional language to articulate his own deepest, most personal feelings. He had forgotten how to be honest, even with himself. He was being "politically correct."

The day before, Gerald Ford had announced, "My fellow Americans, our national nightmare is over." But it was only beginning, because something civic and deeply essential had begun eroding during that time and has not stopped eroding since then. Mr. Smith had seen this, as had Mark Twain in his own time and place. As Huck told Tom Sawyer during a debate over the "politically correct" way to rescue Jim, "Meat first, and spoon vittles to top off 'em." *Substance over style.*

Those who practice contemporary forms of political correctness *ought* to have a hard time with this restored version of *Huckleberry Finn.* Even without its edited passages, it was called, when published in 1885, "trash and suitable only for the slums," and "of a very low grade of morality." This was the outraged voice of the cult of gentility of Twain's day. More recently, the novelist Jane Smiley has written some additional "second thoughts" about Twain's masterpiece. In "Say It Ain't So, Huck," in the January 1996 issue of *Harper's,* she expresses her opinion that *Huckleberry Finn* has little to offer in the way of greatness. There is more to be learned about the American character, she says, *"from* its canonization than *through* its canonization." Ms. Smiley sees the novel as faultily written, as morally unsound, with its place in the national pantheon secured by several generations of white, Protestant, middle-class critics. She writes: "For all his lip service to real attachment between white boy and black man, Twain really saw Jim as no more than Huck's sidekick, homoerotic or otherwise. All the claims that are routinely made for the book's humanitarian powers are, in the end, absurd."

Ms. Smiley makes the case for Harriet Beecher Stowe's

Uncle Tom's Cabin as deserving of canonization, and as a much better novel than *Huckleberry Finn,* because of its clear-eyed look at racism. "When her voice fell silent," she says of Ms. Stowe, "and was replaced by the secretive voice of Huck Finn, who acknowledged Jim only when they were alone together on the raft in the middle of the big river, racism fell out of the public world and into the private one, where whites think it really is but blacks know it really isn't."

The Done Thing

A speech delivered on June 12, 1990,
at the American Center in Tokyo

First of all, may I present two stories from two different parts of my own country.

One month ago, in Iowa, I went with my next-door neighbor, Cheryl Huang, to attend her swearing-in ceremony as a new American citizen. Cheryl is of Chinese ancestry, but was born in South Africa. She moved into the house next to my own about five years ago, and we have become friends. The swearing-in ceremony, in Davenport, Iowa, was an extraordinary affair. The majority of the new citizens were Asians: Koreans, Chinese, Southeast Asians. The Davenport chapter of the Daughters of the American Revolution, an extremely conservative women's organization, went to great lengths to welcome the new people with speeches and a small party. An Episcopal priest tried to define for them the moral implications of their new citizenship. The judge who did the official swearing-in took special pains to assure the new people that being an American meant devotion to an *idea* and not to any sense of racial exclusiveness. He encouraged the new people to hold on to their various ethnic heritages because the culture of the United States was enriched by its diversity of cultures, its differences. A tall, thin, somewhat courtly man, the judge seemed Lincolnesque in his manner. He told the new people that his own wife had been an immigrant to America twenty or so years before, and that his daughter was married to the son of a Korean-immigrant family. Afterwards, he circulated among the new people at the reception given by the D.A.R. He made a point of talking individually with each new citizen. During this reception, the ladies of the D.A.R. gave American flags to the youngest naturalized citizen (the adopted Korean son of a white couple) and the oldest naturalized citizen (an Asian man of about forty-seven). There was an extraordinary degree of human warmth and civility and ceremony in that federal courthouse in Davenport, Iowa; so much, in fact, that I began to feel my own sense of identity as an American being renewed. I remember that I kissed Cheryl Huang on the cheek as we walked away from the reception.

One week later, about three weeks ago, I attended a meeting of a literary panel in New York City. The newspapers and the news programs were full of stories about the outcome of the Yusuf Hawkins murder trial, about the tensions between working-class Italian and African Americans in an Italian community named Bensonhurst; about rising tensions between African and Jewish Americans; and about the tensions between members of the African-American community and Korean shopkeepers. The evening of my arrival in New York, the mayor of that city, David Dinkins, and the governor of the state of New York, Mario Cuomo, attended a mass rally at a New York cathedral. The mayor made a plea for de-escalation of ethnic tensions. Governor Cuomo used the occasion of the rally to make his case for passage of a tough new antibias law, one with stiff fines and penalties for anyone convicted of a hate crime. I watched the governor's speech on the television in my hotel room and wondered whether the rule of law would ever be successful in accomplishing those moral ends sought by Governor Cuomo and by the embattled mayor of New York City. I also contrasted the peace and quiet and absence of such extreme tensions in my home state of Iowa. And I thought back on the swearing-in ceremony in Davenport, Iowa, about one week before. I wondered about what there was in the tradition of one part of the country that made it so receptive to diversity and change. Whatever it was, or is, it seemed not at all apparent in New York and in the larger cities.

The superficial answer is that Iowa is an agricultural state and does not have large groupings of radically different ethnic peoples. The basic stock is Anglo-Saxon and German. Even with gradual increases in the number of Asian, Spanish-speaking, and African Americans, the traditions of the basic stock remain essentially unchanged. But even so, there was an openness to the new people, or at least a *determination* to be open, in the ceremonies I attended at the federal courthouse. I grant that the basic ritual of naturalization was mandated by the rule of law. But the speech by the Episcopal priest, the special efforts made by the ladies of the D.A.R., the judge's own personal comments—these were affirmations of a meaning not mandated by the rule of law. They made their extra efforts out of a sense of obligation to something that could not be required by the rule of law. Perhaps it is *this* special thing which does exist in Davenport, Iowa, but which does not presently exist in New York City that best defines the topic of my talk. Perhaps my own country's present struggle to recapture and to redefine and to better democratize this special thing provides the clearest insights into the present racial and ethnic situation in the United States. The governor of the state of New York seeks to compensate for its absence through increasing use of the enforcement powers of the rule of law. The officials at the swearing-in ceremony in Davenport, Iowa, still retain a sense of this invisible dimension, and they rely on it during those occasions when social or ethnic tensions threaten to disrupt what has already been decided on as a worthwhile way of life. The ladies of the D.A.R. brought cookies and punch and American flags to the ceremony because they considered it the "right" thing to do, or what the British used to call "the *done* thing." They made ceremonial gestures beyond those mandated by the settled rules of the naturalization process. Those rules require only the swearing of a specific oath to uphold the Constitution. No cookies are required.

It has been observed by scholars of human societies that each vital culture attempts to maintain, at all costs, three distinct spheres of human activity. One might imagine these organizational activities as spheres on a spectrum. On one extreme there exists the domain of positive law. This is the domain of absolutes: though shalt not kill, rob, or kidnap businessmen, Japanese or others. Legal codes enforce these prohibitions with the threat of strict sanctions. On the other extreme of this same spectrum, there exists a domain that might be called, by scholars of natural law, the domain of personal freedom. This area, always more idealized than actual, is the area where unquestioned freedom resides. This was the area of human action brought under the protection of the British Magna Carta and the American Bill of Rights. The Western nations have attempted to make this sphere the cornerstone of their vision of what should be unquestionable with respect to the rights of human beings. Great wars have been fought to protect this domain. But between these two extremes on the spectrum, there exists a third domain. It is an ambiguous area, comparable in some ways to your *engawa* in traditional Japanese architecture: not quite inside and not quite outside. This middle area is freedom and *unfreedom,* both at the same time. There are no written rules regulating it, but it is not really part of the domain of absolute freedom.

It is within this middle area that all of the creativity and vitality of a healthy society resides. People act in this area because there is no law saying they *cannot* act. They are "free," so to speak, but at the same time they are not "free." This is so because the gathering of muscular trends in this area (the use of new drugs that could prove harmful, the abuse of the right of free speech, the use of abortion as a simple contraceptive, even too many smokers in a public place) tend to threaten to disrupt the harmonious flow of society. When such trends become too muscular, the domain of positive law moves into this area with another "thou shalt not." When the domain of positive law has usurped all of this area, a society becomes rigid, regulated, and begins to die spiritually. Human beings lose spontaneity and their societies lose vitality. To protect themselves from such legal straitjacketing, the more sensitive societies have encouraged in this middle area, and in the individuals who inhabit it, a set of personal obligations as a substitute for the rule of law. The individual is expected to enforce upon himself a set of obligations that he honors as a way of protecting the moral health and the vitality and the creativity of the entire society. For these reasons, this middle area has been called the domain of obligation to the unenforceable, or the domain of manners, or the area where "the *done* thing" is practiced. The codes internally imposed in this area, whether derived from religion or from tradition, act as a substitute for the strict rule of law. This area provides the basis for the ethos of a society, a source for the spiritual cohesiveness that keeps a society vital and integrated.

In the United States just now, there is taking place an increasing disintegration of this absolutely essential middle area. This disintegration is being caused by a number of factors: the substitution of material goals for spiritual ones over the past decade or so; the revival of the nineteenth-century creed of "rugged individualism" and the consequent fragmentation of communal structures; the elevation of greed and personal gain almost to a moral principle; the erosion of personal trust; the debasement of emotional language and of collective vision; the fear that one man has of his neighbor. Added to this are the traditional racial tensions in American life, compounded by the arrival of many millions of new immigrants whose traditions and habits have not yet been given sufficient study. They are competing with the traditionally oppressed segments of the American population for jobs and status and influence. Such tensions that arise between competing groups are magnified, and probably encouraged, by the rise of ethnic and religious tensions in many parts of the world. To further complicate the ethnic tensions, there has developed in the United States, over the past two decades, an increasing reliance on the courts and the legal system to solve the special problems of groups. Beginning with African Americans, each group has begun its own tradition of petitioning the courts for group-specific remedies. This strategy, while of fundamental importance because of the persistence of white racism, has had two unfortunate consequences. It has encouraged others to begin thinking of themselves in group terms, and it has made litigation into a kind of moral drama in the life of the United States. It would not be unfair to say that our imaginations have been conditioned to view the details of litigation as our only source of civility. All of these factors, and many others, have imprisoned the true sources of American civility within the domain of positive law. In a great many cases, as in the case of legally sanctioned segregation, reliance on the law as a liberating force could not be helped; but this initial reliance on the rule of law as an instrument for eroding negative patterns in American life has become a ritual pattern of patterns followed by other groups, and offered as a way of resolving almost all disputes. This was the ritual pattern alluded to by Governor Mario Cuomo of New York State in his call for a tough new antibias law. Other states have already enacted them, and similar laws are used to police the racial expressions of students on many college campuses. It might be said that our reliance on the rule of law threatens to become our permanent version of "the *done* thing."

And yet there once existed, and still exists in communities like Davenport, Iowa, the spiritual sources of counterrituals,

rituals that move people back toward the middle area I referred to earlier. This is, of course, the source grounded in a fundamental *belief* in the great promise that my country once made to itself and to the rest of the world. I prefer to restate it here in my own personal sense of the meaning of the words:

We hold these articles of faith to be the revealed truth: all *souls* are created equal, and are endowed by God with certain inalienable rights, among which are immortality, free will, and access to grace.

I prefer to call the promise made by these words the "constitutive" dimension of the American Constitution, our own spiritual version of "the *done* thing." Traditionally, our actions have attempted to be premised on the strength of our belief in the *rightness* of this principle. Traditionally, we measured our responses to other people, even strangers, against our commitment to this standard. A person may not be truly valued or thought of as equal, but we have been conditioned to value the human worth represented by that person. We did not lose sight of his human soul. We offered this as a human alternative to the dangerous trends I detailed earlier. It was our pattern of patterns, our very special version of what I have called obligation to the unenforceable. We have not failed in this, but we have temporarily lost contact with some of the spiritual sources of our most fundamental beliefs.

We need to be reminded of them again.

As in my own country, the material aspects of life in Japan

are becoming predominant over spiritual ones. Still, the Nihonjin have a spiritual surplus in the middle area I have called the domain of obligation to the unenforceable, the domain of manners. In the cities of my own country, we have lost personal contact with our spiritual centers. If the group that has invited me to speak here, the newly formed group named JAAS, has any practical purposes, one of them has to be the sharing with my people the surplus of your manners. Since I first visited Japan last year, I have been trying very hard to understand your culture. My friends here have been calling certain books to my attention, and others I have managed to find on my own. I have read enough to know that, until the Modern Period, Japanese society remained close to the traditional model of the village society, in which unquestioned loyalties existed between the individual and his family, his clan, his lord, his *shogun,* his parents and ancestors, his teachers, his associates, and the emperor. This system of loyalties is so intricate and complex that an outsider cannot be certain of whether it is based on racial exclusiveness or on what one writer has suggested is a uniquely Japanese religious feeling which he calls *Nihonism.* Whatever the source of the forms of organization of Japanese life, the Japanese people have remained closer to the ancient and traditional forms of social organization than almost any people in the world. Your culture seems to have an almost biological instinct for harmony at all costs, to make the stream of human intercourse flow gently. Gentleness is even required of your pachinko games.

I have been searching this past year for insights into what gives your society its cohesiveness and vitality; for the fundamental pattern behind the basic patterns of your common life; for the force that feeds your spiritual integration. I think now that a basic clue resides in your predisposition toward ritual and ceremony. There is diffused among your people what in a European community would be called an aristocratic manner, a style based on what I have been calling "the *done* thing." Instead of being the style of an elite, as in my own country, it is the style of an entire culture. I think that the practices of these rituals and ceremonies bind each Japanese to the larger pattern that defines the integrated wholeness of Japanese culture.

I want to give a concrete example of what I mean by attempting to view our American problem from the perspective provided by your culture. I did not know that I would be asked to speak here when I decided to make another trip to Japan. A very nice lady from the JAAS office called me in Iowa only three days before I was scheduled to leave. When I arrived here, I found that she had worked out all the details of my talk this afternoon, and had also scheduled another talk for me in Fukuoka. Last Thursday, she picked me up at the train station near the apartment where I stay here and escorted me by train to the airport. It was a very humid day and both of us were sweating. The lady dabbed her face with her handkerchief, and then she noticed me holding my three bags, and sweating, on the crowded train. She immediately began to wipe my face with her handkerchief. Her sense of the "rightness" of things, given the situation, caused her to forget the fact that I was a foreigner, and an African American at that, aboard a crowded public train. Her impulse— based on human sympathy—and her action flowed *together.*

There was absolutely no hesitation in her gesture. Her one action told me much more about the spiritual integration of Japanese society than I could have read in one thousand books.

I have seen this same integration of impulse and action dramatized many thousands of times during my short stays in your country. I call it the habit of civility. During the time it has taken me to read this much of my talk, at least one million of the twelve million Japanese in Tokyo have bowed; have said "*Soo desu ka?*" ["Is that so?"] and "*Soo desu ne*" ["That's so true"] in place of direct disagreement; have used a special hierarchy of language to address social superiors, social equals, and social inferiors; have said "*Itadakimasu*" ["Thank you for this meal"] before eating and "*Gochisoosama*" ["It was a feast"] afterwards; have been on guard to say "*Kooryoshimasu*" ["I'll take it under consideration"] instead of saying "That's stupid." All this effort and energy amount to something. It keeps the soul of your culture alive. But it also maintains for each individual Japanese a place in your republic of the spirit.

We in the United States, members of all groups, need to reclaim our own ancient promise to ourselves to make and to maintain a similar republic. We cannot imitate the Japanese because our traditions are radically different. But we can learn a valuable lesson from you about the importance of details in the preservation of a spiritually vital common life. I think that one of the many ancient Japanese gods must live in the details of everyday life. If there is to be any lasting friendship between African Americans and the Japanese people, I hope it will not be based on the world's interest in your material affluence or your economic strength. I hope, rather, that you will teach us your daily gestures, your rituals and ceremonies, your respect for human feelings. There is much work that all Americans have to do to revitalize our country's spiritual life, to reclaim from the clutches of the domain of law those heartfelt assumptions that are our own. But there is a *tremendous* amount of work that African Americans have to do to reclaim, perhaps for the entire society, the momentum of the movement toward greater spiritual civility that was the lifework of Dr. Martin King.

We have found ourselves in this position many times before.

I began my talk with two stories and I would like to close with another. This story was told to me several years ago by an African American, a former student, who is a reporter for the *Washington Post.* He said that he observed on a subway in Washington, D.C., an argument between a Japanese businessman and a young African-American male. The young man had thrown some paper on the floor of the subway car. The Japanese man was insisting that he should pick it up. My former student's first impression was that this was yet another expression of the so-called racial arrogance of the Japanese. But as he thought about the incident more, he saw that a basic human value was involved. The Japanese man was insisting that the young man recognize an obligation to the community that existed outside himself. The young African-American man was insisting on littering as a valid expression of his individuality. But the basic truth is that littering causes problems for other people. Far from being an expression of racial arrogance, the insistence of the Japanese man might have been based on his habitual way of conducting himself, whether in Tokyo or in Washington, D.C. He might have been a teacher, a *sensei,* affirming his own version of "the *done* thing." If so, we very badly need to be reminded of all the other details of civility that are presently obscured, and discounted, by the hurry and tension of American life. We need to relearn those old habits before another set of laws is passed *requiring* us to observe them under penalty of law.

I am hoping that your expression of friendship means that we will be able to learn from you much more than we are able to teach.

Three Great Ones of the City
and One Perfect Soul

Well Met at Cyprus*

During the past eighteen months, the complex factual events surrounding the murders of Nicole Brown Simpson and Ronald Goldman in Los Angeles, and the trial of O.J. Simpson for the crime, have been twisted and mutated into what has been called a "media circus," if not a monumental mess. Still, despite the thousands of assertions and counterassertions that the record of this historic trial will comprise, it is possible that, years from now, someone will locate within the factual mess a narrative thread which, when drawn into closer focus, will attempt to make sense of what began as a simple tragedy. As a matter of fact, it was the CBS newsman Dan Rather, who, on June 17, 1994, when the media first focused their full attention on O.J. Simpson cruising along the Los Angeles freeway in his now famous white Bronco, introduced the narrative premise that made most sense to his viewers. Dan Rather spoke, with passion, about William Shakespeare's tragedy *Othello,* and compared O.J. Simpson to that

*Written in 1997.

199

tragic character and Nicole Brown Simpson to the wronged and saintly Desdemona. But soon, after tabloid revelations about Nicole Brown Simpson's personal life, part of this narrative line was edited from the story.

Now, with the tapes of Officer Mark Fuhrman's racial feelings introduced as evidence by Simpson's defense team, a second narrative thread from the same play has been introduced: Officer Fuhrman as Iago, enraged that he, and other Anglo-Saxons like himself, have been displaced by black men, and by women, through the affirmative action industry. If these two narrative threads are eventually knit into the deep emotional structures essential to English-speaking people to provide understanding of the tragedy, it might be fair to speculate, in a comic vein, whether Cato Kaelin will be viewed as a stand-in for Michael Cassio; Prosecutor Marcia Clark a stand-in for Emilia, Iago's wife; Faye Resnick as a stand-in for Bianca; Judge Ito as a stand-in for the Duke; and the mysterious bloody glove, or else the missing eyeglasses, as a substitute for Othello's handkerchief.

Such comic speculations, however, tend to obscure emotional understanding of the human tragedy cheapened in all the media, day after tedious day, for the past eighteen months. The tragic facts are that Nicole Simpson and Ronald Goldman are dead, O. J. Simpson's children are permanently wounded, the families of Nicole Brown and Ronald Goldman are embittered, and the entire media-watching world has relearned that deep, killing racial hatreds are still rampant in this country. But much more tragic, in my view, is that the search for the causal elements at the basis of the tragedy has been relentless in its focus on what is considered the most potentially explosive combination of elements in the emotional imagination of Western physics: the co-joining of a black male and a white female. On its surface, Shakespeare's *Othello* has instructed us in this causality, and we are still slaves to its hidden language. This emotional predisposition is so ingrained in the Western imagination that it is most often employed as a convenient convention, as a substitute for thought.

I relearned the potent power of this hidden language in the early summer of 1994, when a very eager black reporter from *USA Today* called me at home and asked for my perceptions of the events leading up to what is now being called "the trial of the century." At the time I was trying my best to achieve some ironic, if not comic, distance on the tragedy. I noted that the murder, on June 11, and all events following it, represented a narrative commentary on the ritual movements of American society over the past three or four decades, during which time the technological bias of the culture outpaced, and then began to overpower, the *human* capacity to compete with its power to define reality, most especially in the area of communications. I noted that the real underlying issue, apart from the tragedy itself, was the manufacturing of images, and O.J. Simpson's participation in the mechanics of this industry, if not his mastery of the process. To make a joke, I said that he had used his physical grace, and his attractiveness, to turn himself into a marketable image; might have slowly accepted image as reality and lost all the values with which he grew up; might have fallen in love with another image (the nubile, blond, nineteen-year-old Nicole Brown); and might have settled into a lifestyle based on false fronts and "thinness" of personality, of shining surfaces and tinsel, of improvised emotions ungrounded in the deeper stratas of selfhood that is Los Angeles in this postmodern and material age. I went on to say that if indeed O. J. Simpson had committed the murders with which he was charged, I could understand his motivation, no matter how bloody his action. He might simply have grown jealous of other, younger, much more stylish images competing with him for Nicole's attention, and acted out a narrative line from some movie plot inside his head. I added that, given the unreal and unnatural context of Los Angeles, the upcoming trial itself would be steeped in thin images over meaningful substance, because the entire affair was already being drained of human reality, and existed only in the thin and bloodless provinces of the mass media. Continuing with this crazy logic, I told the young reporter that there was still hope for an outcome appropriate to the surreal context of the trial. At around the same time as the murder of Nicole Brown, it should be recalled, the media baron Lawrence Tisch was then negotiating to merge his own Home Shopping Network with the CBS Network. If he succeeded, I noted (as the Disney Company had recently succeeded in its acquisition of ABC), Lawrence Tisch would then be King of Medialand, as well as of all its images. As such, no matter what decision the O.J. jury reached, Tisch, as King of Medialand, and especially of the domain that was the focus of the trial, could say, with media-vested authority, to O. J. Simpson, a simple, wayward image: "*I pardon you.*"

The young reporter made a tape-recording of all my mad speculations. Several days later, his story appeared in *USA*

Today with only one quotation attributed to me: "James McPherson said that O.J. should not have married that white woman in the first place." I then began receiving calls and letters. Producers of a CBS talk show invited me to appear as an advocate of racial purity. So did the producers of *Larry King Live*. My daughter, who, like all teenagers, is captivated by the celestial unreality of the mass media, was very excited to talk with a producer from CBS. She pleaded with me to appear. But by this time it became clearer to me that I had begun to enlist in the spread of a cancer, one with no possibility of complexity or even of isolation, and so I refused both offers to have my own day under the camera lights. Instead, I took my daughter to the Mall of America, in Minneapolis.

It was during this time that I returned to William Shakespeare's *Othello* for a sense of the human complexity that would never surface during the eighteen months of the trial's integration into the mass media. I returned to the play for something deeper than celluloid understanding. I reread it, much more carefully this time, looking for new insights into the issues, racial or others, being raised out in Los Angeles.

William Shakespeare's *Othello* confirms for all English-speaking people, perhaps in keeping with the European mode of causality, a certain narrative line: "Once upon a time a certain combination of elements came together and the results were tragic for all involved. Looking back at that tragic event, one can trace a line of movement from then into this present moment in time; and then, secure within this present moment, one can project the same causality into the future." These are the emotional physics that are imposed on the complex and ever-changing growing edge of human life. These physics may provide those troubled people, who adapt their thinking to this settled emotional order, with a greater sense of security. But at times it becomes necessary to stand apart from the assumptions in which we have been so thoroughly educated, and search for alternative ways of seeing. The European view of causality may well be, as a matter of fact, only *one* of many points of view about the nature of reality, even a reality as thoroughly accepted as the motivations of Orenthal J. Simpson or Shakespeare's great character Othello, the Moor of Venice.

William Shakespeare's *Othello,* after centuries of varied interpretations, has become almost a text in sociology. It has been called a warning to all good wives to look well to their linen. It has been viewed as an object lesson in the negative consequences likely to follow from contacts across racial lines. It has been interpreted as a mediation on the nature of evil. What is not often studied is the context of the play, the backdrop against which the tragedy is played out (the full title of the play is *The Tragedy of Othello, the Moor of Venice*). We have been educated to search for insights into the tragic events in the foreground of the drama rather than in the implied drama, or unstated assumptions, which exist in the background and which influence the actions of the characters. That is to say, there are, in addition to the two different "races" at the center of the drama, the cultural assumptions of each, which assumptions influence the actions of the participants in the drama.

Othello's Venice, one assumes, is the same Venice inhabited by Shylock, another alien, in Shakespeare's *The Merchant of Venice.* In the latter play, the Christian traditions of Venice are at the very center of the actions of the major characters. Antonio, the merchant, and Portia, the heiress, embody values that are employed by Shakespeare to put into contrast the alien values of Shylock. It might even be said that the two different value systems, or traditions, are "actors" in the play, with the Christian values demonstrating themselves to be superior to the Jewish ones. The ruling ethic of the play is derived mainly from the biblical codes drawn from the Gospel of Matthew, Chapters 5 and 6—the core of the ethical teachings of Jesus of Nazareth. Shylock's code, evoked in contrast, is derived exclusively from the Jewish traditions of the Old Testament. The Venice of *The Merchant* is steeped in the ethics of Matthew 5 and 6, so much so that it is the *interface* between it and the written law of Venice that provides the chief dramatic action of the play. This is much the same Venice that Othello inhabits, except that the Christian tradition in this tragedy seems to play no significant role. As a matter of fact, Christian tradition is mentioned only three times in the entire play: once by Iago during his initial complaint against Othello, once by Othello himself as a casual reference, and once by Desdemona in protestation of her loyalty to Othello. There are no references to Jesus of Nazareth and the ethics he taught. One might assume that the Christian ethic is simply "there," implicit in the motivations and the actions of the characters. Or one might assume that they are held in check, in a calculated way, in order for Shakespeare to bring into fuller focus, a focus uncluttered by ethical dogma, his core theme—the contrast between Othello's natural nobility of soul and Iago's natural depravity of soul. It is also of interest to note that although Othello is a Moor, assumedly derived from Levantine traditions, there are no overt references to his being in possession of a different ethical system. Like the Venice he inhabits, he has been stripped by Shakespeare of any connection with an ethical system beyond that of immediate concern to the drama. Othello's Venice, then, becomes only a backdrop, a stage, against which, in contrast to the Venice of *The Merchant,* a very different kind of drama is played out.

That Othello's racial background makes him an outsider in Venice goes without saying. He is black, a Moor, an experienced warrior, and an exclusive servant of the state. His only claims to personal distinction are his nobility of birth, but in another cultural context, and his nobility of soul. There is another very important sociological point of distinction: because of his extensive services to the state, the Duke, who is most powerful, is in his debt. But the Venice over which the Duke presides is a Venice seemingly stripped of the veneer of Christianity that was essential to the action of *The Merchant.* The Duke's Venice seems to be closer to the mode of an ancient European territorial state, and its values, than it is to the Venice of Christian tradition.

The territorial state over which the Duke presides is characterized by common language, blood, and borders. It is dynastic in that it is rooted in family ties that emphasize loyalty and liens of obligation. This web of obligations imposes a series of vertical duties: obligations of obedience upward, obligations of care and responsibility downward. In such a tightly knit living arrangement, issues of right and wrong are reduced to concrete matters of loyalty and disloyalty. To be loyal is right. To be disloyal is wrong. The core ethic in this arrangement is the survival of the dynastic family, or the state, far beyond the lives of its individual members. In this very special and non-Christian sense, purposeful endurance becomes the paramount value of each active member of the community or institution.

Othello, the Moor, did not originate within this community, and therefore has only an outward coating of its innermost values. Shakespeare does not give us very many clues to Othello's place of origin, but the emotional connections he has with Egypt (the place where his mother's handkerchief was made) and the Middle East suggest that he derives, in terms of ethical influences, from the Levantine tradition. This tradition subscribes to its own ethical system. While in the Duke's Venice the paramount ethic is willed, purposeful endurance, whether of the individual, the family, or the state, in the ancient Levantine tradition, the paramount ethic, what is to survive, is the consensus of the faithful, those who have received the same spirit, in the Kingdom of Heaven. Since, according to this ethic, the world itself is sinful but one is obliged to live in it, salvation can only be assured by predestination, by evidence of one's membership in the body of the faithful. The conflict between these two ethical systems, although both are understated and only alluded to, provides, I believe, the basis for the true dramatic conflict in *Othello*.

Iago is the first to tell us, directly, in Act I, scene i, that two sets of values are in conflict, and that the traditional ethic, the liens of loyalty and vertical obligation, are being threatened by Othello's presence. Three great ones of the city, he tells Roderigo, petitioned Othello to make Iago his lieutenant. But Othello rejects their suits and makes Michael Cassio, a Florentine and a foreigner, his second in command. From this experience Iago concludes:

> Preferment goes by letter and affection
> And not by old gradation, where each second
> Stood heir to the first.

As a demonstration that the basic ethic is being eroded, even in the homes of the Venetians, Iago informs Brabantio, who is a senator of Venice, that his own daughter, Desdemona, has proved disloyal, and has demonstrated this disloyalty by marrying Othello. Both Brabantio and Iago then acknowledge recognition of their paramount obligations: loyalty to the existing vertical arrangement. Though Brabantio is a senator, as well as Desdemona's father, he can take no private action without doing violence to this ethic. He must appeal fatherly concerns upward, to the judgment of the Duke. And although Iago has plots of his own, he too recognizes that the authority of the state has a special role to play in whatever fate is assigned to Othello:

> For I do know, the state,
> However this may gall him with some check,
> Cannot with safety cast him, for he's embark'd
> With such loud reason to the Cyprus wars,
> Which even now stand in act, that, for their souls,
> Another of his fathom they have none

> To lead their business; in which regard,
> Though I do hate him as I do hell-pains,
> Yet, for necessity of present life,
> I must show out a flag and sign of love,
> Which is indeed but a sign.

The first scene of Act I sets up the basic dramatic conflict in the play. Venice, a small territorial state, is in a state of war with the Turkish Empire. In such an emergency, foreign mercenaries have been recruited to help the Venetians in their battles. Among these mercenaries are Othello, a Moorish officer and a veteran of many battles, and Michael Cassio, from the rival territorial state of Florence. The necessities of war have compelled the state (in the person of the Duke) to integrate Othello, and then Michael Cassio, into the command levels of the military structure. The existing ethic is applied to them.

The Duke is thus loyal to Othello, and like any other Venetian general, Othello is allowed to exercise his own lien of obligation downward—to choose as his lieutenant the foreigner Michael Cassio, passing over even Iago, a native Venetian who has been proposed for the office in the customary way by men of high status in the dynastic state. Acting on this same sense of status, Othello has courted, and won for his wife, Desdemona, the daughter of Brabantio, a Venetian senator. But these actions by a foreigner, and a Moor at that, have undermined the existing hierarchical order. The liens of loyalty that traditionally flowed downward from the Duke and his nobles and senators to fellow Venetians like Iago, and upward from Desdemona to her father, Brabantio, are threatened with erosion. This is the concern voiced by both Iago and Brabantio—that the "old gradation" has been threatened.

Othello himself appears as a somewhat innocent example of the outsider who has been integrated into a pre-existing hierarchical order, one with its own exclusive ethic. Like the Court Jew, the foreigner or outsider who has been elevated to a position of power within such a structure leaves behind, out of practical necessity, his former loyalties and associates. He becomes "captive" to the power structure that sustains his status. He lacks an infrastructure for the support of his own values. While the pre-existing liens of loyalty may extend downward to him from the ultimate source of power, they do not always extend upward, from below him, with the same degree of obligation. Like the Court Jew, such a person must always depend exclusively on the powers above him for protection, and must be wary of those who are ostensibly under his immediate authority, since they are native and he is not. Unlike Shylock, in this very same Venice, Othello has no co-religionists representing alternate sources of values through which he can sustain himself. Such a figure is totally alone. If the structure into which he has been integrated subscribes to values that are so closely held or assumed that they go all but unspoken, and if the outsider has nothing but a surface understanding of those values, conflict becomes inevitable. If the person has been assigned great authority, and if he assumes a deep personal involvement without a complete understanding of the unspoken values of the world in which he operates, destruction of the self becomes almost an inevitability. Such is Othello's situation.

It is unfortunate that very little is known about the relation of the Western territorial states to the more ancient traditions of the Levantine cultures out of which Othello comes. It is speculated that the culture of ancient Greece was greatly influenced by the culture of ancient Egypt (Immanuel Velikovsky in *Oedipus and Akhnaton* and much more recently Martin Bernal in *Black Athena*). It is known that the Levantine peoples, some of whom are now called Arabs, preserved in their languages the records of the best of Greek philosophy, and it is known that the culture of the ancient Greeks was reintroduced into Western Europe by these peoples. It is known that the essence of Levantine religious thought was distilled in the teachings of Jesus of Nazareth and was adapted, with some significant modifications, by Europeans many centuries later. And it is known that what became the Western tradition of romantic love resulted from the infiltration of Levantine religious rituals and myths into southern France, where it found expression in the religion of the Cathari in the late Middle Ages, and from whom it spread to the troubadours who carried it into all parts of Europe as an expression of a secular art. But for the most part, the deeper influences of Levantine culture on the territorial states of Western Europe have remained obscure. Apart from the scholarship of a few specialists, there is little general understanding of the ethical system that predated that of the West and that once had great influence on Western culture. This deficiency in understanding limits our insights into Levantine peoples when they appear against the backdrop provided by the ruling assumptions of Western tradition. We do not see that they, too, are operating out of an unstated value system, and that this value system, though alien to Western understanding, may play some large part in the choices they make.

While it is presumptuous of any writer to second-guess Shakespeare, I am tempted to speculate, nonetheless, that a character as complex as Othello would be better understood if he were viewed against the backdrop provided by his own ethical system instead of against the backdrop provided, almost exclusively, by the values of the Venice he inhabits. Viewed from such an intimate perspective, Othello's fate, while still tragic, becomes more clearly the result of his own attempt to participate in some private ethic while at the same time serving out his obligation to the state. I believe that it is this conflict between his loyalty to the state and his attempt to be loyal to his own private ethic that is the source of his tragic flaw and his fall from grace.

One sees in Othello the very same merger of noble birth and noble nature that Prince Myshkin, in Dostoevsky's *The Idiot,* possesses. In the Western literary tradition, there is a convention of noble natures appearing in the most unlikely of places. In modern American democracy, we have been conditioned to expect the appearance of such people. From Melville's Billy Budd to Twain's Huck Finn, such natures have appeared, confirming our belief that nature is a wonderful moral factory, capable of throwing up models of moral balance that, in more traditional cultures, would be expected to find expression only in an established aristocracy. In point of fact, as a very practical matter, virtue in pre-Christian Europe was assumed to be invested in dynastic lines and their observances of vertical obligations. Nobility of intention and of action were not so much matters of personal choice as very practical matters of necessity. Othello, although an outsider to Venice, claims for himself a form of nobility that would be very familiar to the Venetian aristocracy. He says in Act I, scene ii, to Iago, in defense of his marriage to Desdemona:

> I fetch my life and being
> From men of royal siege, and my demerits
> May speak unbonneted to as proud a fortune
> As this that I have reach'd.

But Othello also lists for Iago two additional merits, both of which will become active agents in his eventual undoing. He claims a right to fairness of treatment with respect to Desdemona based on his past and present services to the state:

> Let him [Brabantio] do his spite;
> My services which I have done the signiory
> Shall out-tongue his complaints.

His third source of personal merit seems almost arrogant:

> My parts, my title, and my perfect soul
> Shall manifest me rightly.

It is this seeming arrogance in Othello, threaded throughout the play, that proves to be his undoing. In a traditional view of tragedy, it may be construed as his "tragic flaw." Like some royal character in Greek drama, Othello seems to dare to appropriate to himself what should be the exclusive judgment of the gods. He seems to believe in his own mythology, thus running the risk of offending the gods and attracting their jealousy and wrath. It might be questioned, however, whether what Othello expresses is true arrogance or a fundamental belief in a value system, an ethic, that has sustained his life thus far and about which he is merely speaking honestly. The problem raised by this speculation is made even more difficult by the fact that, if indeed there is an independent ethic to which Othello subscribes, its sources are not apparent in the play. Othello's statements provide evidence of its existence, but no full statement of its content, no assertion of its causative principles, is made. Othello merely testifies, throughout the play, to his belief that what he calls his "perfect soul" will not lead him into error. When speaking before the Duke about his courtship of Desdemona, he says:

> She loved me for the dangers I had passed
> And I loved her that she did pity them.

And when he does fall into error, after having been manipulated by Iago, he does not admit to any error on his own part and is still captive to his old sense of his personal nobility:

> Yet, 'tis the plague of great ones;
> Prerogativ'd are they less than the base.
> 'Tis destiny unshunnable, like death.
> Even then this forked plague is fated to us
> When we do quicken.

Even after killing Desdemona, when Othello sees his fatal mistake, he still maintains that the error is not entirely his fault:

> Who can control his fate? . . .
>   When we shall meet at compt [accounting],
> This look of thine will hurl my soul from heaven,
> And fiends will snatch at it.

And when asked by Lodovico how a man as good as he seemed to be could have fallen to such a slavish deed, Othello replies with a peculiar absence of self-blame:

> An honorable murderer, if you will;
> For naught I did in hate, but all in honor.

I speculate that, beneath this seeming obtuseness on Othello's part, there is an unarticulated ethic at work, one upon which he has based a view of the world, the place of loyalty in that world, and his own sense of his soul's worth. I speculate that Othello is operating in accordance with a Levantine ethical system that selects as its core value a passive stance toward matters of personal fate. Whether a person is elected to enter Heaven or doomed to hell is not, in this view of things, a matter that can be influenced by individual action. According to this ethic, an individual is predestined to either join the community of the faithful in Heaven or remain forever outside of it.

Such an ethic based on predestination directly contradicts an ethic based on personal will. It assumes that God predetermines the fates of men and that the will of the individual is meaningless. It assumes that the will of the individual is not under his own control but is only God's instrument in effecting what He has already determined. I believe that it is a subscription to this same ethic, to a belief in his own predetermined election, that motivates Othello. I also believe that the chief dramatic conflict in the drama is the conflict between Othello's private ethic and Iago's personal will.

The nature of this conflict between Iago and Othello might be brought into much clearer focus by being viewed through the dramatic action in the play symbolized by the Signoria of Venice and the island of Cyprus. In the minds of Shakespeare and his contemporaries, the rational world inherited from Greco-Roman tradition tended to make a division between the material world and the irrational forces of Nature. As Edward Said has suggested, the use of the word *Orientalism* is, in reality, an intellectual device employed to block out, or else to reduce in importance, almost anything that is intellectually or emotionally uncomfortable for Western people. Beneath this intellectual device reside the psychological habits that give rise to the accepted divisions between "West and East," "Us and Them," "White and Black." So Venice, in *Othello,* and its senate, embody order, reason, justice, and concord—which binding forces hold the city together. Cyprus, on the other hand, is associated with chaos, violent storms, the Turk, the Ottoman, the unharnessed forces of Nature—the "Other." If one were to reject the conventional interpretation of Iago as a malignant or evil soul in action, and view him instead as an expression of a settled point of view, his interaction with Othello, as I have argued earlier, might then be read as a conflict between two different ethical systems. They are put into contrast by Shakespeare in much the same way, but on a larger scale, the Signoria of Venice and the Island of Cyprus are put into contrast and also into conflict.

The Venice re-created by Shakespeare is the Venice he drew from Giraldi Cinthio's *Hecatommithi,* a collection of one hundred tales printed in Italy in the sixteenth century (1565). One of the tales involves a Moor who kills his Christian wife. All the key elements of Shakespeare's *Othello* can be found in this morality tale: the wicked ensign, a handkerchief ("finely embroidered in the Moorish fashion"), a cruel and vengeful Moor, and a Disdemona, whose dying sentiments are much *unlike* the dying sentiments of Shakespeare's Desdemona:

> . . . and much I fear that I shall prove a warning to young girls not to marry against the wishes of their parents, and that the Italian ladies may learn from me not to wed a man whom nature and habitudes of life estrange from us.

There are mentions of Cyprus in Cinthio's story, but Cyprus is not an active "participant" in his account.

It took the peculiar genius of Shakespeare to transform Giraldi Cinthio's character sketches, as well as his morality tale, into a great drama. Shakespeare added Cyprus to

Cinthio's story, and made Othello an intermediary between these two worlds. This movement on Othello's part, between reason and emotional chaos, is, in my view, at the basis of the tragic events in the play. If it is indeed true, as Jesus of Nazareth taught, that "no man can serve two masters," then Othello's heroism consists, for English-speaking readers of the play, in his resolution of his deep emotional conflict by killing that part of himself which had dishonored Desdemona, as well as her father, and through them the Signoria of Venice. In this conventional view, Othello dies a Christian subject of Venice. It is open to speculation what other part of Othello, an equal partner in his internal conflict, also dies with him.

But Othello is much more than a convert to Christianity. Even before he appears in Act I, scene ii of the play, we are told, through allusions, that he is considered by the Venetians as someone who is alien. This prejudice is expressed in the exchange between Brabantio, Desdemona's father, and Iago, in Act I, scene i:

BRABANTIO: What tell'st thou me of robbery.

This is Venice; my house is not a grange. . . .

IAGO: You'll have your daughter covered with a Barbary (Arabian) horse, you'll have your nephews neigh to you, you'll have coursers for cousins, and gennets for germans . . .

Othello is also called "a lascivious Moor" by Roderigo. And Brabantio, when he confronts Othello, states the Venetian case:

> Damned as thou art, thou hast enchanted her!
> For I'll refer to all things of sense,
> If she in chains of magic were not bound,
> Whether a maid so tender, fair and happy,
> So opposed to marriage that she shunned
> The wealthy, curled darlings of our nation,
> Would ever have, t'incur a general mock,
> Run from her guardage to the sooty bosom
> Of such a thing as thou—to fear, not to delight.

But Othello, in his own self-concept, is certain of his equality of *rank* with Desdemona's family. When Iago orders him to run, Othello says:

> Not I. I must be found.
> My parts, my title, and my perfect soul
> Shall manifest me rightly.

Later, before the Duke, the Venetian senate and the officials, and Desdemona's father, Othello meets anger with reasoned discourse. He gently recounts his courtship of Desdemona. In his famous speech in Act i, scene iii, it should be noted, Othello speaks in the "high" style of the Court, recollecting the incidents of a hero's life, incidents that might have also come from the mouths of Tristram, Lancelot, Percival, or any other knight in that tradition of courtly love so familiar to Shakespeare and his audiences. The speech is beautiful in its childlike simplicity and honesty, but it betrays no sense of psychological depths or insights on Othello's part. He refutes the charges against him, of witchcraft and betrayal of loyalty, by placing his story within a literary convention, or form, familiar to the Duke and his senators:

> She loved me for the dangers I had passed.
> And I loved her that she did pity them.
> This only is the witchcraft I have used.

But the "rational" nature of his speech causes Othello to omit any reference to the handkerchief he has given Desdemona. This handkerchief, of great symbolic significance to the play, is not mentioned, for some reason, until Act III, scene iii, *after* Othello and the Venetians have arrived on Cyprus. It is only then that we learn of its emotional importance to Othello. It is, we learn in Act III, scene iv, a symbol of both the continuity of Othello's own moral identity and of his bond with Desdemona:

> That handkerchief
> Did an Egyptian to my mother give.
> She was a charmer, and could almost read
> The thoughts of people. *She told her, while she kept it*
> *'Twould make her amiable and subdue my father*
> *Entirely to her love; but if she lost it*
> *Or made a gift of it, my father's eye*
> *Should hold her loathed, and his spirits should hunt*
> *After new fancies. She, dying, gave it me,*
> *And bid me, when my fate would have me wived*
> *To give it her. I did so;* and take heed on't;
> Make it a darling like your precious eye.

To lose't or give't away were such perdition
As nothing else could match. [Italics added]

It is on the island of Cyprus that we learn the symbolic importance of this item to Othello. In Venice, before the Duke, the senators, even before Desdemona and Brabantio, her father, there is no mention of it. Perhaps Shakespeare's use of the conventions of courtly love, essential to his viewers for recognition of the emotional understanding expressed by the Duke, negated the introduction of any real evidence of witchcraft. Even though Giraldi Cinthio, in his story, mentions a handkerchief "finely embroidered in the Moorish fashion," Shakespeare delays in raising it to a level of dramatic importance, *at least in Venice,* as Cinthio does in his account. In Shakespeare's version, the handkerchief appears as a central symbol *only after* the action of the play moves to Cyprus. Perhaps it is Othello's loyalty to the rationality of the Signoria that causes him to forget the handkerchief as a symbol of his bond with Desdemona. Or perhaps, in Shakespeare's view, the handkerchief achieves dramatic significance *only* when it and Othello are reintegrated into the "landscape" from which they both derived. Once removed from the rationalizing structure of Venice, in Shakespeare's view, Othello "reverts" to the irrationality represented by "Egypt," Moor, Turk, Ottoman, *Cyprus.* This convention of "place" defining types of responses runs through many of Shakespeare's plays: *Antony and Cleopatra, Troilus and Cressida, King Lear, Henry IV, The Tempest, Richard II, A Midsummer Night's Dream.* But it is in *Othello,* as in *Antony and Cleopatra,* that a far distant landscape—that of an imagined

Cyprus—is employed to suggest the hold of a foreign and alien ethic on a character. The symbolic background, represented by Cyprus, in addition to its emotional correlation with the handkerchief, thus becomes of great importance to the developing tragedy.

Moreover, while he is still in Venice, Othello makes before Brabantio and the Signoria a formal gesture as important as the handkerchief to the tragic developments in the play. Still conforming to the "high" style of the courtly love tradition, Othello has this exchange with Brabantio, Desdemona's father:

> BRABANTIO: Look to her, Moor, if thou hast eyes to see:
> She has deceived her father, and may thee.
> OTHELLO: My life upon her faith.

To Shakespeare's audiences, such an exchange would probably recall to mind the psychological, or emotional, subtext of traditional narratives about the courtly love tradition: The lovers are doomed to *not* live happily ever after. They may separate (as Othello and Desdemona do just after this exchange), and reunite, and maintain their passion for each other, but their fate is *to not be* permanently joined with each other. Rather, their fate is death. Passionate pursuit of the unobtainable "other" leads to death. This was the familiar passion of Tristam and Isolde, of Lancelot and Guinevere, etc. Such is the conventional implication of Othello's foreshadowing "My life upon her faith." But, on a much deeper level, this line, spoken by Othello to Brabantio, the heart-

broken father, might refer back to Othello's initial statement
of his personal ethic, in Act I, scene ii:

> I must be found.
> My parts, my title, and my perfect soul
> Shall manifest me rightly.

Othello's statement to Brabantio may well be an oath that
his personal honor and that of Desdemona have now merged.
He vows to restore the faith that Brabantio has lost in Desdemona. In a deep emotional sense, Othello is making a
"contract" with Brabantio, saying that he will give his life if
what Brabantio perceives as deceit is a true assessment of his
daughter, Othello's wife. Moreover, Othello is making his
vow *through Brabantio* to the entire, ordered, rational world
of the Signoria. Within the context of this reading of the
vow, the significance of the handkerchief, though not mentioned, once again becomes of great symbolic importance. It
becomes a symbol of Othello's own lifeline, though steeped
in "Orientalism"; and, since it is then in Desdemona's hands,
it becomes the symbolic proof of Othello's own faith in their
bond. Othello thus carries to the island of Cyprus, from
Venice, a "rational" contract with Brabantio based on an "irrational" sense of his own parts, titles, and perfect soul. In
this reading of the play, it is Othello's struggle to honor both
the rationality of the Venetian state and the emotional chaos
set off once he is settled into the Cyprus landscape (and what
it represented to the Elizabethan mind) that is at the basis of
the tragic action of the play. It is being suggested that, the

plots and malicious machinations of Iago aside, the tragedy of the play is centered in Othello's own struggle to contain these conflicting obligations inside himself, as these conflicting obligations increase on the island of Cyprus.

Shakespeare's creative genius led him to add the island of Cyprus, its "Oriental" landscape, to Cinthio's story. The conflict between it and the Signoria of Venice parallels, it is suggested, and also contrasts the conflicting emotional states of Othello. It should be noted that, while the Signoria of Venice provides the backdrop of the play for only one act, the backdrop of Cyprus overshadows *four* full acts of the play, as well as its central dramatic actions. Furthermore, the very first scene in Act II, set in Cyprus, raises the possibility of emotional chaos grounded in *natural forces,* the *same* natural forces discussed by Iago and Roderigo in the opening scene of Act I of the play. Act II, scene i, set in Cyprus, foreshadows the commencement of the unleashing of "natural" forces (though "unnatural" to the Venetians) that will dominate the remainder of the play:

> MONTANO: Methinks the wind hath spoke aloud at
> land;
> A fuller blast ne'er shook our battlements.
> If it hath ruffianed so upon sea,
> What ribs of oaks, what mountains melt on them,
> Can hold the mortise? *What shall we hear of this?*
> [Italics added].

Although the raging sea has destroyed the Turkish fleet, it

has also separated Othello from his lieutenant, Michael Cassio, Othello's only official link with Venice. Even Cassio says, "The great contention of sea and skies parted our fellowship." It should be noted that, while the Venetians await Othello's arrival at Cyprus, the "pure" products of the Venetian court —Desdemona, Michael Cassio, Iago, Emilia, Montano, and a second "gentleman"—reconstruct their courtly manners, and their wit, their sense of "breeding." Othello's absence from this scene may be of great symbolic significance to the play. When he does appear upon the stage at Cyprus, he carries in his speech to Desdemona an echo of the storm from which he has emerged as well as a foreshadowing of his own emotional fate:

> If after every tempest come such calms,
> May the winds blow till they have wakened death.
> And let the laboring bark climb hills of seas
> Olympus-high, and duck again as low
> As hell's from heaven.

And of his return to Cyprus, Othello says,

> How does my old acquaintances of this isle?
> Honey, you shall be well desired in Cyprus;
> I have found great love amongst them. O my sweet,
> *I prattle out of fashion, and dote*
> *In mine own comforts . . .*
> Once more well met at Cyprus. [Italics added]

Once again we see Shakespeare searching for a connection

between Othello and the Cyprus landscape. Deeper than this, there is an implication that Othello's "own comforts," whatever they are, are now merged with his bond with Desdemona, as well as with her connection with the Signoria of Venice. A third suggestion that Othello's "own comforts" in Cyprus are becoming alien to the ways of the Signoria is conveyed in two subsequent speeches, after Othello departs with Desdemona. The first is Iago's discourse on unfaithful wives, begun in scene i of this same act, and its continuation with Roderigo. Here Iago's descriptions of Desdemona grow even coarser, and here he discloses his suspicion that *both* Othello and Michael Cassio have cuckolded him with Emilia, his wife. On one level of this speech, Shakespeare is simply deepening the conventional characterization of the stage villain, a stock character familiar to his audiences. But on another level, this full speech to Roderigo, set against the "Oriental" backdrop of Cyprus, suggests that Iago, too, is being drawn under the influence of the mysterious "otherness" that will soon claim the public character of Othello.

An additional narrative suggestion that chaos will soon displace order, that Cyprus will soon threaten the order of Venice, comes just after Iago's soliloquy. This is at the beginning of scene ii in the very same act, when Othello's herald reads his proclamation ordering a celebration of the destruction of the Turkish fleet:

> . . . every man put himself into triumph. Some to dance, some to make bonfires, each man to what sport and revels his addition leads him. For besides these beneficial news, *it is the celebration of his nuptials.* [Italics

added] So much was his pleasure should be proclaimed.
All offices [storerooms, or *ranks of order?*] are open, and
there is full liberty of feasting . . .

It is from within such a context of license, against the
backdrop of Cyprus, that the drama moves toward its tragic
end.

Within such a context, against such a backdrop of what
Shakespeare and his audiences would view as an "irrational"
world, the subsequent contrasts between Iago's ethic and
Othello's obscure one may well be viewed with greater insight and understanding. It should be recalled that it has
been Iago's intention all along to have his revenge on Othello
for preferring Michael Cassio as his lieutenant, as he announced to Roderigo in Act i, scene i:

> Perferment goes by letter and affection,
> And not by old gradation, when each second
> Stood heir to the first.

Iago has also made clear in this speech that he knows both
sides of Othello's nature, both the courtly and Christianized
self, displayed at the Signoria, and the "pagan" side exhibited in other places:

> And I, of whom his eyes had seen the proof
> At Rhodes, at Cyprus, and on other grounds
> Christian and heathen, must be belee'd and calmed
> By debitor and creditor.

It is no accident, I think, that Shakespeare chose the island of Cyprus, and its heathen implications, and not the rational, ordered world of the Signoria, for Iago to act out his will against Othello. On Cyprus, Iago is merely pressing his own case, but against a backdrop which, given Othello's "own comforts" in that landscape—the "pagan" nature of which Cyprus is the symbol—both it and Othello will help further his designs.

Within the specific context of such a perspective, Othello's handkerchief becomes of essential importance. If, as has been speculated earlier, it represents a linkage between Othello and his lineage, as well as his linkage with Desdemona, the deeper importance of this symbol can only be revealed against the Cyprus landscape, the landscape that best connects Othello with his place of origin. As noted before, there is no mention of the handkerchief while Othello and Desdemona are in Venice. But at Cyprus, when Othello and Desdemona enjoy "the celebration of his nuptials," the handkerchief surfaces and is moved to the exact center of the dramatic action of the play. There is, in Act III, scene iii, a fundamental ambiguity, one that might support this specific reading of Othello's ethic. This is the scene in which Iago is insinuating to Othello a hidden love affair between Desdemona and Michael Cassio. Othello doubts it. Then Desdemona and Emilia enter. Othello complains of "a pain upon my forehead."

> DESDEMONA: Let me but bind it hard; within this
> hour

It will be well.

OTHELLO: Your napkin is too little; [stage
directions: He pushes the handkerchief away, and
it falls]

Let *it* alone.

             Come, I'll go in with you.

Whether this "it" refers to Othello's forehead or to the
handkerchief is the fundamental ambiguity in this important scene. As a number of critics have suggested, it makes a
considerable difference in the interpretation of later events
whether this "it" refers to Othello's forehead or to the handkerchief. Given the symbolic importance of the handkerchief
to Cinthio's original version of the story, and given the care
that Shakespeare took to create Cyprus as the dominant
backdrop for most of his play's dramatic action, and considering also the handkerchief's importance to the remainder of
the play, it might be suggested that it is the *ethic* represented
by the handkerchief itself, and not so much Iago's increasing
insinuations and plots, that concerned Shakespeare in all the
scenes after this handkerchief is introduced. It becomes the
first symbol that binds, on Cyprus, *all* the major characters
in the play—Othello, Desdemona, Emilia, Iago, Michael
Cassio, Bianca, Roderigo. In this reading, the handkerchief,
on Cyprus, is an "ordering" force, a symbol of emotional integration, comparable to the reason and courtly manners that
bind together all the people in the Signoria of Venice. But in
the context of Cyprus, the handkerchief binds the characters
to the "Oriental" or unknown mysteries of Egypt, Arabia,
Turkey, the Ottoman Empire—all the potent emotional

powers of the mysterious "East." A comparison could be made here between the rational, unifying intentions of the Western territorial state, in which individuals are bonded by common language, common blood, and common borders (such as Venice), and a Levantine "sect nation," in which a shared belief in a "sacred script," blood and borders notwithstanding, constitute membership. In this reading, the new emotional order introduced by Othello's handkerchief on Cyprus threatens to undermine, if not to destroy, the hold of the rational powers of the Signoria. It is almost as if two *different* models of social organization are being brought into focus, and into conflict, by Shakespeare. And the less familiar, or alien, model of bonding is symbolized by the introduction of Othello's handkerchief into the very center of the drama. The linkage it imposes on the participants in the tragedy also introduces a counterstructure, or an uneasy emotional order, that threatens the traditional order about to be imposed on Cyprus by the rationalizing power of the Venetian state.

But on a personal level, to Othello the handkerchief has something more than organizational meaning. It is the symbol of his own emotional investment, as both an individual man and as a husband, in the continuity of his own version of personal honor. It represents his own pledge to his ancestors and to Desdemona. Also, I suggest, it is Othello's attempt to honor both his sworn obligation to the Duke and to Brabantio, as well as his obligation to the ethic represented by the handkerchief, that leads him to kill himself.

The handkerchief comes "alive" as an additional actor in the play only after its casual introduction in Act III, scene iii.

It is Emilia who first recognizes its importance as Desdemona's "first rememberance from the Moor":

> My wayward husband hath a hundred times
> Wooed me to steal it; but she so loves the token
> (For he conjured her she should ever keep it)
> That she reserves it evermore about her
> To kiss and talk to. I'll have the work ta'en out
> And give't Iago. What he will do with it,
> Heaven knows, not I;
> I nothing but to please his fantasy.

Emilia discloses that, to Desdemona, the handkerchief *is* Othello. But to Emilia it is something to be copied and also a gift for Iago, her husband. To Iago, the handkerchief has no spiritual or ethical content. To him it is a *thing* that can be used to trap Othello:

> I will in Cassio's lodging lose this napkin
> And let him find it. Trifles light as air
> Are to the jealous confirmations strong
> As proofs of Holy Writ.

Once the handkerchief passes from Emilia to Iago, it is increasingly debased and cheapened, losing its original meaning, until it becomes only a trifle for Bianca, Michael Cassio's whore. It would be an instructive exercise to trace the incremental *increase* in Othello's suspicion and "madness" and correlate this with each stage in the debasement of the handkerchief, with each *decrease* in the valuation of the beloved symbol. It is obvious that something changes abruptly in Othello in the very scene (Act III, scene iii) in which Desdemona drops the handkerchief. Emilia picks it up and gives it to Iago just after Othello and Desdemona go offstage. Othello returns almost immediately, but his mood has clearly shifted from the trusting lover of Desdemona to an attitude of deep suspicion. He says to Iago, "Ha! ha! False to me?" Nothing else can account for this abrupt shift in Othello, from doubt in Iago's insinuations to absolute belief in Desdemona's unfaithfulness, unless it is the debasement of the handkerchief that is now beginning. It is significant to note that Othello's deep suspicion begins *even before he knows* that the handkerchief has been stolen by Emilia and passed on to Iago. It is almost as if Othello senses some spiritual loss inside himself. From this point onward in the play, Othello's language becomes debased and angry. He moves away from the courtly language in earlier sections of the play and begins to employ "low" physical images, rage, and vows of retribution.

I suggest that the handkerchief is, to Othello, a symbol of his entire lineage and reason for existence. It moves from being a symbol of self, then to a symbol of his love for Desdemona, then to a symbol of their bond, *in his own ancestral terms,* and from this to a simple trifle with a variety of uses and meanings imposed on it as it passes from hand to hand among an alien people. By losing the handkerchief, and through its cheapening, Othello has lost the symbol of his own election, or predestination, to noble rank. This reading might make much deeper sense of his brooding soliloquy at the beginning of scene ii in Act V. Othello is torn between his loss of self and his remaining love for Desdemona. For him *two* essential concerns—his loss of his symbolic self, the handkerchief, and his dread of losing Desdemona—are *merged* in this speech. Othello is speaking here both to the heavens, from which he once expected protection and salvation, and to himself.

> It is the cause [causality? Loss of the
> ethical meaning of the symbol?],
>   it is the cause, my soul.
> Let me not name it to you, you chaste stars.
> It is the cause. *Yet I'll not shed her blood,*
> *Nor scar that whiter skin of hers than snow,*
> *And smooth as monumental alabaster.*
> *Yet she must die, else she'll betray more men.*
> Put out the light, and then put out the light.
> If I quench thee, thou flaming minister,
> I can again thy former light restore,
> Should I repent me; *but once put out thy light,*
> *Thou cunning'st pattern of excellent nature,*
> *I know not where is that Promethean heat*
> *That can thy light relume.* When I have plucked
>   the rose
> I cannot give it vital growth again;
> *It needs must wither.* [Italics added]

If Othello's speech is read in this way, as a meditation on *both* his own soul's fate and his love for Desdemona, something essential may come into clearer focus. Both this speech and Othello's recollection of the handkerchief's spiritual im-

233

portance in Act III, scene iv contain references to the inextricable integration of the material and the spiritual. The handkerchief is a physical object that contains great spiritual significance for Othello. His speech in Act V, scene ii recapitulates this same close integration. Here, Othello now believes that Desdemona has betrayed him with Michael Cassio, which is the accepted reading of the scene. But which is the *causal* fact beneath his wish to kill her? Is it because through Desdemona the handkerchief has been debased, and through that debasement Othello's own spirit; or is it only that her betrayal has been proved by her loss of the handkerchief? If the latter, then the handkerchief becomes a mere stage prop. But if it is the former, then the handkerchief symbolizes a much deeper causative principle, one which the genius of Shakespeare, despite the intellectual limitations of his historical time and place, was struggling hard to reach and to comprehend.

Othello's handkerchief has passed from Egypt through all the mysteries of the "Orient" into the very "heart" of a European nation-state, as the symbol of a bond between a Venetian senator's daughter and a "pagan" line with claims to a comparable nobility. In that handkerchief both the material and the spiritual are merged. Within the confines of Venice, it is only a material item. But against the Cyprus landscape, Shakespeare shows that the handkerchief is of essential importance to Othello as a symbol of spiritual linkage to both his personal past and to Desdemona. But in the hands of Emilia, Iago, Michael Cassio, and Bianca, it is only a material trifle. And its movement from the spiritual plane to the material one coincides, as has been argued, with Othello's increasing jealousy and "madness." But in Shakespeare's view is Othello truly mad, or is he trying to resolve a spiritual problem that is essential to the life of his own soul, the fate of Desdemona notwithstanding? It is being suggested here that Shakespeare was trying to *imagine* his way toward an ethical basis for Othello's behavior, one far removed from the outward conformity to both the Christianity and the veneer of manners of his adopted Venice. What Shakespeare, possibly, was contemplating was evidence of a form of ethical behavior, and therefore personal transcendence, which, historically, has always been at odds with the material ethic of the West, and most especially the ethic of personal will dramatized by the plots of Iago.

Read in this context, it might be helpful to observe just how Shakespeare treated another "alien" caught up in the ethical structures of this same Venice. This other "alien," of course, is Shylock, the Jewish merchant in Shakespeare's "comedy" *The Merchant of Venice* (1598). Like *Othello* (1604), Shylock is torn between two competing ethical systems, his own Jewish tradition and the Christian tradition of the Venetian state. Perhaps this play is called a comedy because Shylock, the Jew, is shown to be unable to prevail against the expression of personal will, under the guise of Christian ethics, dramatized by Portia. Perhaps the most moving line in the play is Shylock's response to his friend Tubal, when Tubal tells him that his own daughter, Jessica, has sold a ring to Antonio's creditors for a monkey. Shylock responds, in Act III, scene ii of the play, with the most heartfelt emotion:

Out upon her! Thou torturest me, Tubal. It was my
turquoise; I had it of Lea when I was a bachelor. I would
not have given it for a wilderness of monkeys.

There is a parallel, it is being suggested, between both
Shylock and Othello. This parallel has to do with the value
each alien man places on a material item that links each man
to a personal past. In each case, Shakespeare seems to be suggesting, the value invested in the symbol is much deeper
than its surface appearance.

The world to which both Shylock's turquoise and
Othello's handkerchief symbolically link them, in Shakespeare's view, is that unknown and unknowable Levantine
world that enters the historical world known in such scant
detail by Shakespeare only at specific times and places. These
times and places were those chosen by Europeans, selectively,
to construct their ideas about the line of progress of history.
Shakespeare explored the points at which the Western and
the Levantine traditions *met:* Egypt and Rome in *Julius Caesar* and *Antony and Cleopatra.* Historically, the two worlds
met when the sacred texts of Christianity were translated by
Greeks and Jews from their original Hebrew. And they met
again, as has been stated before, when the cult of romantic
love, the courtly love tradition, infiltrated Western Europe,
by way of Levantine influences, during the tenth and
eleventh centuries. There are references to this other, alien
world, in the histories of the Crusades, and in the French
epic poem *The Song of Roland.* But by limiting the knowable
landscape to only these few encounters between the Levan-

tine world and Western Europe, there is a "blind spot," so to speak, in the understanding of cultural traditions that are non-European. This is the geographic place, *the psychological border,* at which reason and unreason, rationality and irrationality, meet and confront each other. The ancient Greeks, those first grand masters of reason, resolved this problem by attributing to the action of the gods a "psychic intervention," or *ate,* which would "rationalize" irrational actions on the parts of their heroes. To the Greeks, *ate* was a state of mind—a temporary clouding or bewildering of the normal consciousness, a temporary insanity—brought on by external "demonic" agencies. Later European societies rationalized the movement of spiritual forces in a variety of other ways. To Christians of the Middle Ages it was the *strigia,* irrational demonic forces, that gave rise to beliefs in witchcraft, as well as to anti-Semitism. In Shakespeare's day, the sources of the irrational became associated with Nature itself. But in *Othello,* Shakespeare seems intent on exploring this intellectual problem through his treatment of his major character. The great writer could only intuit a philosophical system, or an independent ethic, as the basis of Othello's struggle.

To bring into closer focus evidence of what so troubles Othello after his handkerchief is lost, it might be helpful to quote a Muslim theologian, almost a contemporary of Cinthio (1058–1111), who suggests the dualistic nature of the Levantine outlook on the world, its system of symbolic meanings. This is the Sufi philosopher Al-Ghazzali, who, in his *Mishkat Al-Anwar* (*The Niche for Light*), speaks of the meaning of the symbolic language of Levantine tradition, a language that enters Western tradition in John's Gospel, in the stories of *The Arabian Nights,* and, possibly, through Othello's handkerchief:

> The annulment of the outward and visible sign is the tenet of the Spiritualists, who looked, utterly one-sidedly, at one world, the Unseen, and were grossly ignorant of the balance that exists between it and the Seen. This aspect they failed to understand. Similarly, annulment of the inward and invisible meaning is the opinion of the Materialists. In other words, whoever abstracts and isolates the outward from the whole is a Materialist, and whoever abstracts the inward is a Spiritualist, while he who joins the two together is catholic, perfect . . .

This insight suggests that, to William Shakespeare, and therefore to Othello, the handkerchief might have had this very same symbolic meaning.

If the above speculation is accepted, Othello's speech in Act V, scene ii might take on much more significance. Here Othello is trying to reclaim his old ethic, a balance between the "light" once provided by his handkerchief, for both himself and for his bond with Desdemona, and Desdemona herself, who symbolizes his linkage with the Signoria of Venice. This is the terrible "causality" he must contemplate, and this is the foreshadowing of all his subsequent actions. In such a horrible situation, Othello must struggle to remain true to both sources of self-definition, the spiritual and the physical, as well as to the traditions of *both* his places of origin.

> It is the cause, it is the cause, my soul.
> Let me not name it to you, you chaste stars.
> It is the cause. *Yet I'll not shed her blood,*
> *Nor scar that whiter skin of hers than snow,*
> *And smooth as monumental alabaster,*
> *Yet she must die, else she'll betray more men.*
> Put out the light, and then put out the light.
> If I quench thee, thou flaming minister,
> I can again thy former light restore,
> Should I repent me; *but once put out thy light,*
> *Thou cunning'st pattern of excellent nature,*
> *I know not where is that Promethean heat*
> *That can thy light relume. When I have plucked the rose*
> *I cannot give it vital growth again;*
> It needs must wither. [Italics added]

It is in the very last scenes of the play, after Iago's last trick has been disclosed, and after Othello has killed Desdemona, that a *balanced* nobility in Othello does come out. He now recognizes that his "mistake," made when he allowed himself to be manipulated by Iago, resulted from his *unchanging* belief in the rightness and the purity of his own soul, his own source of motivation. But now he has commited murder, has broken the laws of Venice, and has also broken his vow to Brabantio, who, we learn in the same scenes, has died. The unifying power of the handkerchief has been destroyed by being cheapened. The "sect" on Cyprus that has grown up around it has now been supplanted by the authority of the Venetian state. The state has now reintroduced its old hierarchy on Cyprus, and Michael Cassio is put in the place of Othello. Othello is stripped of everything except what in him is literal and irreducible. It is only at this point that Othello's true heroism, his natural nobility, emerges. He has judged others according to his own ethic, and now, to maintain a sense of his own old nobility of purpose, he must judge himself—but on *two different scales of justice.* It is here, in Act V, scene ii, that Othello repeats, in an ironic way, the vow he made in Act I, scene iii to Brabantio:

[Act I, scene iii]
BRABANTIO: Look to her, Moor, if thou hast eyes to see;
　She has deceived her father, and may thee.
OTHELLO: My life upon her faith.

[Act V, scene ii]
OTHELLO: But why should honor outlive honesty?
　Let it all go.

It is only after the acceptance of his fate that Othello reverts to his old "high" speech, the courtly style of speech of personal bravery, such as the one before the Duke back in Venice. He speaks to Gratiano, recently come from the court:

　Behold, I have a weapon;
　A better never did itself sustain
　Upon a soldier's thigh. I have seen the day
　That with this little arm and this good sword

I have made my way through more impediments
Than twenty times your stop. But O vain boasts:
Who can control his fate?

And in this same speech, he says to Desdemona:

　　when we shall meet
at compt [judgment],
This look of thine will hurl my soul from heaven,
And fiends will snatch at it.

But Othello still insists on his nobility of intention when
accused by Lodovico:

LODOVICO: O thou Othello that was once so good,
　　Fall'n in the practice of a cursed slave,
　　What shall be said to them?
OTHELLO:　　　　Why, anything;
　　An honorable murderer, if you will,
　　For naught I did in hate, but all in honor.

There seems to be a contradiction in these two speeches.
On the one hand, in terms of the Christian ethic essential to
Desdemona's fate, Othello sees himself as a sinner whose soul
will be hurled from heaven on Judgment Day. But still, in
terms of his own ethic, he sees himself as acting honorably. It
is this double set of scales, I suggest, that is at the basis of
Othello's last speech. It is a great speech, in the country style
of the Signoria. Its images integrate the divided loyalties of a
noble warrior whose services to the state have always been

based on a belief in the rightness of his actions. But much more important than this is Othello's ambiguous reference to the symbolic meaning of the handkerchief:

> Of one not easily jealous, but, being wrought,
> Perplexed in the extreme; *of one whose hand,*
> Like the base Judean, threw a pearl away
> Richer than all his tribe.

The conventional interpretation is to consider this part of Othello's speech as a reference to Desdemona. But considering the importance of the handkerchief to the tragic development of the play, and considering also that this speech contains a summary of Othello's life, Shakespeare would have been amiss as a dramatist to have not integrated its meaning into Othello's last speech. As said before, the handkerchief represents Othello's *self.* Also, the term *base Judean* is ambiguous. It could refer to Judas Iscariot, or to an "Indian"; but its clear implication is to *infidelity,* to the unbeliever. In this reading of the scene, Othello seems to be saying that he has brought this fate upon himself by throwing away (Act III, scene iii) the symbolic item that had sustained both his life, and his life's meaning, as well as his bond with Desdemona. This is the "recognition," in traditional dramatic theory, of the tragic hero's moral flaw. A reversal of fortunes always comes after this tragic moment of truth.

In Othello's case, the solution is to once again declare his loyalty to the Signoria, by shifting his images abruptly from "the base Judean" and from "Arabian trees" to the history of his past loyalty to the state:

> Set you down this;
> And say besides that in Aleppo once,
> When a malignant and a turbaned Turk
> Beat a Venetian and traduced the state,
> I took by th' throat the circumcised dog
> And smote him thus.

In offering up his own life, Othello affirms his continuing loyalty to the Venetian state. The reference to "a malignant and turbaned Turk" whom he killed is clearly that part of himself that has violated the ethics of the Signoria. Yet if the pearl that has been thrown away is accepted as Othello's symbolic self, and not in total Desdemona, another complexity arises. Is Othello's self-negation so total that he chooses to die to appease *only* the Venetian sense of justice, or has the personal ethic that has sustained Othello all his life, his "perfect soul," his belief in his own election, also found a way to be sustained? I speculate that it is at this extremely important point, and not in the speech that precedes his suicide, that Desdemona again becomes central to the action. As he dies, Othello says to Desdemona:

> I kissed thee ere I killed thee. No way but this,
> Killing myself, to die upon a kiss.

Here Othello seems to be renewing his loving bond with

Desdemona. But this final kiss, a recollection of the intimacy they once had, in Venice as well as on Cyprus, may well be a symbolic reconciliation with Desdemona, and through her with the bond Othello has made with Brabantio, her father. By killing himself, rather than being killed by the Venetians (as was the case in Cinthio's story), Othello has *maintained* his sense of personal honor, and may possibly have also kept alive his old sense of personal rightness, if not predestination. He honors the vow he made to Brabantio back in Venice: "*My life upon her honor.*" This is the other scale of values, his own, that Othello affirms by killing himself. In the act of self-negation, he affirms two sets of loyalties—the one owed to the Venetian state, and the one owed to himself.

In this imaginative reading of Shakespeare's great character, Othello grows even more complex. He is brought closer to our human understanding because he possesses an ethic— a philosophical solution to the fact of death and what should survive it—that is comparable to the Christian ethic held by Desdemona. Othello's suicide might well be, at the same time, an affirmation of his deepest beliefs. If part of his ethical sense originated, with the handkerchief, in Arabia, among the Islamic peoples of the old Levantine world, then Othello's final action might have been a redemptive one, and also an affirmative one, implying that Othello's soul has earned, after all, the transport into the community of the faithful in Paradise. If his ethical sense originated, along with the handkerchief, in Egypt, then Othello's action might have caused his *ka,* his spiritual double, to attain this same afterlife. On this latter point, it might be helpful if we examined two comparable deaths in another of Shakespeare's tragedies—double suicide in *Antony and Cleopatra* (ca. 1608), which also puts into contrast the known world, Rome, and the unknown or "Oriental" world, Egypt. By the last scene in the tragedy, Antony has killed himself, and Cleopatra is to be taken as a prisoner to Rome. Cleopatra determines that she will die at her own hands to escape being degraded by the Romans, *but also to rejoin Antony.* Her speech to Iras, her maidservant (Act V, scene ii), states the nobility of her intention:

> Give me my robe, put on my crown; I have
> Immortal longings in me. Now no more
> The juice of Egypt's grapes shall moist this lip.
> Yare, yare, good Iras; quick. Methinks I hear
> Antony call; I see him rouse himself
> To praise my noble act; I hear him mock
> The luck of Caesar, which the gods give men
> To excuse their after wrath. Husband, I come:
> Now to that name my courage prove my title:
> I am fire and air; my other elements
> I give to baser life.

It is through a comparable action, by kissing Desdemona as he dies, that Othello achieves the same nobility and, it is suggested, the same joy "the gods give men to excuse their after wrath." In this reading of the play, Othello and Desdemona are reunited, at least in the terms that are at the basis of Othello's ethic, *after* their tragic deaths.

Antony's and Cleopatra's deaths took place in Egypt. Oth-

ello died a prisoner of the Signoria of Venice. But Shakespeare's Charmian, an Egyptian, might have said the best final words for the two sets of lovers:

> GUARD: What work is here? Charmian, is this well
> done?
> CHARMIAN: It is well done, and fitting for a princess
> Descended from so many royal kings.

Shakespeare's *Othello* still has very powerful lessons to
teach. Recently, the novelist Scott Turow called the O. J.
Simpson murder trial "the Othello of the twentieth century."
Doubtless, Turow was focused exclusively on the tragic bond
between Othello and Desdemona, between Orenthal James
Simpson and Nicole Brown Simpson. Perhaps, in a superficial sense, Scott Turow is right. But what else does the play
have to teach? For one thing, it provides an understanding of
the psychological tension between the Signoria of Venice
and the island of Cyprus, between rationalized authority and
"irrational" chaos, the deeper emotional meanings between
"us" and "them," suburb and "inner city," between black and
white. The old unstated emotional language of Shakespeare's
day still speaks, though in very subtle ways, from the deepest
levels of this culture. Also—and this is a political point—
this ancient emotional language is likely to resurface, in hysterical ways, as the evolving global economy, structured by
communications technology and the movement of money
and information and peoples, threatens to undermine traditional concepts—common blood and language and borders,
the traditional definition of nation-state sovereignty. The ad-

vocates of nation-state sovereignty will increasingly find themselves confronting ethical systems that are radically different from their own, far, far more different than the Signoria of Venice was from the personality of the island of Cyprus.

These are the growing tensions of this century's end. Of the "trial of the century," only one thing can be said with clarity and certainty. Having made a good living through the commercialization of thin and fashionable images, there was no ancestral handkerchief, either in Orenthal James Simpson's background or in the trust of a beloved, that could keep alive for him a higher meaning in life.

This is the true tragedy of the Simpson case.

Junior and John Doe

In 1961, Ralph Ellison made a prediction. "A period is going to come," he wrote, "when Negroes are going to be wandering around because we've had this thing [the assumption of black American inferiority] thrown at us so long that we haven't had a chance to discover what in our own background is really worth preserving." Nine years later, in an interview, I asked Ellison to elaborate on this prediction. "I think that too many of our assertions continue to be in response to whites," he said. "I think that we're polarized by the very fact that we keep talking about 'black awareness' when we really should be talking about black American awareness, an awareness of where we fit into the total American scheme, where our influence is. I tell white kids that instead of talking about black men in a white world or about black men in white society, they should ask themselves how black *they* are because black men have been influencing the values of the society and the art forms of the society. How many of their parents fell in love listening to Nat King Cole? We did not develop as a people in isolation. We developed within a context of white people."

At the same time that Ellison was responding to me, back

in 1970, the polarization began shifting in the other direction as a deadly racial reaction gathered strength.

I remember San Francisco in 1974. This was the time of the Patty Hearst kidnapping, mass hysteria over an impending gasoline shortage, a time when someone named "the Zebra Killer" was shooting white people. At the height of this hysteria, all black males in the city were subjected to an all-night curfew, by order of the mayor, because the "Zebra Killer" was said to be a black male. I used to defy the curfew by sticking with my personal habit of walking when and where I pleased. One night, on a trolley car, a white male holding the strap next to mine leaned close to my ear and whispered, *"This had better stop! It had better stop before we have to go to war!"* Then, changing the tone of his voice, he said "Good night" to me in a friendly manner, and got off the trolley car.

I remember walking one morning to my favorite black-owned restaurant on Divisadero Street. I liked to go there for breakfast. As I approached the place, I saw seated at a table next to the window a black American friend, a writer, and a white male, an Irishman who lived in that mostly black neighborhood and who had a black girlfriend. I went in and sat down with them. While I had never trusted the Irishman because, officially, he was a policeman whom I considered "slick," I had accepted him as the constant companion of my black friend. My friend seemed especially nervous that morning. And the Irishman seemed especially sour and aggressive. I think he might have resented my intrusion. Whatever the source of his irritation, it soon drew my black friend into a ritual that frightened me. As we sat at the table, the white man would occasionally lift his finger, place it before the eyes of my black friend, and move his finger toward some scene or object on the other side of the café window. "Look at that," he would order. My black friend's eyes followed the directing white finger, almost as if the two organic objects were connected by an invisible string. "See that?" "Look at that!" "What's that?" The orders came again and again, and at each order my black friend's eyes moved with, or his independent will surrendered to, the authority in the single white finger. This single white finger seemed to be orchestrating my black friend's soul. Afterwards, during this same stressful period, my black friend began speeding up his car, in anger, each time he saw groups of black boys taking their time while crossing street intersections.

It was during the early 1970s that I first began to get a new and curious message from black people. It was then that I first began to hear the word *they* being used in an unfamiliar, self-preempting way, a way that suggested that the pressure of the racial reaction had penetrated and was undermining the value sense, or the private idiom, of black Americans. An early warning came from a friend who had achieved early access to a private club habituated by the white upper class. He gave me some advice he had picked up during his rounds: *"They* saw it ain't go'n' be the way it *was. They* say all this bullshit is *over!"* I next heard this new integration of outside essence into personal idiom from a black colleague in response to my description of homeless black people I had seen on the streets of New York. "Poor devils!" this professor of religious studies said. "Well, *they* won't get *me!"* And the next expression came from a personal friend, a poet who had postured militantly during the 1960s. In response to my account of some very vicious treatment to which I had been subjected by some whites, he said, "Maybe *they* don't like what you write. Don't you understand how much they *hate* you? Why don't you just stand pat and take your blows?" Then there was the black woman who stepped out of the crowd at a reading I gave at the Library of Congress. "They've rewarded you," she whispered to me. "Now why don't you make yourself useful?"

Ellison's prediction did not really prepare me for the counterpolarization of black people during the 1970s and 1980s.

Ellison's attempt to define a meaningful identity for black Americans came at a time when the attention of much of the nation, if not much of the world, was still focused on the self-assertions of black Americans. His assessments were made during a watershed period, when certain elites still remained poised to redefine the practical implications of the nation's ethical creed in new, other-inclusive ways. A great number of black Americans, those who were then called "integrationists," represented part of the force pressing for a redefinition of the ethical basis of the society. Traditionally, it has always been black Americans who call attention to the distance between asserted ideals and daily practices, because it is the black American population that best symbolizes the consequences of the nation's contradictions. This unenviable position, or fate, has always provided black Americans with a minefield of ironies, a "knowingness," based on a painful intimacy with the cruel joke at the center of the problematic

American identity. At the core of this irony there used to reside the basic, if unspoken, understanding that identity in America is almost always a matter of improvisation, a matter of process; that most Americans are, because of this, confidence people; and that, given the provisional nature of American reality at almost any time, "black" could be in reality "white," and "white" could be in reality "black." Older Anglo-Saxons used to appreciate a few of the ironies in this minefield, or briar patch. They had, in fact, created the circumstances that had given rise to it. When pressed, or when drunk, one of them might tell you in private, "We're all cousins. The only difficulty is that most people don't understand just how we're related."

The fundamental challenge of the 1960s and 1970s was to redefine this special quality of relatedness. The challenge was a simple but complex matter of articulating, or of dramatizing, how the black American idiom, the special flavor of black Americans, was then redefining in its own terms some aspects of the white American essence. This was the subtle, self-affirming dimension of black American and American experience that could not be comprehended by W.E.B. Du Bois's dualism through its either/or focus. What was needed during and after the 1960s was a creative synthesis, one that would lift the whole issue of black American and therefore American identity to a higher level of meaning based on commonly shared values defined by the experiences of *both* groups. What was needed was a revolutionary model of American identity, an imaginative aesthetic and moral foothold established in the future, with little attention paid to race, toward which all Americans might aspire.

It need not be emphasized that this did not happen.

Because it did not happen, just a few years after Ellison had affirmed his prediction, the minefield of ironies was very suddenly exhausted. Those years marked the true beginnings of the great racial reaction. Stated in terms of tragicomic ritual, or in terms of slapstick, those at the forefront of the charge into the sacred castle suddenly found the drawbridge being raised with most of the invading army still outside. Although no word as harsh as "prisoners" was used, prisoners were indeed taken. They were interrogated in terms of IQ scores, and in terms of the good cop/bad cop ploy of popular melodrama. The "bad cops" (racist social scientists) simply asserted, without any hope of scientific proof, that because of genetic predisposition, black Americans were inferior to white Americans. The "good cops" (sentimental liberals) answered with arguments that black Americans were inferior because of environmental factors. All ironic laughter ceased as this premise was carried forward in the mass media, and all debate about ways to improve the condition of the poor shifted to a discussion of whether or not they are human beings.

Those in the forefront of the movement were stunned, forced now to fight with weapons they had not forged on their own and instead with weapons held within the carefully guarded arsenals of others. The "good cops" won the day, without too many shots being fired. The new black middle class was now isolated from the masses. The resurrected nature-nurture theory had done its work, and was retired to the keep of the sacred castle. Before the experiment in integration, the comic spirit grounded in the realities of the group idiom might have made light of this development with the usual irony. But after Moms Mabley, there was only Richard Pryor to provide the self-affirming communal gestures, grounded in ironic laughter, needed by the group as a safeguard against mechanical or aberrational behavior. Except for the early work of Richard Pryor, during the 1970s reality-based ironic laughter faded out of much black American expression. One result of this was that a large segment of the new black middle class became frightened, conformist, and strangely silent.

Toward the end of the 1970s, I began to hear, increasingly, other-directed allusions being consolidated in our private language. During this period the words *they* and *them* seemed to have become standardized ways of alluding to the relation of our inside world to the larger world outside our group. The old polarity between our idiom and the white American essence seemed to have been thrown into reverse, with the norms of white-middle-class life becoming predominant. Beyond a continuing influence in the areas of sports and entertainment, our private idiom seemed to have lost its capacity to influence the values of the world outside our own. More than this, the passing fashions of the outside world—Du Bois's "tape" of an alien world—seemed to have invaded our very souls. The erosion of something fundamental and sacred began then, and has not stopped since. This great reversal of influences may not have destroyed the group idiom, but it did encourage many of us to allow our eyes to follow a directing white finger; and it did cause

many of us to begin to express contempt for poor or unconscious black people who did not know enough to get out of
the path of a speeding luxury car.

Sometime toward the beginning of the 1980s, all the
"theys" seemed to me to have coalesced into a code of conduct, an acceptable guide to black behavior, the script of
which existed outside of the group. This model of acceptable
behavior began slowly to function as an internalized norm,
causing some of us to begin policing the behavior of others in
the group. This new norm was of very special interest to me.
I had not realized just how powerful it had become until
around Thanksgiving of 1980, when one of my earliest black
teachers and his wife visited my home in Charlottesville,
Virginia. My former teacher, an elderly man, had a nightmare during his first night in my home. All his life he had
been sensitive to the nuances of naked white power. Only
such a man could have drawn up into his dreams the unre-
fined images of white supremacy. On Thanksgiving morning, he reported to me the contents of his nightmare. He said
he had dreamed of interviewing a black newspaper reporter
who had just covered a top-level briefing of the military high
command at the Pentagon. My former teacher reported to
me what "they" said: "We should kill a million or so of them,
just so the others will understand we mean business and
won't start moaning about their 'civil rights.' "

My former teacher was, those many years later, still my
teacher. He was prophetic in his expression of the deep fear
that invaded the black American soul during the 1980s.

By the first years of the 1980s, I began to appreciate, in a
deeply personal way, the consequences of the penetration of

this new norm, this new sense of self, into the very core of the
black American idiom. I saw the disintegration of whatever
sense of self we still possessed. I saw the enthusiastic inter-
nalization of the assumed assumptions of "them," and I saw
the beginnings of what has become an unending, self-
negating, if not self-hating, conformity to the externally imposed model of an acceptable black self. Initially, I took an
ironic stance toward this somewhat comic transformation.
But when it began to condition the emotional and ethical responses of my family and my oldest black friends, when I saw
that white hostility toward me was a signal for black hostility toward me, I abandoned some of my family, and many of
my oldest black friends, and accepted a condition of internal
exile in a small, isolated town in Iowa as the only way I knew
of maintaining myself whole. I accepted this burden of guilt
as the price I had to pay for my own psychological freedom.
But much deeper than this was my *fear* that the pointing
white finger, the one I had observed in San Francisco and in
other places, might direct a hostile and inwardly dead set of
black eyes at me. For the first time in my life, I began to fear
my own people.

Over the past twelve or so years, here in Iowa, I have often
wondered whether I might have overreacted in putting great
distance between some of my family and my oldest black
friends and myself. There is always the temptation, if you are
a writer, to be suspicious that your imagination might be
overactive. But on the other hand, during these same years I
have had to deal with black men and women whom I sometimes considered alien. I have seen a colleague fly into a rage,
using the appropriated language of his white peers, over my

expression of independent thought. There were too many "theys" in his tirade for him to name. Another acquaintance, when I reported to him the way a black female student had used the bogus charge of racism to browbeat a "liberal" to give her a scholarship, laughed approvingly and said, "She's slick. She'll go far." Like my other colleague, he merely applauded *her* acceptance of the prevailing morality. But the very ease of *both* their acceptances was evidence that something was terribly wrong. Something humanly vital in them had been defeated, and they were involved in a constant process of self-improvisation, an improvisation relying on the "tape" provided by some external script.

I do not believe that Du Bois, or even Ellison, could have anticipated the extent to which black people conformed to the white American model during the 1970s and 1980s. Both their analyses assume a limited absorption of white influences into the black American idiom. But traditionally, with black people, this reverse integration has been a highly selective process. Only those traits of the "other world" that could enhance the group's sense of self were selected by black people to be incorporated into the group's ongoing process of self-making. It was only under a new set of historical circumstances, during the past two decades, that a large segment of the newly created black middle class assumed that it had much more in common with that idealized other world than it had with the vernacular sources of its own vitality.

During these decades, a very large group of black people took a side trip, so to speak, by attempting to standardize an identity apart from the concrete conditions of the group

ethos. Many stopped negotiating the complex balance between the moral and aesthetic feeling tones of our own ethos
and the influences, or trends, abstracted from Du Bois's
"other world." Many allowed an assumed corporate white
consensus regarding the nature of reality to predominate
over our own instinctive sense of reality. What was once
viewed as a spectrum of choices, some of which were to be rejected and some of which were to be selected for incorporation because they "fit" (an enterprise undertaken by any
group involved in the process of self-making), became for
many an opportunity to embrace an abstract white-middle-
class model in its entirety. Whereas our ancestors had abstracted and recombined with great discrimination and care,
many of us accepted unthinkingly the images and trends paraded before us. In doing this, we won with ease our cen-
turies-long battle against "discrimination."

But we also disrupted our historical process of making a
usable identity, and many of us have settled for a simple standardization around the norms, racist and other, of middle-
class American life. One advocate of this standardization is
Shelby Steele, who sees something heroic in conformity to
middle-class norms. Another advocate is Clarence Thomas,
whose story about his rise from the outhouses of his youth
(*Up from the Outhouse?*) conforms to the middle-class model
of heroism, but stops there. It makes all the difference in the
world, at least in the storybooks, whether the hero confronts
the dragon or joins him. It makes all the difference in the
world what is chosen as the basis of the happily-ever-after. Is
it the self-making, self-affirming challenges of the quest, or
is it the creature comforts of consumerism and conformity?

The issue of race aside, does the basis of ultimate security and identity reside in process or product?

If the answer to this question is the former, then perhaps another, very basic question should follow. What, in the nature of a group ethos, or an idiom, have we managed to bring forward from our failures in the 1970s and 1980s? The visible "leaders" of the group are always bemoaning the fact that we are losing our "gains." But beyond those material things that can be measured, what else, of much greater value, have we lost? I believe that we have lost, or are steadily losing, our sense of moral certainty, the ability to distinguish between right and wrong. I believe that this moral certainty once was, among the best of us, an ethical imperative, one passed along as a kind of legacy by our ancestors. This was our true wealth, our capital. The portion of this legacy that fueled the civil rights movement was a belief that *any* dehumanization of another human being was wrong. This moral certainty once had the potential to enlarge our humanity. Beneath it was the assumption that the experience of oppression had made us more human, and that this higher human awareness was about to project a vision of what a fully human life, one not restricted by color, should be. We seemed to be moving, on an ethical level, toward a synthesis of the "twoness"—the merger of the double self into a better and truer self—that was the end Du Bois had in mind.

Because of the complex ways in which the black American idiom relates to the white American essence, there were certain whites who anticipated the projection of a new *human style,* one which finally transcended race, rising from our struggle. This did not happen. What happened instead was

that the process of making a usable identity was minimal-
ized in its ambition: from the humanly transcendent to the
material plane, from an ethic based on possibility to an ethic
grounded in property. The historical moment had provided
us with a choice between continuing a process of human redefinition of an evolving sense of self, with all its pains and
risk and glory, and entry into a prearranged set of social for-
mulas. The choice was between process, which is on the side
of life, and product, which goes against the fundamental
ends of life. Many of us chose the latter option, and something of very great value in us began to die.

While our slave ancestors would no doubt be proud of us
as skillfully crafted copies of white people, they would not
really recognize many of us as blood kin, as products of the
process they initiated. The very first articulation of language
in their idiom, as expressed in their songs, had sufficient vitality to look beyond the trends of the moment and identify
with an age that was yet to come. The best of them looked
back on their own degraded status from the perspective of a
future time when their own process of self-making was complete. Denied recognizable human souls by the society that
enslaved them, they projected their full souls so far into the
future that they became content to look back on their en-
slavers with laughter, and with pity. This was one measure of
their full and self-confident humanity. Where once we
shared in their ethical critique of the moral defects in the
"other world" of Du Bois's dualism, many of us have now
abandoned, or trivialized, this resource. One result of this
mass defection is that we now lack a moral center, an independent ethos, a vital idiom. Another result is that the coun-

try itself now lacks the moral dimensions once supplied by our critique. It lacks our insights into what is of truly transcendent value. On this essential level of moral abstraction, in those places where *meanings* imposed by the black American group had value far beyond its immediate experience, the group is at risk of losing the catholic dimensions of its ancient ethical struggle for identity.

As a substitute, we now compete with white Americans for more creature comforts. Many of us now eat and dress in extraordinary style. We can lie and lie with greater and greater facility, and can even compete with whites in this enterprise. Back during the late 1970s, the comedian Richard Pryor captured the bleakness of our choice in graphic vernacular language. In one of his routines he portrays a black wino standing on a street corner, humming hymns and directing traffic on a Sunday morning. The wino sees a junkie coming up the street. He says, "Who's that boy? Is that Junior? Look at him. In the middle of the street. Junkie motherfucker. Look at him. Nigger used to be a *genius,* I ain't lyin'. Booked the numbers, didn't need paper or pencil. Now the nigger can't remember who *he* is."

My assertion is that something very tragic happened to a large segment of the black American group during the past two decades. Whatever the causes of this difficulty were, I believe that they were rooted more in the quality of our relation to the broader society than in defects in our own ethos. That is to say, we entered the broader society just at a time when there was the beginning of a transformation in its basic values. The causes of this transformation are a matter of speculation. In my own view, we became integrated into a special kind of decadence, which resulted from what has been termed *false consciousness,* one that leads to personal demoralization.

The basic pattern of this erosion was outlined, early in this century, by the Spanish philosopher José Ortega y Gasset, as he contemplated a similar development in his native Spain. "This degradation," he wrote, "merely follows from the acceptance of misgovernment as a constituted norm even though it continues to be *felt* as wrong. Inasmuch as what is essentially abnormal and criminal cannot be converted into a sound norm, the individual chooses to adapt himself to the abnormality by making himself a homogeneous part of the crime weighing upon him. The mechanism is similar to that which gives rise to the popular saying 'One lie breeds a hundred.' "

To fully appreciate the implications of Ortega's insight, one would be required to abandon Du Bois's dualism altogether and view black Americans as simply Americans who, like all others, are open to personal corruption as a consequence of living in a corrupt society. We are required to make the same personal adjustments as others in order to ensure our survival. In this broader sense, the movement of black Americans follows the pattern of other inspired movements to raise the moral tone of an oppressor through an appeal to some transcendent principle. Usually, those armed with only the slogans of liberalism, when they actually confront cynical and entrenched power, reach an impasse. After failing again and again to reform that which is incapable of reformation, such movements tend to regroup in such a way as to leave the sacred ideology intact. Whereas once there was an effort to raise everyone to the same level of equality by pointing to the moral failings of the oppressor, those faced with failure in this tactic often fall back on a much more cynical argument. Since it is not possible to force others to behave as they *should* behave, it is accepted that everyone has the right to behave as the oppressors *do* behave. This leaves the old moral ideology intact as a deadly form of cynicism.

But in the case of black Americans, this cynicism is proving to be much more deadly than the cynicism embraced by other groups. A great many black elites, like other elites, rushed to embrace the fashionable public behavior of the 1970s and 1980s. Part of the appeal of the Reagan years was the reemergence of the ideology of extreme individualism—the main chance, the reification of the bottom line, the location of an ethic in ownership, the elevation of individual concerns over the common concerns of the group. Many black elites embraced a public philosophy that helped to justify, for the first time on an inverted scale, our old "crabs in a barrel" mentality: those at the top of the barrel should try to *push down* those trying to climb out. This new sense of irresponsible individualism contributed to the growth in the sale of drugs as the main concern of a new underground economy in the black community.

And then there was the almost religious identification with politics. Democratized by Jesse Jackson, a crude political style seeped into many aspects of black American life. Lying and manipulation in personal relationships became fashionable. What made these masquerades so pathetic was the shallowness of the lies and the poor quality of the manipulations. It was as if mentors for the development of these skills had been selected from among those whites who were themselves on the margins of an increasingly sophisticated bureaucratic culture. Flabby tricks seemed to have been learned from those whose own political skills had become obsolete. This was a product of our racial marginalization. During the 1980s, whenever I heard a black bureaucrat depicting with pride the trick he had used to manipulate toward some end, I silently compared it with some much more subtle manipulation I had already witnessed on a much higher level of white society. I imagined this seemingly "new" manipulation as the brainchild of some tired and lackluster white bureaucrat now lost in the mists of time. My silent response was always something like "Crafted by John Doe, Assistant Clerk, Water Works Commission, Cleveland, 1913."

I believe that these preoccupations with fashionable individualism and with small-time politics, toward the end of survival during decadent times, invaded the very centers of our lives. In order to make room for these fashions, we tore down, tossed out, and discarded some of our most basic beliefs. But a very high price was paid for this trade-off. The acceptance of one fashion after another tends to draw the fashionable mind farther and farther away from the sources of its own vitality, its own feeling tones. A preoccupation with public fashions also erodes the unstated values, what the Japanese call "belly language," which provides the foundation for any group consensus. It seems to me that by the end of the 1980s black Americans had become a thoroughly "integrated" group. The trends of public life had successfully invaded, and had often suppressed, the remnants of our group ethic. Our ancient process of self-making had at last found a resting place, a point of consolidation. We were, at last, no better than and no worse than anyone else.

I am remembering now a very serious discussion I had with one of my mentors one rainy night in San Francisco many years ago. He had been after me for my usual crime: speaking my mind to the head of an institution because I thought that what the institution was doing was wrong. My mentor said, "Man, can you afford to *buy* [a certain institution]? Well, *they* can afford to buy integrity a dime a dozen!" After all these years I have reason to concede the truth of my old mentor's assessment. He understood, as I had still to learn, the extent to which ethics and ownership are interrelated in this culture. He was speaking as a learned student of European and therefore American history and culture. And yet I still think he was not quite right. Something happens to the *meaning* of integrity when it becomes a property. It ceases to be an active agent, its value content is cheapened, if not destroyed, and all that remains is an empty fashion. The authentification of such empty fashions by society leads to moral dandyism—a public moral stance or style without private substance. We learn to feign a serious preoccupation with what is assigned value as a current moral fashion, and we learn to view with watchful contempt that which is outside the prevailing consensus of public concern. The result is integrity by consensus, as opposed to the much more willful, much more meaningful kind. It represents the difference between looking outside oneself for clues to what *should* be a current concern and turning within to some private scale of values. It represents the difference between a shifting value sense dependent on outside verification and a value sense that is self-reifying, one that is beyond the control, or the measurement, of time and place. My old mentor was right. Integrity can be measured at a dime a dozen. But the attempt to encase it in material terms, paradoxically, causes it to become even more rare.

Our slave ancestors were familiar with this distinction. Their very lives depended on the ability to distinguish between moral fashions and meaningful actions. They survived by having sufficient vitality of imagination to pass over the present scene, if its currents were not moving in their direction, and identify their meaning with an age that was yet to come. In this way they kept alive the hope of eventually being able to continue moving toward their own goals. In this way a defeated people kept alive a sense of integrity, a sense of self, even if their bodies were bought and sold. During the worst of material times they provided a standard for the best of material times.

I am painfully aware that I may be much too critical of negative developments that might have been inescapable for all black people, myself included. I sit here in Iowa City in almost complete isolation from the flow of black American life. My telephone and my letters have provided a lifeline during all these years. On the other hand, I read a great many books and magazines, and I talk on a regular basis with selected friends in other parts of the country. I am beginning to sense that, just now, the group is engaged in a search for something that has been lost. Many of us are looking again to the past. Many of the new middle-class people are trying to fill a void in their lives by embracing a connection between the languages and the cultures of African peoples and our old black American traditions. Some of our children are learning to salute African flags. There is among us now the belief that, like immigrants from other nations, we must have a homeland to look back on before we can resume the process of making our identity. I have no arguments, now, with the choices being made by others.

But it does seem to me that our slave ancestors resolved this issue many centuries ago, long before most of the immigrants arrived in the United States. In the words of Howard Thurman, our slave ancestors were stripped of everything except what in them was literal and irreducible. Out of this raw and wounded humanity there began to be projected a new people, a people whose only vital lifelines were the roots they planted in the future. All the ancestors who came after them were linkages in the ongoing process of self-making. The present generations are likewise extensions of this same imaginative projection. Many of us have already tried to opt out of this process by attempting to standardize an identity around the norms of middle-class life at a time when the authenticity and the vitality of those norms were questionable. For many, this excursion has proved unsatisfactory. What seems to be gathering strength now is a comparable excursion, this one toward the traditions of ancient Egypt and Africa. Because I am isolated here in Iowa, I think I will sit out this second side trip.

If my years in this place have taught me anything, it is to be even more wary of abrupt shifts in the language and habits that appear around me. I have learned to continue with my own process of making, in my own way. I have learned, mostly on my own, that when the lifestyle out of which the idiom of a people grew is changed or altered, the idiom can break down. Such breakdowns provide the excuses needed to abandon a lifestyle based on a meaning that has been called into question by outside reality. But if the idiom has been identified with the essence of one's own life, and the former lifestyle was merely its transitory expression, then the old values at the basis of the idiom *hold* their essence of identification. Sometimes this holding action can go on for years during a period of readjustment. But afterward it is possible for a *new* lifestyle to grow out of the experience of the old values with a new reality. This is how human beings change with the times while remaining themselves.

What was only an abstraction for me became concrete when watched the retirement of Thurgood Marshall from the U.S. Supreme Court and the elevation of Clarence Thomas to Marshall's seat. I was interested in Thomas because both of us were raised in Savannah, Georgia, in extreme poverty, and both of us attended schools in the same Catholic system there. When Thomas publicly thanked the nuns in that school system, I could remember names and faces. But as the Senate hearings dragged on, and especially after Anita Hill's allegations, I found myself identifying less and less with Clarence Thomas, as well as with Ms. Hill. Both of them seemed to me to be captives of ideology. At one of the low points in the hearings, after Ms. Hill had testified, my older sister called me from Connecticut. She said, "James, Clarence Thomas didn't attend the same Catholic school we did in Savannah. If he had, he would have remembered the first thing the nuns taught all the kids." And then she recited the first lines of a poem: "I have to live with myself and so,/I want to be fit for myself to know."

When the lifestyle out of which the idiom of a people grew is change or altered, the idiom can break down. But if the idiom has been identified with the essence of one's own life, and the former lifestyle was merely its transitory expression, then the old values at the basis of the idiom hold their essence of identification. And afterward it is possible for a new lifestyle to grow out of the experience of the old values with a new reality.

Such a process of continuation and change is an essential part of one's *meaning* as a human being. A reclamation of essential meaning, for black Americans, has very little to do with the other side, the white side, of Du Bois's dualism. But at the same time, considering the white American context of our idiom, it has *everything* to do with it. Once again, we must consider the special interrelatedness of the two groups. Among white Americans, as among black Americans, there is now a desperate hunger for every value once included in the rhetorical category called "ethics." As the responses of "John Doe" to the Thomas hearings must have made clear to a great many people, the current fashion in moral dandyism and lying is about to run its course. The hunger for moral certainties provides much of the appeal of David Duke and Ross Perot. Beneath the open racism of Duke's supporters, one can perceive the first stirrings of a response to the metaphysical problems shared by all people, black Americans included, who have become personally demoralized by living with a false consciousness. For better or for worse, there is now a public lust for moral clarity. This hunger permeates all groups, and transcends the special interests of any one.

I would not advocate a return to a strict religious tradition, but I would hope that the group try again to understand some of the old definitions of the words *truth* and *meaning* and *honesty* and *love* and *integrity.* I am grateful to be hearing, these days, much more familiar language working its way through the black American community: "If you want to talk that talk, you have to walk that walk." I consider this first step toward the reassertion of the old idiom downright refreshing. And I am attempting to consider something refreshingly radical: Since every other attempt at "integration" has failed, perhaps we have one last chance to help each other, through our divided black and white vocabularies, work toward some common and solid definitions.

I want to believe that the spirits of our black ancestors, from the safe perspective of their long-imagined bridgehead someplace in the future, would somehow expect this effort on our part as a final affirmation of the self-definition, the process of making, they initiated those centuries ago. All I have been struggling to say is this: the implication of Du Bois's dualism notwithstanding, we should remember the uniqueness of our origins and locate, within our own idiom, sufficient courage to affirm this uniqueness as the only possible positive norm. Perhaps we should consider doing this as a way of keeping faith with our ancestors. It may well be that the uniqueness of our uniqueness, along with the implications of that, is our most basic value and is the most meaningful asset we have. If so, we ought to find ways of affirming it.

Ukiyo

... How one positions oneself in the world will always reflect to some degree the seminal experiences and indoctrinations of class, race and gender, but may also ... float above them, wondrously unanchored in categorical imperatives, mysteriously untraceable in derivation.

Martin Duberman on Paul Robeson,
The Nation, December 28, 1998

In early November of 1998, after sustaining a fever for almost two weeks, I developed a case of viral meningitis. This disease attacks the brain by way of the spine and can be fatal, especially to memory. I have been told that Jim Galvin, a friend and a colleague, was sent to my home to see about me when I did not answer my telephone. I am told that he found me unconscious, that he called my physician, that an ambulance was summoned, and that I was taken to Mercy Hospital. There I went into a coma that lasted eleven days. The doctors at Mercy decided that I should be placed in intensive care.

Rachel, my daughter, told me that when Richard, my brother, arrived in my room, my eyes opened wide for the very first time

But a friend in Cambridge, Jim Freedman, a former president of the University of Iowa, made a number of long-distance telephone calls and used his influence to have me transferred to the much better equipped intensive care unit at University Hospital. When the doctors there determined that I would probably not live, a number of friends called Rachel, at her dorm at Tufts University, and told her that she had better come. Jim Freedman called my sister, Mary, in Stamford, Connecticut, and advised her of my condition. Mary called my brother, Richard, in Atlanta, and advised him to come. Jorie Graham, Jim Galvin's wife, was then on a reading tour. She mentioned my condition to people during her reading at Ann Arbor, and one of them, a former student and friend named Eileen Pollack, quickly made plans to come. I am told that the students in the Writers' Workshop prayed for me. Connie Brothers, the administrative assistant in the Workshop, told me that so many calls came in, and so many students went to the hospital, that the staff imposed a quota. Only Rachel and Richard were allowed to spend any length of time in my room.

I do not remember any of it.

Howard, my neighbor across the street, gave Mary, my sister, a loaf of bread and a quart of fresh milk when she arrived at my home. Howard says he and Laurel, his wife, had watched me carry a suitcase and a video camera to the waiting ambulance.

When I did regain consciousness, for the very first time in

my life I had to rely on *others* to disclose to me my own personal details for nearly two weeks. There was, in my hospital room, a packed suitcase and a video camera that I had borrowed from Rachel earlier in the fall. Jim Galvin told me that when he had found me in my home, I had refused to leave. Perhaps I was so deranged that I could only be convinced to leave if I fantasized that I was going, once again, to see Rachel. Another friend, Fred Woodard, told me that when he visited me in intensive care, I had pleaded with him to help me get out. I had apparently tried to leave so many times that my hands and feet were tied to the bed. Jim Galvin said that I told him, "If you were a true friend you would cut these straps!" Rachel said I called the nurses and doctors "fascist bastards" (a line I remember from Lenny Bruce's routine "White Collar Drunks") when they refused to let me go out for a smoke. Rachel said that I was unconscious most of the time, that I was literally covered with tubes and needles and lights. Rachel said my eyes were swollen and discolored, and that she recalls my opening them twice. Once was when she and Marian Clark, another friend, were standing outside my room looking at me through a plastic curtain. I opened both my eyes a little and waved both my hands as high as the straps would allow. Rachel said the lights, when I moved, made me look like a Christmas tree. She said I said, "You are so beautiful!" The second time was when Richard was there. Rachel said I opened my swollen eyes as widely as I ever had and stared at Richard. "I guess you opened them so wide because he was standing over you and he is so tall," Rachel told me.

*Ted Wheeler, a track coach, cooked a meal and brought it to
me for a special lunch
Dentia MacDonald, a former student, baked an apple pie
for me and took it to the hospital just after I had checked
out
Jeannette Miyamoto called me from California
Suketu Mehta called from India
Indera called from India*

To this day, I have no clear memory of any of it.

For most of December, while recovering, I sat in a rocking
chair by my fireplace in the living room of my home, trying
to pull together the details of those lost days. The record of
the interior persistence of my life existed only in the memories of other people. Their recollections told me that my
sense of humor had remained intact, as had my smoking
habit, my sense of duty toward Rachel, and most especially
my desire to be free. Moreover, I could still recognize and appreciate beauty, and remained capable of opening my eyes
wide if the image coming into view was potent enough to
touch me at the deepest level of consciousness. As for my *own*
memories, I recall from this great encounter with the edge
only a kind of metaphorical wandering, or flights of imagination, or of landings, from the open heavens to the shifting
sandbeds of the sea. Perhaps it was Richard's image in the
outside world floating above me, the shadowy world that the
Japanese name *Ukiyo,* that led me to sitting with some of my
father's relatives, females mostly, in a living room in a place I

know was South Carolina. We were discussing some dis-
puted facts about our family history. I had promised to make
something right for them, something that was of great importance.

One of the nurses, after an embarrassment, washed down my
body and then hugged me

I believe now that the promise that I made to those
women had to do with my relationship with Richard. Before
my illness we had been estranged for many years. When he
called me at my home after my release from University Hospital, he told me, "You have so many friends. I was amazed
by all the friends you have out there." And I told Richard,
"That's what Daddy always taught us."

I was referring to the way our father, James A. McPherson,
Sr., had operated even within the tightly segregated world
that Savannah, Georgia, was during the 1940s and 1950s,
when we were growing up. Both Richard and I can remember his believing that the entire system of segregation was a
joke. He maintained many heartfelt relationships across
racial and class lines. He possessed a generous heart, but
liked to drink and gamble, and was always in trouble with
the law. I have two very painful memories of emotional dis-
locations between Richard and me, after our father's death in
1961. The first is from the time of the funeral, a few days after our father died. I was seventeen, Mary was eighteen,
Richard was sixteen, and Josephine, our youngest sister, was
fourteen. We sat as a family with our mother on a bench in

the Sidney A. Jones Funeral Parlor while a minister preached our father's funeral. I can still feel the pain his words inflicted on all of us. He said, "We all knew Mac, and we all know he's better off where he is now." The fact that I walked out of the funeral must have hurt my family, but especially Richard. The second memory derives from a time twenty years later. I had been in his home in Atlanta, and we had had an argument. He had told me, "Remember when I visited you in Berkeley in 1971 and you gave me a reading list? Well, you know what I read? Airplane repair manuals!" And I told him, "Richard, you are an ignorant man."

Richard had ordered me out of his home.

The code sustaining the world that floats at the foundations of the world is based on predatory violence and exquisitely good manners

The exterior news in December 1998, while I sat by my fireplace and healed, was about the impeachment of William Jefferson Clinton. Slowly, there began to form in the various media a consensus that the animosity toward Clinton had grown out of the unfinished business of the 1960s. That is, his public persona remained imprisoned within the popular images that linger in consciousness from that period: draft resisting, flirtations with drugs, sexual adventuring. It seems that an entire generation, those born a few years after me, still remained in the public stocks of suspicion. Those who mistrusted them most were older people, but there were also those of that same generation who had followed orders, who had done their duties, and who had remained loyal to convention. They filtered through the media the voice of Shakespeare's Henry IV as he reprimanded Prince Hal for his youthful dalliances with Falstaff, Bardolph, Gadshill, Poins, Peto, and with Mistress Quickly.

My brother might have been of this group.

I have always maintained that there were two 1960s, one for black people and another for white people. Simply put, the black people were trying to achieve full citizenship, to get into the mainstream. The young white people, having already experienced the loneliness and the uncertainties of middle-class life, were trying to get out. The black people came from tightly structured communities in which interdependence was essentially a matter of life or death. The white people came out of communities in which the myth of individualism had imposed a norm of habitual suspicion. The white side of this divide was explained to me once, out in Santa Cruz, by a very gentle friend named Don Ferrari, who had been an early inhabitant of the Haight-Ashbury district of San Francisco, before it became a commercial legend. He talked about the spirit of generosity and interdependence that the early residents there tried to achieve. I have since read an old book, based on a series of articles published in the *Village Voice* during the early 1960s. The book, *Moving Through Here,* by Don McNeil, details the noble ambitions of this wave of pioneers against the mythical landscape of the West. The black side of this spiritual divide, set during this same period and against the very same landscape, was told to me by Anne Thurman, the daughter of Howard Thurman, who was one of Martin Luther King's mentors at Morehouse. Thurman had moved to San Francisco to start his own "universalist" church. His daughter, Anne, then a teenager, had found employment in a bank. She had been the only black employee in the bank, and she received what she perceived as brutal treatment. She complained to her father, and the very wise Howard Thurman focused on the inevitable paradox in the quest for greater civil rights. He told her, "Annie, what makes *you* think that they would treat *you* better than they treat *each other?*"

Howard Thurman wisely saw that noble rhetoric must lead to steadfast human *action*.

Konomi Ara sent a message and then a gift from Japan
Takeo Hamamoto called from Japan
Benjamin called from Los Angeles

My brother and I grew up together in a segregated Savannah, Georgia. We had enjoyed a thin cushion of middle-class stability early on, when our father worked as an electrical contractor, the only black master electrician, at that time, in the state of Georgia. But he lost his status, as well as control over his life, before Richard and I were adolescents, and the two of us had to go to work to help our mother take care of our two sisters. This training to be supportive of others, especially of needy women, I think now, shaped both our inner dramas. Both of us have what health professionals now call a neurotic need to rescue women. But back then we did not understand the nature of the path we were taking. Richard and I worked very, very hard to get our family off public welfare. In 1961, when I completed high school, I was lucky enough to get a National Defense Student Loan, which enabled me to attend Morris Brown College, a black Methodist college in Atlanta. In 1962, when he finished high school, Richard joined the air force, with ambitions to become a pilot. He visited me once at Morris Brown College before he left for Viet Nam. He had been diagnosed as color-blind, so he would not be trained as a pilot. But he later distinguished himself in Viet Nam, was promoted in rank, and was able to sit out the last years of the war at an air force installation in Athens, Greece.

Between 1961 and 1971, a mere ten years, I had experiences on every level of American society. While in Atlanta, I worked part-time as a waiter at the exclusive Dinkler Plaza Hotel, at the post office, and at the extremely exclusive Piedmount Driving Club (of Tom Wolfe fame) in Buckhead. During the summers I worked as a dining car waiter on the Great Northern Railroad and was able to explore Chicago, St. Paul and Minneapolis, the Rocky Mountains, and Seattle. I remember watching King's March on Washington, in August of 1963, on a great wall of television sets in a department store in St. Paul. I spent my junior year in Baltimore, at Morgan State College, learning about history and politics and literature. After graduating from Morris Brown, I entered the Harvard Law School. I worked there as a janitor, as a community aide in an Irish-Italian Settlement House, and as a research assistant for a professor at the Harvard Business School. In the summers I took writing classes. In the fall of 1968, I moved to Iowa City, enrolled in the Writers' Workshop, and completed all my coursework in one year and a summer. In the fall of 1969, I took a teaching job at the University of California at Santa Cruz. I lived in Santa Cruz for nine months, and then I took an apartment in Berkeley, and then another apartment in Berkeley. I had begun to publish stories in the *Atlantic* in 1968, and I published a book of stories in 1969. While at Iowa, I had spent my weekends in Chicago researching a series of articles about a street gang named, then, the Blackstone Rangers. I had met and interviewed, in New York, Ralph Ellison, and had just completed an essay on him when my brother and his fiancée visited me, in the fall of 1971, in Berkeley. Both Richard and I had experienced very different decades. He had returned to Savannah from Athens. He had then found employment with Delta Airlines as a mechanic. He had moved from Savannah to Atlanta where he had met, ten years or so after graduation, a high school friend named Narvis Freeman, who was then working toward her master's degree. He and this hometown girl dated, recognized that they liked each other, and decided to get married.

But like my eleven days in a coma, neither of us knew the internal details of the other.

I know now that, to Richard, I must have seemed a product of the popular images of the 1960s. By this time I *had* inhaled marijuana, but I had not enjoyed it. This was because a gun had been at the back of my head while I inhaled. A Blackstone Ranger was holding the gun while we raced along Lake Shore Drive in Chicago. This had been a test. If I wanted to observe the gang and write about it, the gang had to have something incriminating on me in case I was a "snitch." The Rangers had their own code. I had also been a draft-dodger. My local board in Savannah had been trying to draft me since my third year in law school. It did not seem to matter to them that Richard was already in Viet Nam and that I was enrolled in school. What seemed, in my own mind, to matter to them was that my name had been listed on the welfare rolls of Chatham County, Georgia, and that I had gotten as far as the Harvard Law School. Given the norms of white supremacy, this must have been considered "wrong." Moreover, on a deeply emotional level, ever since I had walked out on my father's funeral I had kept my vow that no one would ever say over my body that my life had not been worth anything. I had also vowed that I would never allow *any* circumstance to force me into the hands of people who might do me harm, as my father had been done harm. So I remained in school, communicating with my local board from Cambridge, from Iowa City, and from Santa Cruz. Finally, my boss at Santa Cruz, a writer named James B. Hall, wrote a letter on my behalf to my local board. "You don't want this man," he wrote with his usual irony. "I happen to know that he's crazy." This was sometime in 1970, when the Santa Cruz campus, as well as the campuses of Berkeley, Harvard, Columbia, and Iowa, were exploding with antiwar protests.

Beginning in Cambridge, when I was twenty-two or twenty-three, I began to have a sex life. But I was never a fiend. The old pattern of being a caretaker to wounded females had persisted, and so I rejected one woman who wanted to give to me emotionally in order to bond with one who was needy. I repeated this pattern in Iowa City and again when I lived in Berkeley. It took a very bad marriage to help me break this pattern. This experience also helped me to better understand some of the emotional and psychological damage that the caretaker can inflict on the person who is "rescued." It freezes the helpless person at a permanent point of neediness, and it keeps that person confined in this role. Although the act of rescue may seem heroic at its outset, the interplay between one's own neurosis and the human need of the rescued person's desire to grow can become a battle, if not an endless war.

But when Richard and Narvis came to visit me in Berkeley in the fall of 1971, I was very much unconscious of my *self*.

Richard Feldman came by with his juicer and several packets of fresh carrots in his backpack and made a glass of carrot juice for me

Stephanie Griffin sent me a tin of homemade cookies from upstate New York

Ms. Miwa sent me a Japanese calendar from Oxford, Mississippi

I considered myself, at that point in my life, primarily a teacher. At Santa Cruz I taught writing and literature to mostly young white people from the upper middle class. I was living, then, in the basement apartment of a Japanese landlady, in Berkeley, and I had a Japanese girlfriend. When Richard and Narvis visited me in that apartment, I know now, the only experiences we had in common were our mutual memories of childhood and adolescence in Savannah. We could talk about family matters, about people from back home who were still close to us, but Richard's experience of Southeast Asia and of Athens, Greece, contained strands of memory so deeply private that they could only be shared, over a great number of years, inside a close relationship like a marriage. My own experiences were just as private. But, I still want to believe now, I tried to do the best I could to bridge this gap. I had invited Ishmael Reed to give a talk to my students at Santa Cruz. I invited Richard and Narvis to drive there with us. As I recall, we had a wonderful class. Ishmael was full of gruff humor and street smarts, and the students were receptive. When we returned to Berkeley in the evening, the four of us went to a bar and talked some more. Then I invited Richard and his fiancée back to my apartment.

Greg Downs sent me by mail a chocolate orange

Opal Moore called from Richmond

Stuart Harris flew in from Richmond and brought a book on Japanese aesthetics and some cookies baked by his fiancée. Stuart hugged me

Mitzi Clawson sent a box containing dried beans and the makings for fish stew

Craig Awmiller sent from Oregon several CDs and then, by Air Express, some frozen fish cakes

I have now in this house and in my office and in storage close to five thousand books. I left home for college with a single suitcase containing clothes and a National Defense

Student Loan. But my love for books had grown the more I read and the more I traveled. When I lived in Cambridge I used to joke that I was amazed to see so many people walking pridefully into bookstores or reading books openly in cafés and restaurants. I noted that where I came from such actions constituted an open invitation to be beaten up. As a teacher, books, back then, became my life, an extension of myself. They were a necessity for a very special reason. I had been raised in almost complete segregation, had attended a second- or third-rate college, and had been admitted to the Harvard Law School where I had been exposed to the legal and intellectual institutions that governed the country. I had left the law school knowing only two levels of the society: the extreme bottom and, much more abstractly, the extreme top. This was still segregation of a kind. Only the experience of reading, I determined, could help me integrate the fuzzy middle areas so I could have a complete picture. Paul Freund, who taught me constitutional law at Harvard, used to say that his students knew all the answers without knowing any of the basic questions. I think now that I was trying to learn the basic questions through reading so that, when combined with my own experiences, I could develop a national mind—a sense of how the entire culture, regional, ethnic, class, institutional, functioned together, as a *whole.* At the basis of this idea, I concede now, were ideas I had absorbed from conversations with Ralph Ellison and Albert Murray. I know it was this very issue of identity that caused the black 1960s and the white 1960s to come together.

At a time when black nationalist rhetoric had become the new political fashion, I began consciously bonding across racial lines. I thought that the real end of the civil rights movement—beyond economic and political empowerment —needed, if it were to succeed, a moral component that transcended race. It was simply a matter of trying to follow the Golden Rule. This was the open but complex and untested area that lay beyond access to once-closed institutions. It was the human problem raised by Howard Thurman in his question to Annie, his daughter. The search for this moral feeling tone was what the white 1960s had been all about. It was what Martin King envisioned would happen, would *have* to happen, after the once-closed institutions became open and allowed free-and-easy access to what was unquestionably of transcendent *human* value. These were some of the intellectual abstractions through which I faced my brother in Berkeley that evening in 1971.

I gave him some of my precious books, as I had given books to students and friends for many years before that evening.

My next-door neighbors, two women, plowed my sidewalk and front steps during the terrible late-December snows and freeze

Almost ten years later, this time inside Richard's home in Atlanta, the long-delayed confrontation took place. I was then going through a crisis, and it seemed that every place I turned toward those people I had known the longest, there

came the same refrain, *Remember that time?*, with some incon-
sequential slight or omission on my part attached to the
sound of an old friendship breaking. I managed the crisis as
best I could, finally deciding that the only way I could survive, as a whole human being, was to make a break with
those people who bore such hidden grudges. This meant, in
fact, that I had to make a clear break with an entire region of
the country. It meant I had to turn my back on my entire
family. I was willing to pay this price. So in 1981 I settled in
Iowa City, made a new home for myself, and in 1989 I went
to Japan for the first time. I made new friends there, friends
who came often to this country to explore its culture. In
about 1992, ten years after I had left the South, two of my
Japanese friends were planning to visit Atlanta. I called up
Richard, and I asked if he or Narvis, his wife, would greet
my two Japanese friends when they arrived at Hartsfield Airport. But Richard told me, "No!" He added, "Remember
that ten years ago you drew a line in the sand against the
whole South? Well, now I'm drawing a line against *you!*
Scratch my name, address, and telephone number out of your
address book and never call here again!"

A white lawyer, an old classmate at law school, agreed to
go to Hartsfield Airport and greet my two Japanese friends.

I know now that Richard had, by this time, good reason for
this total dismissal of me. It seems to me now that I had violated the ritual bond that we had shared since childhood.
Our mother had been very ill during those ten years, and it
had been Richard who had traveled to Savannah each week-

end to see about her. It had been Richard who had brought her to Atlanta to see medical specialists. And when she was no longer able to live alone, it had been Richard who closed down her apartment in Savannah and had moved her into his own home in Atlanta. It was Richard who had cooked for her, had given her daily baths and shots of insulin for her diabetes. And it had been Richard, finally, who was by her bedside in the hospital when she died.

I recognize, now, that I had dishonored our mother for the sake of a lonely principle, and since those years I have been struggling with what I thought had been vital in that principle. To make this clear, to myself as well as to Richard, and to earn the forgiveness of our mother, I have had to imagine the shadowy dimensions of the William Jefferson Clinton drama that is now occupying so much of public discourse. At its basis, as I have said, is the lingering animosity toward those who represented the counterculture of the 1960s. But there was, and is, something much more subtle at work. The moral energy generated by the civil rights movement benefited black people like Richard and Narvis, his wife. Simply put, a black middle class, with some economic stake in the system, was created. The proper ritual stance, for all such beneficiaries, is gratitude and economic self-celebration. But before the largesse flowed, there had been a much larger goal, one articulated by King as the creation of a "beloved community," one that intersected, at certain points, with the communal goals of the white counterculture. Both movements, at their high points, were beginning to formulate an answer to Howard Thurman's question to Annie, his daughter: "What makes you think that they would treat *you* better than they treat *each other?*" Both King and Gandhi, his mentor, would have answered, "Because they have been practicing *swaraj*—self-rule. Because it is only through wishing for the best for others that can one become and remain truly human." Aristotle called this special kind of emotional relationship "perfected friendship." The Japanese term relationships that are grounded in such natural feelings "*shizen na kamoche.*" I believe, in justification of myself, and also of my father, that it is only in locating these emotional resources inside ourselves, as well as inside other people, that one can create meaningful communities, even across racial lines.

The South, as I had experienced it while growing up, and as I had reexperienced it in Charlottesville, Virginia, during the late 1970s and the early 1980s, just did not offer normative opportunities for this kind of human growth. For me, the goal had never been economic success. For me, it had *always* been a matter of personal growth within a communal context unstructured by race. It is a very hard fact of life that there exists no such community in any part of the country. But, at the same time, it *does* exist in every part of the country, among selected individuals from every possible background. But this community is a floating world, a *ukiyo,* sustained, incrementally, by letters, telephone calls, faxes, e-mail, visits from time to time. It is not proximity that keeps it alive, but periodic expenditures of human energy and imagination and grace. This is what I have now, as a substitute for a hometown. I find it more than sufficient.

This is the thing I wanted very badly to explain to Richard, my brother, after I came out of my coma.

*There is a very peaceful spirit contained in a fire that is kept
alive day and night and day and night and day and night*

After our mother's death, Mary, our older sister, began to grow closer to our father's family, the core of which still survives in a little community named Green Pond, South Carolina. Mary began attending reunions there. Then she became active in helping to organize the reunions. Rachel attended one such reunion in Atlanta in the early 1990s, and several years ago I attended another reunion in Detroit. It was a loving affair. Richard was there, and though we were wary of each other, we got along very well. Also attending was my father's half-brother, Thomas McPherson, and his wife, Vanzetta. She is a federal district court judge in Birmingham, Alabama. Thomas's sister, Eva Clayton, was also there. Eva represents a district of North Carolina in the U.S. Congress. There was no sense of rank or of status among us. We were simply family, simply community. When I began telling jokes, Eva told me that I should never call her up in Washington, as I habitually called up Mary in Stamford, to recite my latest one-liners. She said that they might, if overheard, land her in trouble.

We took a group trip deep into Windsor, Canada, across the river from Detroit, in order to visit a station on the old Underground Railroad. The tour guide detailed the complex history of this station, one grounded in a communal effort that had transcended race. He noted that a great number of wooden carts, piled high with manure used for fertilizer, would stop periodically at the station. And hidden in the false bottoms of those carts, beneath the great piles of manure, would be fugitive slaves. We were all in good spirits, so I decided to try a one-liner on Richard. I said, "Richard, those carts are the ritual basis of our old Negro expression, 'Nigger, you ain't shit!' Only we have forgotten the celebratory tone that used to go with it. Our fugitive slave ancestors really said when they opened those false bottoms, 'Nigger, you *ain't* shit. *You're a free man!*'

Richard laughed then, and the years of ice began to melt.

Last year Mary attended another reunion, again with members of our father's family, in Patterson, New Jersey. She sent me a news article about one of the young men descended from this line who, Mary says, is our third cousin. His name is Leonard Brisbon. He is a major in the air force and is the co-pilot of Air Force One. He is an honors graduate of the Air Force Academy and has won many awards. In the article he talked lovingly about his parents and their values, and about his family roots in Green Pond, South Carolina. His lifelong ambition, he said, was to go to Mars. I plan to travel to the next reunion of this branch of my family, no matter where it takes place, in order to meet this cousin. I hope that Richard will also be there. I know he would be very proud of how high this cousin in our family has risen in the air force. In the meantime, I am practicing a new one-liner, one that I plan to try on Leonard Brisbon. I plan to say to him, "You crazy Negro. There ain't no collard greens on Mars!" I am hoping that Leonard Brisbon will laugh, along with Richard. I hope both of them will be able to see me as I *am*.

I also hope to have a much better funeral than my father had.

Perhaps this is what, in my coma, I promised those ladies who sat in a room in South Carolina

Workshopping Lucius Mummius

"As for the shows," said objectors, "let them continue in the old Roman way, whenever it falls to the praetors to celebrate them, and provided that no citizen is obliged to compete. Traditional morals, already gradually deteriorating, have been utterly ruined by this imported laxity!" . . . Two hundred years have passed since the Triumph of Lucius Mummius—who first gave that sort of show here —and during that time no upper-class Roman has ever demeaned himself by professional acting.

Tacitus, *Annals of Imperial Rome*

I lived for a while in a town house behind the private gate of an upper-class community in Los Altos, California. Although there was no official gate, a sign posted on an arch at the entrance warned that only residents and their guests were entitled to drive up the private road leading to the town houses. I spent my nights secure inside my own rented town house several hundred feet from the protective gate. My days were spent beyond the protective barricade of another gate. This metal gate guarded the very beautiful hilltop quarters of the Center for Advanced Studies in the Behavioral Sciences at Stanford University. Atop this hill were the offices of an assembly of academics from the best universities in the country, as well as from abroad. We met for lunch each day at noon and discussed, during intense conversations, our various projects. My colleagues, who were mostly social scientists, used a highly refined and specialized language. Phrases like "statistical models" and "variations" were employed with the ease of a priestly caste reciting incantations. There was another word that aroused extreme suspicion among the social scientists. That word was *narrative.* This word was intended to evoke the "anecdotal" evidence that was not susceptible to rigorous analysis. This evidence was viewed with suspicion because it was contained in stories that did not have any scientific value. Over the course of nine months, I was able to understand, and to even respect, the scientific rigor that had been evolved to achieve the respectability now enjoyed by the social sciences. But I soon began to miss the emotional muscle, the complexity of feelings, within the "narratives" that were so suspect within the intellectual precincts beyond that particular gate.

Each Thursday at 3:00 P.M., inside the private clubhouse of the gated community in Los Altos, I met with a group of elderly people who had begun a writing circle. The idea had originated with Leon Wortman, a retired businessman, who had grown dissatisfied with the quality of exchange among the people in the writing circle sponsored by the Senior Citizens' Center in Palo Alto. Leon had circulated a proposal among the occupants of the town houses, and soon a small group of elderly people, all of them retired, began to meet. Leon himself was writing a novel based on his exploits as an undercover operative in the O.S.S. during World War II. Ida, another member of the group, had been crippled since birth, had no children, and was trying to recapture the emotional texture of the Jewish immigrant experience in New York. Another woman, a retired teacher, was reaching back in memory to connect emotionally with communal life of small towns in Oklahoma, Kansas City, and Texas, where she had grown up, and where she had had roots. Another man, retired from teaching in a prep school in Washington, D.C., was writing, for his sons and daughter, a memoir about the early years of this century and the high points of his life with his deceased wife. All of them were looking back toward substance. As a longtime teacher, one with a conditioned hunger for "workshopping," I tried as best I could to help my neighbors refine their narratives in ways that would improve their writing styles. But the greatest pleasure, for me at least, resided in the opportunity to encourage the freedom of narration within a context in which anecdotal evidence, the emotional texture of the lives people had actually lived, was not suspect.

These contrasting memories of narrative "sites" remained with me when I returned to my regular teaching duties at the University of Iowa Writers' Workshop. I returned to my spacious office in the elegant Dey House, the new home of the master in fine arts program, the mother of all such programs, to a context in which "narratives" are still held in high regard. Such is the influence of the Iowa Writers' Workshop that its graduates now staff most of the other writing programs in the country. News reports, arriving on almost a weekly basis, testify to Iowa's great influence. The Art Institute of Chicago has launched its own writing program, one staffed by Iowa graduates. The *Writers Chronicle,* the official newspaper of the Associated Writers Programs, lists writing programs from Alabama to Wyoming, all soliciting applicants, sponsoring workshops, listing names of famous graduates. That there are so many programs is a testimony to the fact that universities, for both commercial and aesthetic reasons, have made homes for aspiring writers, meeting the need once met by newspapers. The success of such programs, at least as providers of space for writers, is noted, even with only wry humor, by John Updike in his collection of stories *Bech at Bay*:

> There are these facts, this happened and that happened, all told in this killingly clean prose. They have advanced degrees in creative writing; they go to these workshops and criticize each other; there is nothing left to criticize, but something is missing. I don't know what it is—a love of the world, some hope beyond the world.

Reading this comment by John Updike reminded me of the disjuncture I had sensed, last year, between the scientific techniques of the social scientists at the Center for Behavioral Studies and the rough but heartfelt prose of the senior citizens in the town house of my gated community. The one group of specialists had succeeded in reducing the human complexity of life to statistical models, while the older people were wise enough to still remain in awe of its magical and improvisational nature. The one group focused on surfaces, the other group focused on human essentials based on lived experience. The one group evolved a technology in the sense defined by the Swiss novelist Max Frisch—"the knack of so arranging the world that we don't have to experience it." The other group had already experienced the world and was trying to evolve forms that would make that experience of value, and useful, to others. While I do not agree with Updike's insinuation that workshops help to evolve techniques that tend to substitute for deeply felt emotional realities, I do believe that writing workshops can be influenced by cultural trends that flow into them from the outside world. To the extent that they do, the quality of the fiction written within such sites can be undermined.

The cultural critic Roger Rosenblatt, in a television review of the film *Saving Private Ryan,* offered his perception of the basic problem:

This art of persuasive appearance is true of the work of an entire generation, who have mastered the trappings of things but not the center. What has happened, I think, not just in movies but in books, theater, architecture, even government, is that technique has replaced meaning. Technique is so polished, so expert, it *becomes* meaning. . . . Many books have a center because there will always be authentic writers. But too many are made, as if with Lego parts, so much exposition, so much violence, so much sex. Books are acquired, not edited. They come prefabricated and presold. Magazines are made. Name your niche and fill it. Buildings are made to look like buildings. . . . Political candidates are built out of appearance, voice, the ability to

deliver one-liners, out of everything except what is inside them. The inside of the candidates, the reason for
the person to behave as he or she does, is not considered
an element of the product. . . . The best in art and life
comes from a center—something urgent and powerful—an ideal or emotion that insists on its being. From
that insistence a shape emerges and creates its structure
out of passion. If you begin with a structure, you have
to make up the passion. And that's very hard to do.

Roger Rosenblatt's critique of the current culture's devotion to technique over meaning raises serious questions. Just
how much are the many writing workshops, with their heavy
emphasis on technique over passion, contributing to an aesthetic that celebrates the outside, the surface of things, while
obscuring the essential inside world, the subjective world,
that is essential to good fiction? But much more important,
what can writing workshops offer as creative solutions to this
entrenched cultural problem?

I am imagining that, as a workshop teacher, I have enrolled
in my class a descendant of Lucius Mummius, that illustri-
ous Commander Lucius Mummius who, during the Third
Punic War between Rome and Carthage, had sacked
Corinth, the last of the free Greek city-states, and had hauled
cartload after cartload of sacred relics back to Rome. He received a triumph for his ostentatious display of loot, believing, along with the mob, that he was now in possession of
"culture." He did not know, or even suspect, the relations of
the treasures, torn from their ritual basis, to the religious and

ethical life of the Greeks who had made them. To Lucius Mummius, they represented only a surface displace of his journey from warrior to *novus,* a "new man" now in possession of refinement and taste. In the reign of the Emperor Nero, the writer Petronius Abiter would write satires about such *novii* as Lucius Mummius and Trimalchio in his *Satyricon.* Many centuries later, the American writer F. Scott Fitzgerald would reexamine the old problem of surfaces obscuring substance in "Trimalchio in West Egg," later renamed *The Great Gatsby.* But Fitzgerald, the great writer, would never have envisioned the time when most meanings surrounding the writer would be surface meanings, a time in which the passionate subjective voice of Nick Carroway would find no place in fiction.

To help instruct my wealthy student in the true meaning of his cultural artifacts, I would expose him first to a book, *The Death of Adam,* by Marilynne Robinson, who raises this issue in her brilliant essays. She argues for the preeminence of meaning over fact. That is, beyond the fact itself there should exist a fundamental principle grounded in the essentials of human life; a principle with which one can identify, when the identification with the undefinable is complete, a meaning that defines one's own meaning. Ms. Robinson's argument is not just that of a "contrarian." Even the right-wing press, specifically *Chronicles of Culture,* supports Ms. Robinson in her assessment of the current state of things:

As our lives become drabber and less substantial, we become obsessed with celebrities—body-sculpted starlets, basketball players, and jet-setting politicos. *People* magazine is our Bible and Larry King is the greatest prophet. Every day, American life becomes less and less like something the authors of the *Federalist* would have understood and more and more like scenes from Petronius' *Satyricon,* where sex substitutes for love, profits for productivity. Petronius lived in the time of the Emperor Nero, when the Romans no longer voted for their consuls but were content to worship whatever buffoon had been selected to be the god-man who ruled the world's only remaining superpower.

I would add to my lecture that Daniel J. Boorstin made the same points in his book *The Image,* as long ago as 1961. But when Boorstin wrote, there did not exist then the technological processes that have now helped to revolutionize the transformation of emotional language into thin images. In Boorstin's time there still existed, beneath the various surfaces, a core of commonly held values that taught what it meant to be human. Now we are not so sure of this. Issues of multiculturalism and relativism aside, there seems to be under way a steady retreat from engagement with these core values. Instead, there is a proud celebration of the image, the polished surface, that is offered without irony of hesitation, as a *substitute* for the core value. This sea-change has encouraged the development of a new art speech grounded in technology: "buzz," "spin," "image-rehabilitation," "synergy." While such developments were not encouraged by the numerous workshops, the aesthetic, commercial, and most especially the technological preoccupations of the world outside the workshops tend to filter into such specialized enclaves. I recall an incident from nearly twelve years ago when a student came to my home in tears. He showed me a letter from a senior editor at a prestigious magazine, an editor who had been encouraging the young writer's work. The editor now informed the writer that his magazine was no longer publishing "minimalist" fiction. I recall attending a lecture about five years ago given by an editor at a major publishing house. She advised the students that publishers were no longer accepting stories or novels about incest. A comparable commercial reaction has already been mounted against the memoir form. And then there is the new synergetic operation now managed by Ms. Tina Brown, a literary outlet that will transform stories from magazine-to-book-to-film with the wave of a high-tech wand. Subjected to the shifting commercial tastes of publishers and editors, young writers are being encouraged to perform "dog tricks"—to make radical adjustments in the ways their passions connect with artificial forms. They can be tempted to please commercial Sirens whose songs may mislead young writers trying to follow their own passions toward some home port that is familiar to their own feelings.

This fascination with the surface beauty of things is what inspired L. Mummius to haul into Rome, in 146 B.C., cart after cart of the spoils of Corinth. He had no understanding of the aesthetic sensibilities, level of taste, and meaning that have gone into the creation of these artifacts. Mummius represented the triumph of a civilization with a technological bias (military, architectural, roads, arches, camps) that was beginning to be troubled by a void in its spiritual life. Possession of the artifacts, then, symbolized a connection with the meaning of the culture that had produced them. But this assumption of connection and of meaning was left to those who viewed the artifacts from outside their settled ritual context. To such perceptions they represented only wealth. But to the Greeks who made them, they represented a deeply serious connection to the city-state of Corinth, to the meaning of the *polis,* to civic concerns and, ultimately, connections to the gods. The Greeks were serious spectators, ever on the lookout for the ideal, the universal, the perfected form of something great. To them, beauty was an everyday necessity because the experience of it led to an appreciation of truth, and an appreciation of truth led to goodness. Perfectionism, then, was the aesthetic standard. One should never pay attention to the trite, the aesthetically unpleasing, because what one paid attention to could shape one's character. To such sensibilities, art served as a prop for living the highest kind of life. Mummius brought cart after cart of Greek artifacts into Rome. But he had amassed only the surface of the culture from which they had come. He had the material wealth to put on display, but he lacked the inner refinement to actually *look* at, to appreciate on the deepest levels of his self, the aesthetic ideals they represented.

Facile analogies to the moral and aesthetic condition of Rome during its decadence are very easy to make, so I should be cautious with my generalizations. I would, nonetheless, like to continue with the idea of the ancient Greek as spectator, because it suggests a somewhat comparable development in America culture, one which exists outside the communities of the workshops but which, like trends in publishing, affects the quality of work done by young writers. It seems to me that the electronic media have now appropriated the word-of-mouth process that has always existed at the basis of storytelling and have transformed it into only another thin surface. It also seems to me that the news media now dramatize in a scene-specific way the deepest and most complex of human feelings, but almost always in a fashion that is emotionally numb. I watch news stories about disasters—earthquakes, fires, bombings, hurricanes, murders. The victims of such disasters, having already been instructed in the limited range of emotional responses required by a sound bite, have learned to script and economize their televised grief-stricken responses. This is for all the other spectators who will be watching them. But their efforts to be brief, instead of conveying a tragic sense, can become comic. One female victim of a tornado, several years ago, gave such an economic and tearful account of her losses that it prompted the on-site television reporter to say, "*Wonderful!*" Then there are the televised stories that are becoming a staple feature on both local and national newscasts. "Everyone has a story to tell," the wandering reporter advises. And then he throws a dart into a wall map of the country and chooses one town in one state. Going there, he locates by random one name and address from the telephone book and calls up that number. The person contacted then has an opportunity to pull one emotional thread out of a highly complex life history, a story line that must end on an optimistic note, as required by the production values of the network. But the most obscene expression of the American as spectator, of the technological crafting of stories, was the House and Senate impeachment trial of Bill Clinton. During the final days of the Senate hearing, after the videotaped depositions of Monica Lewinsky, Vernon Jordan, and Sidney Blumenthal, the television-viewing world of spectators was invited to view the chamber of the United States Senate as a magisterial writing workshop. A series of managers, acting as narrators, attempted to pull together a "story" about the interactions of the three deposed witnesses with Bill Clinton. Video clips of individualized question-and-answer sessions with the three witnesses added "dialogue." The spectators observed a "story" being written, but one with no real meaning or moral value, given the trivial matter at its basis.

The ancient Greek was a spectator of a different sort. He attended the theater on a weekly basis in order to contemplate the fundamental ethical issues of his reality being dramatized by Aeschylus, Aristophanes, Euripides, and Sophocles. He watched to see who and what he was and what life itself meant. The Greeks had an earnestness and great intensity, and a deeply tragic sense of life. They avoided the trite and the commonplace and anything that had nothing to teach.

It may well be that the young writers now entering workshops have already been trained, by the technological media, as spectators. But this does not make them Greek-like. While it remains a human truth that people live in terms of images, it is also true that where there are no good images there will always be bad ones. And the images that, day after day, condition all of us are mostly drawn from the extreme, unmetaphorical range of the visual spectrum, evoking no recognition of moral complexity or depth. We have come to accept the mundane image, and its lack of human vitality, as

only what should be expected, and are sometimes even bothered by the passionate, the perfected, the aspiration toward
the ideal. The general culture has forged a kind of unconscious consensus with respect to the proper precincts in
which beauty, and therefore truth and goodness, may be located. Given this reality, it seems to me that there should
arise a challenge to this status quo from within those communities of writers whose job it is to expand the spectrum of
acceptable images steeped in moral and metaphysical meanings.

Opportunities for such expansions can come from the
most unexpected of places. A few summers ago, for example,
the major newspapers carried a story and a picture of a young
black woman in Ann Arbor, Michigan, who threw herself
across the body of an American Nazi and took the blows that
a group of attackers had intended for him. This image came
into general consciousness and then faded out of it very
quickly, but it told a story as deeply felt as the trials in Jasper,
Texas, in 1999. The roots of both stories go deep, and only
radical acts of human sympathy could provide them with
meaning and value. Once again, any effort to understand
both incidents would require the writer to consider the increasing role now being played by the electronic media in as-
signing values to human groupings. I am alluding here to
the increasing commodification of the "moral voice" by the
mass media. Very serious concerns—the moral legacy of
Martin Luther King, issues of sexual and personal identity—
are reduced to one-dimensional images and marketed to targeted groups as products. Perhaps it is this commercially
driven reinforcement of group-specific demographics that

has encouraged the reappearance of phratric communities—blacks, gays, feminists, white males, senior citizens—many of which groups, like the citizens of Corinth, Athens, and Sparta, were uncomfortable with each other. In Jasper, Texas, in 1998, a human being, called a white supremacist, helped to drag a black man to his death. In Wyoming, also in 1998 and also just as impersonally, a group of teenagers killed a young gay man. The phratric community represented by the antiabortionists maintains a Web site listing the names of the doctors who perform abortions and their families, members of an opposing phratric community. Each time an abortionist is killed a line, a very impersonal one, is drawn through his/her name on the Web site. Such events are usually casually reported and are received with numbness except by those belonging to the group being victimized. Each collectivized communal voice is given sufficient time to vent, or rant, their rage. Such ritual moments become, after a while, almost normative in their flatness or thinness, even to writers whose craft encourages them to wrestle their imaginations into such moments in order to locate whatever meaning, tragic or otherwise, resides in them.

The riot at Ann Arbor, in other words, was a typical confrontation between members of two radical phratric communities—the American Nazi Party and the remnants of the New Left. Ever since the early 1980s the American Nazis, almost always on the cutting edge of new trends, concluded that they were not recruiting enough new members through simple mailings of party propaganda. The Nazis were the first to foresee the propaganda potential in the new technologies—computers, video cameras, the Internet, the hunger of the media for unusual images. During those years the Nazis began targeting those campuses said to be populated by liberals. These sites were targeted as backdrops against which racial demonstrations would be made. The ruling assumption behind this strategy was that the liberal elements would turn out en masse and subject the Nazis to violent attacks, which would be dutifully filmed by the media and used to recruit new members to the party. This strategy worked all during the 1980s and 1990s until the Nazis ran into *meaning* in Ann Arbor, in the person of a young black woman who might have been a *spectator* in a comparable engagement in the South or elsewhere. Perhaps it was the moral training that a comparable spectacle had induced in her that she had the courage to turn away from it. Her body, thrown across the back of a fallen Nazi, said a resounding "No!" to the theatricals of both the liberals and the Nazis. Because she remained human for a moment, her gesture, for a while, reminded a great number of people that transcendent loyalties could still exist outside of the phratric sense of self. She made a genuinely *human* gesture, one worthy of literary engagement, because it restored something of beauty to the world.

Some years later, the citizens of Jasper, Texas, faced with the consequence of another calculated gesture, affirmed the rightness of the Ann Arbor woman's gesture. Assigned the role of spectators, they chose to remain conscious of transcendent images, of justice or of compassion, toward the other extreme of the media-saturated spectrum, where adequate images reside.

. . .

A Region Not Home

In late May of 1998 I drove from Bristol, Rhode Island, to Cambridge, Massachusetts, with a group of Japanese friends. We had lunch in a restaurant just across from Harvard Yard and then walked around Harvard Square. Over in Harvard Yard, just at that time, President Neil L. Rudenstine was giving his commencement address. There was a great crowd of people, students and their families, packed into the Yard. As my friends and I walked along the edge of the crowd, I listened to President Rudenstine's voice over the public address system. I kept hearing him repeat the word *values*. I had not attended my own graduation from Harvard in 1968, and so, thirty years later, I lingered on the edge of the crowd, listening to the speech and pretending that it represented the distillation of wisdom I had missed back in 1968. After I returned to Iowa City, I received in June a copy of *Harvard Magazine* containing the full text of the speech. It was called "The Nature of the Humanities" and in it President Rudenstine expressed his fear that the humanities are in danger of being eclipsed by the natural sciences and the social sciences. He made an eloquent case for the essential place the humanities have for the health of society as a whole. While conceding that the humanities are untidy, offering knowledge not susceptible to elegant proofs, and thrive on the pattern, texture, and flow of experience, they nonetheless provide the most vital signs of human experience compared to any other representation. Rudenstine added:

> The purpose is not so much closure along a single line of
> inquiry—as we might find in the sciences—but illumi-
> nations that are hard won because they can only be dis-

covered in the very midst of life, with all its vicissitudes. If we are fortunate and alert, we may gradually learn how to see more clearly the nature and possible meaning of events; to be better attuned to the nuances, inflections, and character of other human beings; to weigh values with more precision; to judge on the basis on increasingly fine distinctions; and perhaps to become more effective, generous and wise in our actions. . . .

He also made a case for the interrelatedness of great literature to the more practical work of a society, that reading Plato's *Republic* opens questions about political theory and practice and law and civic obligations. "When it comes to central questions of the meaning of human life," he told the audience, "neither the humanities, the sciences nor the social sciences can be sovereign."

President Rudenstine's speech led me to reconsider my own role as a teacher in a workshop setting, where I have been making a living for well over twenty-five years. During those years of contact with young writers from a great diversity of ethnic, educational, and regional backgrounds, I have had to educate myself, over and over, in the cultures and values of people from points of origin differ from my own. I have had to do a great amount of reading, of self-education, in order to better communicate with the students whom I profess to teach. Since I began my teaching career at the University of California at Santa Cruz, back in 1969, I had developed the habit of spontaneously lending books to students. At first such gestures might have grown out of my own desire to be professorial ("I'm the teacher because I've read the book!"). But gradually, over the years, I have come to realize that by maintaining a "floating library" of books lent out, I was sometimes able to touch a student just at a time when an insight expressed in a specific book might be of help in the clarification of values. More than this, the great range of academic backgrounds brought by young writers into the workshops made it easier for a physics major to discuss theories of causality with a major in religion. It became easier for a writer trained in the exact language of law to learn the emotional language of fiction and poetry from a peer. A medical doctor could learn mythology from a classmate who had been educated in the classics. A writer with a background in engineering could, just by conversing with a music major, learn how American technology and American music derive from the very same idiom. A student with a background in film could help his classmates master the essentials of narrative pacing. Best of all, I, as a teacher, could gain wider knowledge from such a diverse body of students.

This is the kind of cross-fertilization, or of abstraction and recombination, that writing workshops can offer, even at a time when the outside society is becoming increasingly specialized and technological in its aesthetic and spiritual precincts. Such enclaves represent the ideal places for the conferring of affirmative action on people who have possession of the artful artifacts, like Lucium Mummius, but who need to learn just how they relate to rituals grounded in passion and the quest for what is beautiful in life, especially in a life as relentlessly materialistic as American life currently is. Once again, it is only a matter of clarifying the often ignored spectrum of adequate images, and investing them with meaning and with value. An example comes to mind from an incident a few years ago. One student had asked me to work with him in an independent study on religion. After I agreed, several of his peers asked if they could join us. Then other students asked to join the group. Marilynne Robinson, my colleague, agreed to help me teach what was becoming a class. A sign-up list was posted on a bulletin board, and it was soon filled with the names of young fiction writers and poets. Even some Mormon missionaries came to the classes. As for myself, as one of the teachers, I was obliged to study in order to increase my own knowledge of religion. The larger point is that, within all such gatherings of talented and curious people, such extensions of the spectrum of adequate images can take place. In such projections of communal imagination, deeper meanings can be explored, meanings that may give beauty and passion and depth to the fiction written out of this experience of exploration.

Finally, such communities of talented writers have an opportunity to impose their own values on the technological and marketing revolutions that have already taken place. Once a new technique has been introduced, it can either be ignored or else it can be embraced and made to serve one's own purposes. The new technology, as always, is neutral; it is, finally, the user who must determine its highest value. For example, the marketing of books by Amazon.com on the Internet and the trade in sharply discounted books by Barnes & Noble and by Daedalus, while putting great economic pressures on independent booksellers, also make many important books cheaper to purchase. Once again, the encouragement of levels of taste, or the discernment of beauty, encourages an appreciation of books that are outside commercial concern but are simply available. Great classics can easily be purchased at discount. The purely commercial books can be ignored. Similarly, the introduction of the VCR has encouraged many classic films to be remastered, reedited, and made available, also at great discount. Anyone can now build his own library of great films, once again ignoring those without sufficient aesthetic or moral content. The same is true of the relation of the compact disc to the cultivation of taste in music. The basic fact is that no one is really obliged to compromise a passion for aesthetic perfection, a passion for the ideal, on the altars of commercial taste. One can simply look the other way, toward where the ideal should reside.

These are some of the benefits of the new technology for writers and artists. For better or for worse, it has provided twenty-first-century people with what André Malraux called, two generations ago, a "museum without walls." That is, most people now have at their disposal reproductions of much of the great art produced in human history—books, paintings, music—as well as an understanding of the rituals and meanings behind them. Marilynne Robinson would caution here that during the last decades of this century we have begun to celebrate merely the surface of those meanings without any understanding of their content, historical or otherwise. But perhaps this is only the nature of change, only the lapse in time between the triumph Lucius Mummius received when he hauled his carts of loot into Rome from destroyed Corinth. It is possible that in succeeding years, sensibilities superior to the Roman general's developed a deeper appreciation of the culture that produced the beautiful artifacts. Perhaps, finally, this is the role that the many, many writing workshops are destined to play. In my view, they will remain the places where the best of the literary resources of the humanities will remain available to those who want to develop refined levels of taste and meaning that will help to define some ultimate meanings, no matter what else is being marketed outside such enclaves. It will be simply a matter of imagining the other way.

Permissions Acknowledgments

"Grant Hall" is reprinted from *Graywolf Forum Two: Body Language: Writers on Sport,* edited by Gerald Early, published in 1998 by Graywolf Press, Saint Paul, Minnesota.

"Disneyland": From *Fathering Daughters,* edited by Dewitt Henry and James Alan McPherson. Copyright © 1998 by DeWitt Henry and James Alan McPherson.

"The Done Thing," by James Alan McPherson, originally appeared in *Ploughshares,* vol. 16, nos. 1 and 2.

"Three Great Ones of the City and One Perfect Soul: Well Met at Cyprus" is reprinted from *Black Writers on Othello,* edited by Anada Kaul, published in 1997 by Howard University Press, Washington, D.C.

"Workshopping Lucius Mummius" is reprinted from *The 11th Draft,* edited by Frank Conroy, published in 1999 by HarperCollins Publishers, New York.

About the Author

James Alan McPherson is the author of *Crabcakes, Hue and Cry, Railroad,* and *Elbow Room,* for which he won a Pulitzer Prize in 1978. His essays and short stories have appeared in numerous periodicals—including *The New York Times Magazine, Esquire, The Atlantic Monthly, Newsday, Ploughshares, The Iowa Review,* and *Double-Take*—and anthologies such as volumes of *The Best American Short Stories, The Best American Essays,* and *O. Henry Prize Stories.* McPherson has received a Guggenheim Fellowship and a MacArthur Prize Fellows Award. He is currently a professor of English at the Iowa Writers' Workshop in Iowa City.

FOL

MAY 1 4 2024